JUDAISM AND ISLAM

THE LIBRARY
OF
JEWISH CLASSICS

Edited by

Prof. Gerson D. Cohen

VI CONTENTS.

JUDAISM AND ISLAM

BY

ABRAHAM GEIGER

PROLEGOMENON BY

MOSHE PEARLMAN

KTAV PUBLISHING HOUSE, Inc.

NEW YORK

1970

FIRST PUBLISHED 1898

BP134
J4
G4313
1970

NEW MATTER
© COPYRIGHT 1970
KTAV PUBLISHING HOUSE, INC.

SBN-87068-058-7

LIBRARY OF CONGRESS CATALOG CARD NUMBER: 79-106524
MANUFACTURED IN THE UNITED STATES OF AMERICA

TABLE OF CONTENTS.

PROLEGOMENON

A series of curious circumstances surround the history of the epoch-making study by Abraham Geiger herein being reissued. A pioneering work that quickly achieved recognition as a major contribution to the field of Islamic studies, the book was actually composed almost by accident. It was, moreover, the first real scholarly effort of a very young author which, while crowned with success, was never followed by him with another in this field. Although it was translated into English, the English edition became a rarity almost from the moment of its publication and has remained all but inaccessible to most English and American students to this very day. All this, despite the fact that the work has never lost the high regard in which it was held by its first readers.

*   *   *

Abraham Geiger's study on the Jewish foundations of Islam was originally composed in Latin and submitted to the University of Bonn in 1832 in response to a contest announced by the Faculty of Philosophy on the subject: An enquiry into those sources of the Koran, that is, the Muhammadan law, which were derived from Judaism. ("Inquiratur in fontes Alcorani seu legis Mohammedicae eas qui ex Judaismo derivandi sunt.") Presumably, the subject of the contest was formulated by Professor Georg Wilhelm Freytag (1788-1861), who was a disciple of the renowned French Arabist Antoine Isaac Silvestre de Sacy (1758-1833) and who himself was a distinguished authority on Arabic poetry, editor of basic medieval Arabic texts and compiler of the monumental

Arabic dictionary, *Lexicon Arabico-Latinum*. The award to young Geiger thus constituted a stamp of approval by one of the most accomplished orientalists of his day. The University of Marburg subsequently accepted the essay as a thesis and awarded its author a doctoral degree in June 1834.[1]

One year after it had been compiled the essay was published in German, "at the expense of the author," under the title *Was hat Mohammed aus dem Judenthume aufgenommen?*, the title page indicating that the essay had been crowned with a university prize.[2] In 1896, F. M. Young, "a member of the Ladies' League in Aid of the Delhi Mission" stationed in Bangalore, India, translated the work into English in the hope that it would be of assistance to Christian missionaries in their "dealings with Muhammadans." Two years later the translation was published in Madras by the Delhi Mission of the Society for Promoting Christian Knowledge. The English translation adhered faithfully to the original, diverging only to the extent of relegating Hebrew and Arabic quotations to the footnotes in order to allow for greater clarity in the body of the exposition.

*   *   *

At the time that Geiger wrote this first of his scholarly masterpieces he was but twenty-two years old. This study was but the first achievement in the author's remarkable career. Subsequently he was to distinguish himself in the rabbinate as one of the fathers of Reform Judaism and as a Judaic scholar and theologian whose astounding erudition, penetrating perception and critical acumen were applied to a variety of historical, philological and theological subjects. Geiger proved to be equally at home in the areas of biblical, talmudic and medieval research in such diverse subjects as Jewish lore, philology, history, literature and philosophy.

Born into a strictly orthodox family and milieu in Frankfurt, he was instructed in Bible from the age of three and launched on the Talmud at the age of six. Although secular studies were relegated to the background, he absorbed German and classical languages and literature in due course and, at the age of nineteen, began his university studies at Heidelberg and later repaired to Bonn. Beginning his career as a rabbi in 1833, he served at Wiesbaden, Breslau, Frankfurt and Berlin; simultaneously, he engaged in a variety of scholarly and communal activities—published a learned journal of his own, contributed to various periodicals, authored distinguished works, and taught in his last years, until his death in Berlin in 1874, in an institution of higher Jewish studies which had been established under his influence and guidance. In the Jewish community at large he was remembered as the moving spirit of several historic rabbinical conferences and of on-going discussions on the problems of contemporary Jewish life.[3]

So much has been written about Geiger's Jewish scholarship and communal leadership that little notice need be taken here of this aspect of his work, which in fact constituted the overwhelming bulk of his activity, writing and thought. Suffice it to say that his driving conviction was the need for a new adjustment of the eternal ethical verities lying at the root of Jewish faith to the changed and ever-changing social realities of the modern world. Indeed, in his view, this continuous process of readjustment and adaptation constituted the very essence of the course of Jewish history. This process of adaptation and metamorphosis in response to the needs of contemporary society was reflected in the literary heritage of the Jews, which contained the record of adjustments and reforms that were often conscious, systematic and fundamental. In Geiger's view his own program of reform was but one more link in the long chain of Jewish historical experience, a link that would, in turn, provide the foundations for further reform and new adaptations, one, in any case, that was indispensable to any continuity worthy of Jewish faith and ethic. Much of his scholarship represented an effort to document these convictions and to provide the scientific support for his theological stance.

Inevitably, then, the subject of his writing moved far afield from that of his first major scholarly effort. While he continued to betray deep interest in the Arabic-Islamic phase of Jewish history, it was only in his work on the Jewish foundations of Islam that he delved into the field of Islamics itself. While the study remained but a first effort beyond which he never attempted to go in this area, the work elicited high appreciation from authorities in the field.[4]

*   *   *

Before proceeding to analyze some of the major themes in Geiger's treatment, as well as some of the subsequent contributions to this aspect of Islamic research, it is appropriate to record the reactions of some of the major Islamists of the nineteenth and twentieth centuries testifying to the view that the work remains a pillar in its field.

One of the first to take notice of the book was the renowned De Sacy himself, who accorded it a full review in the *Journal des Savants* (1835, pp. 162-174) and who recommended it highly, Geiger's discussions of Muhammad's borrowings from Judaism, he felt, "rend presque superflues . . . toutes les discussions précédentes que je pourrais appeler préjudicielles." Curiously, he could not go along with Geiger's view that Muhammad had been a sincere religious enthusiast. To the nineteenth-century French scholar, Muhammad appeared to remain "un imposteur adroit, préméditant toutes ses démarches, et calculant de sang-froid tout ce qui pouvait favoriser et assurer le succès de ses projets ambitieux."

Similar reservations had been registered in a somewhat earlier and much briefer appreciation by Heinrich Ewald (1803-1875). The simple designation of Muhammad as a sincere enthusiast (*Schwärmer*), he felt, did not make for greater clarity in understanding the prophet's activity. Muhammad reflected a different personality at various moments in his career. He also thought that Geiger missed the point in his explanation of the connections between Judaism and Islam on the basis of certain historical conditions. In Ewald's view, these connections derived from ancient bonds between Hebrews and Arabs, which were reflected in common origins, customs and religion. Despite these differences of opinion, he, too, felt that Geiger's main conclusions were cogent and that the work opened many new vistas for further inquiry.[5]

A signal honor was accorded the work with the appearance of a detailed analysis of the Arabic materials in Geiger's study from the pen of the foremost German Arabist of the second half of the nineteenth century, H. L. Fleischer (1801-1888). Characterizing Geiger's work as genuinely scientific, Fleischer indicated that his critical remarks were in no way intended to detract from the recognition that the work deservedly enjoyed. He concluded his study by "taking leave of Dr. Geiger with sincerest thanks for the wealth of new and valuable data gleaned from his book."[6]

Later, Theodor Noeldeke (1836-1930), who ranked as the leading Semitist and Arabist of his day, registered, in his renowned history of the Quran, his appreciation of the "epoch-making work whose findings rapidly became the common stock of scholarship." Noeldeke indeed went out of his way to express his regret that rabbis of the generation following that of Geiger were not responsive to the challenge implicit in Geiger's study to carry his researches further. An up-to-date revision of the book, he felt, was an urgent desideratum for Islamic studies.[7]

Since this task has not as yet been undertaken, scholars continue to consult Geiger's as a comprehensive treatment of all aspects of the subject. Even in recent times, Heinrich Speyer, who re-examined thoroughly the Biblical motifs in the Quran, could observe that Geiger's great and enduring merit lay in the fact that while he drew on minutiae embedded in classical materials, he was nevertheless able to see beyond the isolated details and to give an insight into the total conception that the Prophet of Islam had had of the Biblical narrative and its personages. Finally, Rudi Paret, in his study on the teaching of Islam in German universities, pointed out that modern historical-critical research on the origins of Islam as a whole must be considered to have been initiated with the works of two Jews with Talmudic training,

Abraham Geiger and Gustav Weil (1809-1889). "The essay
by Geiger," he felt, "is distinguished for its clear structure,
its thorough treatment of source material and its sureness of
method."[9] His achievement looms even greater if one con-
siders the paucity of materials at Geiger's disposal. The renowned early authoritative Muslim sources which contain the
crucial material for a study of the problem (Ibn Ishāq,
Wāqidī, Ibn Saʿad) had not yet been published, nor had Ta-
bari's invaluable history and commentary on the Quran been
recovered from the oblivion into which they had fallen.

In a word, for all their reservations about the work and
their feeling that the subject required further treatment, the
outstanding students of Islam have, for more than a century,
been virtually unanimous in their acclaim and high esteem
of this pioneering effort.

*   *   *

The early history of Islam was nothing short of cyclonic
in the speed of its development and in its effect on every
area which it mastered. The rise of the new faith, its rapid
success in gaining adherents, its swift development into a
theocratic state, centered in Medina and under the guidance
of the prophet Muhammed, its successful assertion of its
dominion over the Arabian peninsula within a decade of its
emergence, its lightning campaign and spread abroad immediately following the death of its Prophet, the quick and
efficient liquidation and take-over of the Sassanian empire,
the conquest of Byzantine holdings from the Taurus to
Libya within a dozen years of its first campaigns outside
Arabia, the consequent entrenchment of the new imperial
power, religion and language over the vast areas of the Near
East and Mediterranean littoral—all these will forever remain
a chain of events constituting one of the most remarkable
upheavals in history, an eternal reminder of the possible
swiftness and permanence of fateful change. However, under-
lying and forever hovering over each of these developments
was the central figure of the Prophet and his revelation. Mo-
tivation, élan and legitimacy flowed ultimately from his teach-

ings, as enunciated either in his recorded prophecies or in the traditions of law, theology and practice associated with his "attested" statements or acts.

The core of his revelations to mankind became embodied in the holy scripture of the new faith, the Quran. While Arabic literature, especially in the form of poetry, had been transmitted orally long before Muhammad, the compilation of his prophecies was more than a religious landmark. The Quran became actually the first written Arabic *book*. With its rapid dissemination to millions of new believers and with the daily emergence of new challenges to the leaders of the young community, the many obscurities of the book evoked constant interpretation, discussion and debate over its numerous and often baffling allusions and references.

For all its enigmatic characteristics, the overall message of the Arabic scripture is clear and unmistakable. The Quran sets the prophet Muhammad in a framework of universal sacred history. To Muhammad God revealed anew what he had oft disclosed to prophets and believers of more ancient times: God, Creator of the universe as a whole and of mankind in particular, revealed such truths as the existence of God, human dependence on Him and man's duty to worship Him. Through Muhammad, and in the Quran, God further revealed the essential facts of man's past—the development of mankind under divine supervision, and the succession of prophets and scriptures, culminating in the revelations to Muhammad and in the Quran itself as the acme and "seal" of prophecy and prophetic ministry. In short, sacred history proceeds from Adam to Muhammad. Accordingly, Judaism and Christianity are construed as but steps in mankind's progressive march to Islam. Indeed, the two earlier monotheistic faiths constitute in this scheme but varieties of one and the same revelation of the One God.

The Quran, therefore, abounds in echoes of the earlier revelations, of the Hebrew Bible and the New Testament, each of which had appeared centuries before the Quran. However, since the latter makes frequent references to the contents of these earlier scriptures, the immediate question

facing the reader of the Quran is the extent to which the allusions and references of the latter are in consonance with the
actual contents of the Hebrew and Christian scriptures.

As every reader of the Quran quickly learns, the Muhammadan scripture is often an opaque body of literature. Its
meaning is most clear when it recites Biblical data known to
us from clear and attested texts. Frequently, however, the
reference in the Quran is quite obviously to some report or
body of lore unknown to us from explicit classical texts.
Whence did the Prophet derive his unprecendented information? It is at this point that scholarship entered the picture
to try and unravel the sources of Muhammad's inspiration.

However numerous and puzzling the frequently astounding
references to Jewish and Christian religious antiquity, the
student is never in doubt that both the Quranic conception
of history and the manifest significance of a host of details
establish a clear and definite nexus between the Quran, on
the one hand, and Jewish and Christian lore, on the other.
The reader of the Muslim scripture finds himself in the
world of Adam and Noah, Abraham and Lot, Jacob and
Joseph, Nimrod, Pharaoh and Haman as well as in the
presence of Mary and Jesus, the Baptist and the Seven
Sleepers. While the evidences of "borrowing" or "influences"
are obvious, the knotty problems associated with the references to, and the associations with, these figures are equally
inescapable: What exactly did the Prophet appropriate from
these earlier religious traditions, and how much did he deliberately or even unconsciously modify? What determined his
selection and rejection of materials from the earlier lore?
What, above all, were the sources at his disposal?

While in theory orthodox Muslims might well reject such
questions out of hand—for the Quran, after all, is the re-
pository of God's verbal communications to the Prophet, and
"borrowing" is, therefore, out of the question—in reality, very
early in the history of Islam, Muslim scholars were already
displaying interest in what could be gleaned from *the people of the book"* to elucidate and illuminate obscurities in

the text of their scripture. Evidence of this interest is attested in the early commentaries as well as in the body of tradition with its multitude of stories (*hadit*) about the Prophet and his Companions.

While the notion of borrowing forces itself upon any student of the Quran almost at once, Geiger determined to test the notion punctiliously with respect to Quranic borrowings from Jewish sources. Geiger, to be sure, was aware that Biblical lore could just as well have been gleaned from Christians as from Jews, and that, accordingly, the claim of specific sources of influence would have to be justified at every step and with respect to every single item. Needless to say, only those Jewish sources and tenets that unquestionably antedated the rise of Islam could legitimately be invoked. Conversely, only those parallels to Judaism that made their appearance in the earliest stages of Muslim history and development could serve as a proper field of investigation, for such borrowings that became manifest at but a later period might be challenged as later accretions. Geiger preferred to remain on sure ground that could not be explained away as post-Muhammadan borrowing or influence. Above all, he was aware, the analysis would perforce have to relate the suggested sources of influence to the environmental background of the Prophet's life and activity. The circumstances, occasion, purport and overall significance of each case in which borrowing or influence seemed plausible would have to be cogently set forth in order to make the proposed background of Muhammad's new faith convincing to the critical student of history.

*   *   *

The principal characteristics of the environmental seed-bed in which Muhammad matured had long been evident from the Quran itself and from attestations in pre-Muhammadan literature. The Arabian peninsula of pre-Islamic times had a substantial Jewish settlement, which exercised considerable influence on the general population in many respects—

economically, politically, intellectually. In the south, a century before Muhammad's activity, aggressive kings who were
adherents of some form of Judaism ruled in the Yemen. To
the north, in a number of towns, such as Medina and Khay-
bar, Jewish settlements figured prominently in agriculture and
handicrafts. Organized in their settlements 'very much like
the Arabs as independent tribes, these Jews were, nevertheless, quite conscious of their relationship to Jewish groups
elsewhere and were possessed of considerable religious
learning.

When Muhammad began to entrench himself in Medina,
he sought to win their adherence to, or at the least their
sympathy with, his young cause. From the text of the Quran
itself as well as from subsequent traditions it is virtually certain that discussions were held between the Muslims and
their Prophet, on the one hand, and the Jews whom they encountered, on the other. The Jews found themselves unable
to take the prophetic claims of the newcomer from pagan
Mecca seriously, and they were quick to express their derision for the howlers he expressed with his references to
Jewish lore. To the modern student it is clear that Muhammad had absorbed his notions of Jewish lore from oral communication and impressions gleaned by ear, rather than from
any study of the text of Scripture or any other authoritative
Jewish text. The Prophet was certainly not a scholar, and it
is very likely that many of his informants were not either.

After repeated rebuffs from the Jews, the mounting irrita-
tion of the Prophet finally turned into outright hostility. He
soon turned against them openly by denouncing them and ex-
horting the faithful to avoid contact with them as a group
hell bent on conspiring to lead genuine believers astray. Indeed, he now set himself to widen the gulf between the two
groups. The emphasis was now to be on the differences between the two religions rather than on their affinities in faith
and usage. Abandoning his original practice of facing in the direction of Jerusalem at the time of prayer, he now ordered
the Muslims to orient themselves to the ancient Arabian shrine
of Mecca. Theory was quickly devised to keep abreast of

practice—Abraham was now declared to have been neither
Jew nor Christian, and the Ka'ba, the sanctuary of Mecca
with its venerated stone, was designated as the place hallowed
by Abraham and his son Ismail.

From the speeches of Muhammad in the Quran, it is also
evident that the prophet felt that his message was unfairly rejected by the Jews, since his was merely "the truth confirming
what is with them" (Quran 2.85). More than once the Prophet himself had suggested that he had learned much of what
he taught from others, presumably Jews of the Arabian peninsula. On the other hand, it should be evident that differences between Muhammad and his Jewish interlocutors were
virtually inevitable. At the root of the chasm lay not so much
Muhammad's bizarre construction of early Jewish history as
his essential purpose in preaching: his mission as a prophet,
as the messenger of God and as legislator in Medina. His
essential purpose brought him squarely into conflict with basic
Jewish commitments. To the Jewish postulate of the permanence of the Torah and its law, Muhammad countered with a
theory of abrogation. Jewish messianic expectations, he
claimed, were now to be regarded as fulfilled in him. But
given the deep affinities between his teachings and those of
his Jewish neighbors, he failed to see the reasons for their
intransigence.

Geiger set out to trace with precision and exactitude those
elements that the herald of Islam had appropriated. Among
elements borrowed from Jewish sources that could be traced,
Geiger pointed to the notions and terms of the Ark, Eden,
Hell, Rabbinic scholars (aḥbār), divine presence (sakīna;
variation: assistance, calm), and so on—fourteen ideas and
terms in all. Turning to abstract religious ideas, Geiger found
that the basic concept of Islam, the unity of God, must have
been óf Jewish rather than of Christian origin. Bliss in the
hereafter is characterized in similar phrases in the Quran and
in Talmudic lore (although in the latter earthly pleasures do
not figure). The same was true of the ideas of the cata-
clysms announcing the end of the wicked world and the advent of the Messiah.

The Quranic notions of resurrection, divine spirit, and Gabriel, to be sure, could well have derived from Christian influence, and Muhammad's notions about the angels may go back to Persian sources. Although the Quran's ethical and legal stipulations and general notions about life at first blush show considerable affinity with those in Judaic sources, Geiger was aware of the possible methodological pitfall; much could have been due to a common Near Eastern social background. Accordingly, half his book is devoted to tracing the Judaic sources of the Quranic story material.

Geiger's emphasis on the Biblical narrative as an index of the avenue of influences on Muhammad's thinking was predicated on plausible methodological considerations. More than any other literary form, the *tale* appealed to Muhammad's poetic imagination and certainly suited the simplistic level of his audience far more than abstract doctrines and arguments. In Geiger's judgment the tales of the Hebrew Bible pointed to Jewish sources rather than to Christian informants, for Christians of that period placed greater emphasis on materials of the New Testament. Moreover, Christian points of stress in the Old Testament, such as the notion of original sin, are singularly absent in the Quran. The Quran, to be sure, displays no knowledge of the history of the Jewish people. However, this ignorance cannot serve as evidence against Geiger's thesis. Muhammad's interest was focussed on a limited number of personages of the biblical narrative. Moreover, in his version of the narratives connected with these figures, the biblical stories are innocently intertwined with post-biblical haggadic embellishment and are invoked as prototypes of Muhammad's own fate.

On occasion, indeed, an obscure passage in the Quran becomes quite clear only if read in the light of its Jewish antecedent. "Because of that We have prescribed (as a law) for the children of Israel that whoever kills a person otherwise than (in retaliation) for another person, or for causing corruption in the land, shall be as if had killed the people in a body, and he who brings life to one shall be as if he had brought life to the people as a body" (Quran 5:35; Bell's translation). Geiger rightly points out that the verse in its present context is virtually unintelligible unless one assumes the association of ideas in which Muhammad heard its background expounded. The *form* of the Mishnaic proposition of this idea, on the other hand, makes the verse quite lucid. According to Mishna Sanhedrin 4:5 witnesses in capital cases were admonished before they gave their testimony with the following words: "Know, indeed, that capital cases are not as non-capital cases: in non-capital cases a man may make atonement (for false testimony) by making restitution. However, in capital cases the blood of the condemned and of his (unborn) posterity to the very end of time is on the head of the witness. For so we learn in connection with Cain, who slew his brother and to whom it was said: 'The cry of your brother's *bloods*' (Gen. 4:10). Scripture did not say 'Your brother's *blood (dam)*' but 'Your brother's *bloods (demay 'ahika)*,' meaning *his* blood and the blood of his *posterity.* . . . It was on that account that but one man was first created, to teach you that if a man destroys a single life, Scripture reckons it to him as though he had destroyed a whole world; and if a man preserves a single soul, Scripture reckons it to him as if he had preserved a whole world."

How pervasive this Jewish influence was may be seen from the fact that even some early post-Quranic Muslim exegesis on occasion reflects such sources of inspiration.

In some instances biblical data are transmitted in distorted form. Abraham, in particular, appears as a prefiguration of Muhammad. While Isaac and Jacob are but pale images in the Quran, Joseph stands out as a substantial figure reflecting the possible traces of midrashic stories that Muhammad heard but that have since been totally lost to us. However, the figure towering above all others, the one with whom Muhammad most evidently identified himself, is that of Moses: the messenger of God, who, rejected by his people, finally prevailed despite many tribulations. The embellishments on the Moses story reflect Jewish influences and the large corpus of haggadic reflections and fantasies about the "father of prophecy."

Having absorbed a considerable amount of lore from others, Muhammad aimed at bringing about a fusion of existing creeds within his own new one. It was the Jews who, more than any other faction in Arabia, stood in the way of the fulfillment of this aspiration. Accordingly, Muhammad felt obliged to denounce their adherence to many peculiar and cumbersome laws. He further proceeded to reinterpret native Arabian customs and, after purifying them of blatant pagan overtones, to associate them with the name of Abraham.

The actual confrontation with the Jewish tribes, the continued scoffing and derision of the Jews, alienated him further. As a consequence of his denunciations the Jews soon came to be viewed by the young Muslim community as enemies of all believers, killers of prophets, arrogant claimants to divine favor and to all of paradise, if not, indeed, as syncretists of a sort. The Jews were soon characterized as worshippers of Ezra as the son of God, and as people who relied on the intercession of the pious of the past, falsified scriptures, and converted tombs of prophets into sanctuaries. It was right and incumbent on the Muslim to differ from them, and the Prophet, therefore, encouraged departure from Jewish custom and law in such matters as prayer, marriage, dietary restrictions, and the law of retaliation. These very stipulations, on the other hand, give evidence of Muhammad's acquaintance with Jewish usage through personal experience and observation.[10a]

In sum, Geiger could conclude that Muhammad had appropriated much from Jewish sources by means of oral communication, frequently without being aware of the difference between sacred text and later embellishments or exegetical comment, between primary stratum and secondary conflation, between biblical and post-biblical materials.

*   *   *

For all the detail and conviction that went into the presentation of his case, Geiger never lost sight of the possibility of an entirely different construction of the origins of Islam. He was keenly aware of the actual or possible Christian influences on Muhammad, of a possible Near Eastern substratum to his faith, and of the indubitable legacy of pagan Arab lore. Such an evaluation was, indeed, not long in making headway. In subsequent research, especially since the third quarter of the nineteenth century, scholars in ever growing numbers did actually come to the conclusion that Muhammad's development owed far less to Jewish influences than to Christian sources of information. Such a construction, they felt, would account for Geiger's findings as well as for much for which he had failed to account. The assumption of a Near Eastern Christian impact, for example, could well explain the transmission of patently Christian elements as well as those considered to be characteristically Jewish.[11] Thus, it was clear that the Quran reckoned Jesus among the prophets, indeed as an exceptional and outstanding messenger of God. What is more, biblical names and terms appear in the Quran in forms that have a decidedly Greek imprint: *Fir'aun,* Pharaoh; *Yūnus,* Jonah; *Sulaymān,* Solomon; *Ilyās,* Elijah; *iblís,* a devil (besides the more Hebraic form *shaytān*). The fear of imminent doom and of the end of the world permeates the early strata of the Quran and points to a religious mood far more in consonance with Christian apocalyptic than with Jewish attitudes. It is noteworthy, too, that the persecuted followers of Muhammad sought refuge in Christian Ethiopia. This new explanation also dovetailed with what was known of the dissemination of Christianity in the Arabian peninsula. Christianity was the prevailing faith, or at least was widespread, in many parts of Arabia and the surrounding areas of Byzantium and Ethiopia, in areas forming part of the Sassanian sphere of influence, where Arabic-speaking people were governed by the princes of Ḥira, in the lands of the Ghassanids living within the Byzantine framework, and in the Yemen. With so strong and numerous a Christian presence in the area, the infiltration of Christian influences into pagan Arabia was virtually inevitable. This influence could well have left an imprint not only in the form of ideas expounded through religious teaching and preaching but also in actual names and terms, locations and dictions, words and images that an occasion penetrated regular Arabic usage.

The studies of Julius Wellhausen, Richard Bell, Tor Andrae and K. Ahrens succeeded in gaining greater sympathy for the view accounting for the birth of Islam as a consequence of Christian Aramaic inspiration and information. This view gained its widest currency in scholarly circles in the 1920's and after. And while Charles C. Torrey's attempt to reestablish *The Jewish Foundations of Islam* was far from convincing, the "Christian" thesis also sustained serious blows. With further research, the Jewish factor in pre-Islamic Arabia was more fully demonstrated and elucidated by such scholars as J. Horowitz and Z. Hirschberg. Plausible, and on occasion less than plausible, hitherto unknown points of contact with a Jewish background were suggested by Hartwig Hirschfeld, D. Kuenstlinger and R. Lesczynsky. The biblical elements in the Quran were submitted anew to a searching examination by H. Speyer, and a cumulative "Jewish" commentary on the second and third suras of the Quran was composed by Abraham Katsh.[12]

Nor did a middle position fail to gain support in some scholarly quarters. A. Sprenger, the first major biographer of Muhammad, suggested that since neither Jews nor Christians could evidently be at the root of the Meccan revelation, the only plausible explanation lay in seeking for some group that combined elements of Judaism as well as of Christianity. Taking a cue from research on sectarian and dissident groups in Christendom, this view found support among several scholars who traced the origins of Islam to sectarian and heretical Christian groups with strong Judaizing tendencies.

In recent years the whole subject was given a fresh stimulus by the researches of Shlomo Dov Goitein. In his earliest investigations on the subject, he noted the clear affinities between the Quran and elements of Syriac church poetry. On the other hand, out of purely textual considerations he

stressed that it was implausible to posit Christianity as the
principal source of inspiration of Islamic revelation. In a
close examination of the earliest forty-eight suras of the Quran
Goitein could not find a single reference either to Jesus or to
any other patently Christian element. The six references to
Jesus in Meccan suras—as against 108 explicit references to
Moses, not to mention many more allusions to him—are
scattered and vague in their import. This is noteworthy, for
the figure of Jesus would have suited Muhammad's needs far
better than that of Moses. Jesus, after all, had had to contend
with opposition from within his own people, whereas Moses'
principal task was to take on alien tyrants. Jesus had preached
the Kingdom of Heaven, while Moses had led a people in an
exodus from the country of their enslavement. Goitein, accordingly, suggested that inasmuch as the bulk of the early
data pointed to a Jewish source of inspiration, while at the
same time traces of Christian piety were also in evidence, the
material pointed to the influence of local, Arabian Jewish
groups that combined these Jewish and Christian elements. It
was in all likelihood these very elements that introduced into
their environment tales of Arabian prophets of more ancient
times whose chastisements went unheeded. The local ruins
were cited by these groups as evidence of the fruit of ignoring
prophetic admonitions. From these, accordingly, Muhammad
appropriated his basic orientations to religion and to ancient
religious history. Only later did he learn about Christianity,
Jesus and the Gospel. Muhammad may have at some time in
his career have been especially moved by a Christian homily
such as that contained in Paul's Epistle to the Galatians (3 f.)
on Abraham as the forefather of all true believers. But the
initial and formative influences in Muhammad's prophetic
development, on the one hand, and his later contacts with the
Jews of Medina, on the other, combine to point clearly to
the dominance of the Jewish sources of inspiration in his
preaching. Goitein even ventured to suggest that the early
impulse to Muhammad's religious activity was stimulated by
a proselytizing Jew or Jewish group who was also fired by

the notion of Christian monastic pietism. (Such a combination is not unattested in Jewish history; German Jewish pietism of the eleventh and twelfth centuries betrays the manifest influence of the Christian pietist trends of its age and environment.) However, when Muhammad later repaired to Medina he encountered a strictly orthodox Jewish community that saw in his doctrines little more than blasphemous heresy. It was this group that caught him unawares with its total rebuff and generated his later intense hostility to the Jews and Judaism.[13]

After the "first *hijra*," when some of the persecuted followers of the Prophet left for Abyssinia, the Christian influences to which they were now exposed were bound to gain greater weight in the new community. With their return to the peninsula, the first Muslims must have brought with them a host of Christian notions and a body of information about the Christian faith. To this new lore the Prophet felt compelled to respond ambivalently, with expressions of reverence for Jesus himself and with a rejection of the latter's divinity and his death on the cross.

Further research has suggested the influence of other streams of religious thought, such as that represented by Manichean and Gnostic groups. However real these influences may have been, they remained marginal at best and can hardly serve to account for the preponderant Jewish and Christian strains in the Quran.

Quite obviously the inquiry into the religious and literary origins of Islam is by no means over.[14] Whatever the results of these new researches, they can in no way detract from the genius, originality and personal contribution of the Prophet of Islam to the treasury of human experience. To whatever materials he encountered and approximated, Muhammad gave fresh design, and to the course of history he generated a new direction.

Moshe Pearlman
University of California
Los Angeles, California

March 15, 1970

NOTES

1. L. Geiger and others, *Abraham Geiger, Leben und Lebenswerk* (Berlin, 1910), pp. 17, 33 f., 400.

2. The title page read: *Was hat Mohammed aus dem Judenthume aufgenommen?* Eine von der Königl, preussinchen Rheinuniversität gekrönte Preisschrift. Von Abraham Geiger, Herzogl. nassauischem Rabbiner zu Wiesbaden. Baden, 1833. Gedruckt auf Kosten des Verfassers bei F. Baaden. The work was reprinted in Leipzig in 1902, and a new issue of the German original has recently been announced.

3. For summaries and appreciations of his activities and scholarship, see the work referred to in n. 1. For the latest treatment of his thought, see M. Wiener, *Abraham Geiger and Liberal Judaism* (Philadelphia, 1962).

4. For a listing of the critical reviews of the work, see V. Chauvin, *Bibliographie des Ouvrages Arabes ou Relatifs aux Arabes Publiés dans l'Europe Chrétienne de 1810 à 1885,* X (Liege-Leipzig, 1907), pp. 4-5. For a survey of the early modern literature on the subject of Geiger's work, as well as on other aspects of Jewish influences in Arabia and on Islam, see G. Pfanmüller, *Handbuch der Islam-Literatur* (Berlin, 1923), pp. 98 f.

5. *Göttingische gelehrte Anzeigen,* 1834, vol. I, pp. 438-440. The review is signed by H. E.

6. H. L. Fleischer, "Über das Arabische in Dr. Geigers Preisschrift: *Was hat Mohammed dus den Judenthume aufgenommen?,*" *Der Orient: Literaturblatt des Orients,* II (1841), nos. 5, 6, 8, 10, 12; reprinted in the author's *Kleinere Schriften,* II (1888), 107-138.

7. The first edition of Th. Noeldeke, *Geschichte des Qorans* (Goettingen, 1860), p. 5 n. 2, refers to Geiger's, "scharfsinnige Untersuchungen," and accepts one of the points made by Geiger, *ibid.,* p. 77 n. 4. The remarks cited in the text appear in the second edition of Noeldeke's work (edited by Fr. Schwally), II (Leipzig, 1919), 208 f.

8. Cf. H. Speyer, *Die biblischen Erzaehlungen in Qoran* (Berlin, 1931; reprinted in Darmstadt, 1962), pp. vii-viii.

9. R. Paret, *The Study of Arabic and Islam at German Universities* (Wiesbaden, 1968), p. 9. Cf. Johann Fück, *Die arabischen Studien in Europa* (Leipzig, 1955), pp. 174-5.

10. The 1902 reprint of Geiger's book evoked a review by Hubert Grimme in which he characterized the work as an achievement in its own day that had become obsolete; *Orientalistische Literaturzeitung,* VII (1904), col. 226 f. Similar sentiments were echoed by J.H. (Horovitz?) in the *Zeitschrift fuer Hebraeische Bibliographie,* VI (1903), 10, who caviled about the dry style of the study. More pertinent to the real issue was his observation that Geiger had ignored the apocryphal and pseudepigraphical literature of the Jews with its wealth of relevant data.

10a. Cf. J. Waardenburg on Qoranic polemics in *Liber Amicorum* in honor of C.J. Bleeker (Leiden, 1969).

11. Cf. A. Jeffery, *The Quran as Scripture* (New York, 1952).

12. Cf. A.I. Katsh, *Judaism in Islam* (New York, 1954).

13. Cf. S.D. Goitein's preliminary edition of a Hebrew volume on *Muhammad's Islam* (Jerusalem, 1956); *idem,* "Who were Muhammad's Chief Teachers?" [in Hebrew], *Gotthold E. Weil Jubilee Volume* (Jerusalem, 1952), pp. 10-23 with a summary in English; *idem, Jews and Arabs* (New York, 1955), ch. 4, especially pp. 52-58; and the opening chapters in *idem, Studies in Islamic History and Institutions* (Leiden, 1966). In the *Encyclopaedia Judaica, s.v. Koran* he surveyed the older literature on the subject.

14. Cf. J. Obermann, "Islamic Origins," *The Arab Heritage,* edited by N.A. Faris (Princeton, 1944), pp. 58-120; J.K. Henninger, *Spuren christlicher Glaubenswahrheiten in Koran* (Schoeneck/Beckenried [Schweiz], 1951); G. Widengren, *Muhammad, the Apostle of God, and His Ascension* (Uppsala, 1955); S.W. Baron, *A Social and Religious History of the Jews,* 2nd ed., III (Philadelphia, 1957), 61-72, 75-86, 256-268; Y. Moubarac, *Abraham dans le Coran* (Paris, 1958); F. Altheim and R. Stiehl, *Die Araber in der alten Welt* (Berlin, 1964); C.D.G. Mueller, *Kirche und Mission unter den Arabern in vorislamischer Zeit* (Tuebingen, 1967). On the problem of the originality of Muhammad, cf. J. Fück, "Die originalitaet des arabischen Propheten," *Zeitschrift der Deutschen Morgenlaendischen Gesellschaft,* XC (1936), 509-525; G. von Grunebaum, "Von Muhammads Wirkung und Originalitaet," *Wiener Zeitschrift fuer die Kunde des Morgenlandes,* XLIV (1937), 29-50; C. Issawi, "The Historical Role of Muhammad," *The Muslim World,* XL (1950), 83-95. On recent trends in research on the rise of Islam, cf. M. Rodinson, "The Life of Muhammad and the Sociological Problem of the Beginning of Islam," *Diogenes,* no. 20 (Winter 1957), pp. 28-51; *idem.,* "Bilan des études mohammediennes," *Revue Historique,* CCXXIX (1963), 169-220; K. Rudolph, "Die Anfaenge Mohammeds im Lichte der Religionsgeschichte," *Festschrift Walter Baetke* (Weimar, 1966), pp. 298-326. See also the survey of recent research by F. Rosenthal in his introduction to the reissue of C.C. Torrey, *The Jewish Foundation of Islam* published by the Ktav Publishing House (New York, 1967).

TRANSLATOR'S PREFACE.

I undertook to translate this Prize Essay by the Rabbi Geiger at the request of the Rev. G. A. Lefroy, the Head of the Cambridge Mission at Delhi, who thought that an English translation of the book would be of use to him in his dealings with Muḥammadans. The Rev. H. D. Griswold of the American Presbyterian Mission at Lahore has very kindly put in all the Hebrew and Arabic citations for me, and has also revised my translation.

F. M. YOUNG.

BANGALORE,
March 17th, 1896.

PREFACE.

I VENTURE to offer to the general public a work which was primarily undertaken with somewhat scanty materials. The question propounded by the Philosophical Faculty at Bonn, viz., "*Inquiratur in fontes Alcorani seu legis Mohammedicae eas, qui ex Judaismo derivandi sunt*," served as an inducement to the undertaking. The point of view from which the subject was to be approached was left by the terms of the question entirely to the different workers; and that from which I have regarded it must be considered, in order that a right judgment upon my essay may be formed. It is assumed that Muhammad borrowed from Judaism, and this assumption, as will be shewn later, is rightly based. In this connection everything of course is excluded which appears only in the later development of Islám, and of which no trace can be met with in the Qurán; but on the other hand all such religious ideas and legends as are hinted at in the Qurán, and are explained and developed at the hands of later writers, deserve and receive consideration. Secondly, a comparison between Jewish sayings, and those of the Qurán, in the hope of setting forth the former as the source of the latter, can take place only on condition that the Jewish sayings are actually found in Jewish writings prior to Islám; or unless it is certain that such sayings, though only recently recorded, existed earlier in the synagogue.

But this certainty cannot easily be attained, and historical criticism must find its doubt as to this the more deeply rooted in proportion to the number of times in which the sayings are found among those of other creeds, from which there is probability that they were adopted. Thirdly, those who undertake this work must consider seriously the question, whether a mere similarity in the tenets of two different religious sects establishes the fact that an adoption from one into the other has taken place. There are so many general religious ideas that are common to several of the positive religions existent at the time of the rise of Muḥammadanism, that we must be very careful not to assert rashly that any one idea found in the Qurán is taken from Judaism.

I have therefore given in the different sections the marks and indications, and in the case of some points of greater difficulty, the reasons also, from which I believe myself justified in the conjecture that there has been such a borrowing.

For these three reasons many citations which I might have made from later Islám and later Judaism are excluded, and in like manner many statements also, which do not bear the impress of a borrowing.

On the other hand, the first division had to be added, in order to shew the basis on which the probability of a general borrowing from Judaism rests. After I had once settled the subject in this way, the arrangement of the whole, and more especially of the many disconnected divisions and sub-divisions, gave me no less trouble. The borrowings are of details not of anything comprehensive; they are fragmentary and occasional in that they were chosen according to what Muḥammad's reporters knew, and according to what was agreeable to the prophet's individual opinion and aim, consequently there is no close connection. How far I have succeeded in reducing these details to order the reader may see and judge from the book itself.

The materials at my disposal, when I first undertook this work, were only the bare Arabic text of the Qurán in Hinckelmann's edition from which the quotations are made,*

---

* In the translation the quotations are made from Fluegel's edition.

Wahl's Translation of the Qurán, and an intimate acquaintance with Judaism and its writings. A transcript from Baidháwi's Commentary on the Qurán on some passages in the second and third Súrahs, which Professor Freytag made for himself and which he with his usual kindness allowed me to use, was the only help outside the Qurán. I had thus the advantage of having an unbiassed mind; not, on the one hand, seeing the passages through the spectacles of the Arabian commentators, nor on the other finding in the Qurán the views of the Arabian dogmatists, and the narratives of their historians. I had besides the pleasure of finding out independently many obscure allusions, and explaining them correctly, as I afterwards learned from Arabic writings. In this form my work received the prize, and only after that had been gained was I able to collect more materials, and to use them for the remodelling of the work in German. To these belong especially the valuable Prodromi and Comments of Maraccius in his edition of the Qurán, the Commentary of Baidhâwi on the 10th Súrah (in Henzei's *Fragmenta Arabica*), and two parts of an excellent unpublished Commentary by Elpherar which begins with the 7th Súrah and was bought by the famous Seetzen at Cairo in 1807, and is now in the library at Gotha, whence I received it through the kind mediation of Professor Freytag at the expense of the University Library at Bonn. To these may be added Abulfedæ *Annales Maslemitici* and *Historia Anteislamica,* the works of Pococke, D'Herbelot's *Bibliothéque Orientale,* and many other works which will be found quoted in the book itself. All observations drawn from writings to which I first obtained access while the work was in the press are given in an Appendix. The advantages of a three-fold register, viz., of the explained Arabic and Rabbinical words, of the cited passages of the Qurán, and of quotations from other Arabic authors (with the exception of the constantly-quoted Elpherar and Maraccius) need not be dwelt upon in detail. The Jewish writings which I have used consist almost entirely of the Bible, the Talmud, and the Midrashim, and in accordance with my determination to reject all Jewish writings later than Muhammad's time, they had to be thus limited. The few passages which are taken from other writings, of which the age is not so exactly known, such as the sections of Rabbi Elieser, the Book *Hayyáshár*, and the two differing Recensions of the Jerusalem *Targum* on the Pentateuch (which are placed in a somewhat later period than that of the composition of the Qurán by the learned Zunz in his latest valuable work *Die Gottesdienstlichen Vorträge der Juden historisch entwickelt*: Berlin, 1832, A. Asher) are all of such a kind that one can generally point to some decided declaration in Holy Scripture itself from which such opinions and traditions may have arisen, and therefore their priority of existence in Judaism can be accepted without hesitation.

I must publicly offer my thanks to Professor Freytag for the many different kindnesses he has shown me in connection with this work, and also to my dear friends S. Frensdorf and J. Dernburg for their help in the correction of the proofs. Finally, I here express my heartfelt wish that this little work may be true to the spirit of our time, the striving after true knowledge, and that learned men may give me the benefit of their criticisms upon it.

THE AUTHOR.

WIESBADEN,
May 12th, 1833.

CORRIGENDA.

		Page						
For eas		,,	V line 5			*read* eos		
,,	Henzei's	,,	VII ,, 20			,,	Henzii	
,,	Maslemitici	,,	VII ,, 27			,,	Moslemitici	
,,	' Ábid ben ' Umr	,,	11 note 2	(l. 5)		,,	' Abíd ben ' Umya	
,,	Súra XII	,,	20 ,, 1	(l. 1)		,,	Súra VII	
,,	قَاسَلْ	,,	28 ,, 3			,,	قَاسَلْ	
,,	גֻּמָא	,,	31 ,, 4			,,	גֻּמָא	
,,	وَقَامَةْ	,,	33 ,, 1	(l. 3)		,,	وَقَامَةْ	

Transpose وَقَامَةْ and عَدْنَ ,, 33 ,, l.

For	עֵם	,,	35 ,, 5			,,	עֵם	
,,	ו1	,,	38 ,, 1			,,	כו	
,,	הַנִּכְבָּד	,,	39 ,, 3	(l. 2)		,,	הַנִּכְבָּר	
,,	שֻׁבָּת	,,	39 ,, 3	(l. 3)		,,	שֻׁבָּת	
,,	שֶׁכְּתָב	,,	48 ,, 1			,,	שֶׁכְּתָב	
,,	תִּנָּח	,,	48 ,, 4			,,	תִּנָּה	
,,	בֵּן אָחָר	,,	49 ,, 1			,,	בֵּן אֶחָד	
,,	Derabbi	,,	50 ,, 5			,,	Rabbi	
,,	מזו	,,	51 ,, 2			,,	מִזּוּ	
,,	וְאַחֲרִיתְךָ	,,	57 ,, 4	(P. 56)	,,	וְאַחוִיתְךָ	
,,	III. 2	,,	60 ,, 4			,,	111. 2	
,,	LXXIX. 11 ff.	,,	62 ,, 3			,,	LXXIX. 1 ff.	
,,	בָּנִין	,,	72 ,, 1	(l. 1)		,,	בָּנָיו	
,,	נֶאֱמָר	,,	81 ,, 1	(l. 1)		,,	נֶאֱמַר	
,,	وَرَفَعْنَاهْ	,,	82 ,, 3			,,	وَرَفَعْنَاهْ	
,,	*even to*	,,	110 line 2			,,	*as also did*	
,,	אֶלָּא	,,	138 note 4	(l. 2)		,,	אֶלָּא	
,,	תְּשׁוּבָה	,,	138 ,, 4	(l. 4)		,,	תְּשׁוּבָה	
,,	שׁוּתִּין	,,	146 ,, 3			,,	שׁוּתִּין	
,,	בְּיָדָה	,,	147 ,, 1			,,	בְּיָדָה	
Delete self		,,	158 line 7					

JUDAISM AND ISLÁM.

INTRODUCTION.

It will be found, speaking generally of the whole sphere of human thought, whether we consider matters which have already become the clear and certain possession of mankind, or those which are left for the future to unveil and to determine with scientific precision, that almost always a correct intuition precedes scientific knowledge, so that a generally correct idea, though not yet supported by adequate evidence, obtains some hold on the minds of men. In this way the thesis of this treatise has long been recognised as probable, namely that Muḥammad in his Qurán has borrowed much from Judaism as it presented itself to him in his time, though for this opinion no sufficient grounds have hitherto been advanced. And the very endeavour to give this just conjecture its place among scientific certainties seems to have produced in the faculty the wish to see the subject accurately and thoroughly worked out by scholars, conversant with both the Qurán and Judaism in their original sources; and to meet this wish I take up my present task, conscious indeed of feeble powers, but determined to use unsparing industry in the steadfast pursuit of my purpose. This is the end which we have in view, to wit, a scientific presentation, and not a mere list of apparent adaptations from Judaism, nor a statement of isolated facts dissevered from their historical connections. For this we must study the connection of the facts to be demonstrated with the whole life and work of Muḥammad, as well as with those events of his time, which either determined his actions or were determined by him. And so this treatise falls into two divisions, of which the first has to answer the following questions :—

Did Muḥammad wish to borrow from Judaism? Could Muḥammad borrow from Judaism? and if so, how was such borrowing possible for him? Was it compatible with his plan to borrow from Judaism? The second division must bring forward the facts to prove the borrowing, which has been stated on general grounds to have taken place. Only in this way can an individual proof of the kind referred to acquire scientific value, partly as throwing light upon the nature of Muḥammad's plan, and partly as showing the intrinsic necessity of the fact and its actual importance by virtue of its connection with other facts of Muḥammad's life and age. To this an appendix will be added, in which will be given a collection of those passages in which Muḥammad seems not so much to have borrowed from Judaism, as to have reviewed it and that too in a hostile spirit.

FIRST DIVISION.

*Did Muḥammad wish to borrow from Judaism? Could Muḥam-
mad borrow from Judaism? and if so, how was such
borrowing possible for him? Was it compatible with
Muḥammad's plan to borrow from Judaism?*

It is not enough for us to give a dry meagre summary
of the passages which appear to have some connection
with Judaism, in order to shew that Muḥammad really
possessed a certain knowledge of it, and used it in the
establishment of his new religion, and that, further, a
comparison with it makes clear many passages in the
Qurán. Rather is it our task to shew how it was bound up
with the spirit, the striving and the aims of Muḥammad, with
the mind of his time and the constitution of his surround-
ings, and thus to demonstrate the fact that, even were we
deprived of all proofs which undeniably shew Judaism to
be a source of the Qurán, the conjecture that a borrowing
from Judaism had taken place would still have great
probability. Thus it is necessary for us first to account
for this as the philosophical development of a process,
afterwards to be confirmed by historical evidence.

Three questions come prominently forward here :—

First: Did Muḥammad really think he would gain
any object by borrowing from Judaism? or, in other words,
Did Muḥammad of set purpose borrow from Judaism?

Second: Had Muḥammad means, and what means had
he, of attaining to a knowledge of Judaism? *i. e.,* Could he
thus borrow? and if so, how was it possible for him?

Third: Were there not other circumstances which
militated against, or at all events limited such a borrowing?

Was it compatible with the rest of his plan so to borrow ?
Was it permissible for him, and if so on what grounds ?

These three enquiries form the different Sections of the
first division.

FIRST SECTION.

Did Muḥammad wish to borrow from Judaism ?

Although we may by no means ascribe to Muḥammad a
special liking for the Jews and for Judaism and indeed in his
life, as well as in the writings which he left behind him as
laws for posterity, there are traces of hatred against
both ;—still it is evident that, on the one hand, the power
which the Jews had obtained in Arabia was important
enough for him to wish to have them as adherents and, on
the other, that they were, though themselves ignorant, far
in advance of other religious bodies [1] in that knowledge
which Muḥammad professed to have received by Divine
revelation,[2] as indeed he liked to assert of all his knowledge.
The Jews, moreover, gave him so much trouble with witty
and perplexing remarks that the wish to propitiate them
must certainly have arisen in him.

That the Jews in Arabia at the time of Muḥammad possessed considerable power is shown by the free life of many
quite independent tribes, which sometimes met him in open
battle. This fact is known especially of the Banu Qainuqá' [3]
in the second or third year of the Hijra, also of the Banu
Nadhír [4] in the 4th year. The latter are spoken of by

---

[1] See Jost's Geschichte des israelitischen Volkes, Vol. II. pp. 207. ff.

[2] Súra XXIX. 47 وَمَا كُنْتَ تَتْلُو مِنْ قَبْلِهِ مِنْ كِتَابٍ وَلَا تَخُطُّهُ بِيَمِينِكَ
' Thou didst not read any book before this, neither couldest thou write
it with thy right hand." (i. e., the Word of God). Sale's Translation.

[3] بَنُو قَيْنُقَاعَ Abulfeda (Vita Moḥammedis ed. Gagnier, p. 67).

[4] بَنُو نَظِيرَ In Pococke (Specimen Historiae Arabum p. 11) نضير See
also Commentators on Súra lix. and also Vita Moḥammedis p. 71.

Janáb as a great family of the Jews.[1]   This fact is further
known of the Jews in Khaibar[2] with whom he fought in
the 7th year.   The Banu Nadhír are supposed to be referred
to in Qurán lix. 2.   They are there described as so powerful
that the Muslims despaired of their conquest, and the
fastnesses which they possessed would have banished
thoughts of a capture, if as Muḥammad with probable exag-
geration expresses it, they themselves had not destroyed
their houses with their own hands, or if, as Abulfeda with
greater historical probability asserts, they, fearing a long
siege, had not withdrawn themselves and turned to quieter
regions.   The want of settled civil life, which continued in
Arabia till the rule of Muḥammad, was very favourable to the
Jews, who had fled to that country in large numbers after the
Destruction of Jerusalem, inasmuch as it enabled them to
gather together and to maintain their independence.   A
century before Muḥammad, this independence had reached
such a pitch that among the Himyarites the Jewish ruler
actually had jurisdiction over those who were not Jews; and
it was only the mistaken zeal of the last Jewish Governor,
Dhú Nawás,[3] which led him to a cruel attempt to suppress
other creeds (which attempt is pictured for us with the
very colours of a martyrologist), that brought about
the fall of the Jewish throne by the coming of the
Christian Abyssinian King.[4]   Although it seems to me
altogether improbable that the passage in Qurán lxxxv.
4 refers to this event, partly because of the indefin-
iteness of the allusion and partly because on this supposition
the Christians are called " the believers,"[5] which is never
the case elsewhere, though as a rule Muḥammad's treatment

---

[1] قبيلة كثيرة من اليهود

[2] خيبر Pcc. Spea. p. 11.

[3] ذو نَوَاس

[4] Comp. Assemani Bibliotheca Orientalis I. 361 pp. and Michaelis
Syrische Chrestomathie p. 19 ff.

[5] Qurán LXXXV. 7. ٱلْمُومِنُون

of the Christians was indulgent ; and although I give an
entirely different interpretation to this passage—an interpretation borne out by every word, [1] nevertheless this very
mistake of the commentators shews the importance which
the Arabs attached to this conquest of the Jewish ruler,
and is a proof of the greatness of his former power. That
the remains of such a power, even when shattered continued
to be of importance is plain in itself, and is moreover
clearly shown in a passage soon to be quoted,[2] where
the Himyarites are depicted as particularly unbelieving.
An Arabian author [3] mentions other tribes beside the
Himyarites as adherents of Judaism, *viz.*, the Banu Kinána
Banu Hareth ben Kab, and Kinda. [4]

While this physical power of the Jews inspired partly
fear, partly respect in Muḥammad's mind, he was no less
afraid of their mental superiority and of appearing to them
as ignorant ; and so his first object must have been to
conciliate them by an apparent yielding to their views.
That the Jewish system of belief was even then a fully
developed one, which penetrated the life of each member of
the community, is proved both by its antiquity and by the
fact that the Talmud had already been completed. Though
the Jews of that region were among the most ignorant, as is
shown by the silence of the Talmud concerning them, and
also by that which was borrowed from them and incorporated

---

[1] See Division II, Section II, Chapter II, Part IV.

[2] Baidháwi on Qurán II. 91.

[3] Vide Pococke Spec. p. 136.

[4] A good voucher for the importance to which some Jewish families had
attained might be found in a poem of Hamasa (ed. Freytag p. 49), which
is full of the spirit of chivalry and self reliance, if only the evidence that
the family referred to was a Jewish one were sufficiently certain. The
only thing for it is the name of the author ٱلسَّمَوْأَل which, as a commentator cited by Elpherar remarks, is a Hebrew name (السموال ابو العلاه) ,وقال ابو العلاه السموال
(اسم عبرانى وليس بعربى but which might easily have come into use
among the Arabs. Even in the verse هڠونا page 52, where the pure and
unmixed descent of the family is praised, and where one might expect a
mention of its Jewish origin, no such allusion is found.

in the Qurán, yet very many traditions and pithy sayings survived in the mouth of the people, which doubtless gave to the Jews an appearance of intellectual superiority in those dark times and regions of ignorance, and so gained for them honour in the sight of others. Thus it came about naturally that Muḥammad wanted to learn their views and to include them in his community. It was not only the idea of swelling his society with these numbers of adherents[1] that produced this wish in him, but also the way in which they defended their own cause and their mode of dealing with him. The fact that Muḥammad very often came off second best in religious disputes is evident from several sayings, and particularly from the following very decided one :—" When thou seest those who busy themselves with cavilling at Our signs, depart from them until they busy themselves in some other subject; and if Satan cause thee to forget this precept,[2] do not sit with the ungodly people after recollection." This remarkably strong statement, in which he makes God declare it to be a work of the devil to be present at controversies about the truth of his mission, shews how much Muḥammad had to fear from argument. Intercourse with the Jews appeared to him to be dangerous for his Muslims also, and he warns them against too frequent communication or too close intimacy with the Jews.[3] He naturally puts this forward on grounds, other than the right ones; but the real reason for the warning is obviously that Muḥammad feared the power of the Jews to shake the faith of others in the religion revealed to him.[4]

---

[1] מוֹרָשָׁה קְהִלַּת יַעֲקֹב

" An inheritance for the assembly of Jacob." Deut. xxxiii. 4.

[2] وَاَمَّا يُنْسِيَنَّكَ ٱلشَّيْطَانُ Súra VI. 67.

[3] لَا تَتَوَلَّوْا

[4] Súra LX. 13. On this Elpherar remarks:

و ذلك ان ناسا من فقرا ٱلمسلمين كانوا يخبرون اليهود اخبار ٱلمسلمين
يتواصلونهم فيصيبون من ثمارهم

Most characteristically, and doubtless quite in accordance with the intellectual manner of the Jews, this is shown in a witty and satirical play of question and answer, about which Muḥammad complains bitterly, and which often gave him apparent weapons against the Jews, in that he regarded their utterances as bona fide expressions of opinion and not as mere teasing mockeries.

Thus, in order to gain reputation, and also because he was under the impression that, if some (he says ten) of the Jews would join him, all the rest would become his adherents,[1] he made the attempt with some, who either did not have the courage to withstand him, or else did not wish to enter upon a long dispute with him. They either got rid of him with an answer which he could not gainsay, or they mixed up the words which he required from them with others of similar sound, but of different and even contrary meaning. Thus they said to him once :—" we can do nothing for our unbelief, for our hearts are uncircumcised."[2]   On another occasion they advised him to go to Syria, as the only place where prophetic revelations were possible, according to the Jewish saying :[3] " Prophecy is not found out side the Holy Land." This is given by some expositors as the cause for the revelation in Súra XVII. 78[4], but others assign a different reason for the verse.   Further the

---

" This (was revealed) because some of the poor Muslims instructed the Jews in the doctrine of the Muslims, so that there was unity between them and the former received of the fruits of the latter."

[1] Comp. Sunna 445, Fundgruben des Orients, Vol. I. p. 286.

[2] Súra II. 82 غُلْفٌ قُلُوبُنَا اَنَحْنُ لَب עָרְלֵי Comp. Deut. x. 16. " Circumcise therefore the foreskin of your heart and be no more stiffnecked."

[3] אֵין הַנְּבוּאָה שׁוֹרָה בְּחוּצָה לָאָרֶץ

[4] Jalálu'd-dín (Maracci in loco).

نزل لما قال اليهود ان كنت نبيّا فالحق بالشام فانها ارض الانبياء
" This verse was revealed when the Jews said ; If thou art a Prophet, then go to Syria, for Syria alone is the land of prophets." So Elpherar et al.

commentators cheerily relate many anecdotes by way of explaining the reason for certain passages, which appear to the unprejudiced quite in the same light. As the occasion of Qurán II. 91, Baidháwi relates the following tale:[1] " It is said that Omar went once into a school[2] of the Jews and asked them about Gabriel. They replied: ' He is our enemy, he reveals our secrets to Muḥammad, he is also the messenger of wrath and punishment; Michael on the contrary brings us prosperity and plenty.' Then Omar said: ' What is their position with regard to God?' and the Jews replied: ' Gabriel on His right and Michael on His left, but between these two there is enmity.' But he said: ' God forbid that it should be as you say; they are not enemies, but you are more unbelieving than the Himyariks.[3] Whosoever is the enemy of either angel, he is the enemy of God.' Then Omar went away and found that Gabriel had preceded him with a revelation, and Muḥammad said to him, ' Thy Lord has already agreed with thee, O Omar.' "

Although what is here brought forward is to some extent what is really held by the Jews, as *e.g.* that Gabriel is the messenger of punishment,[4] and although accordingly there is much of truth in this narrative;

---

[1] قيل دخل عمر رضى الله عنه مدراس اليهود يوما فسالهم عن جبريل فقالوا ذلك عدونا يُطلع محمدا على اسرارنا و انه صاحب كل خَسَف وعذاب وميكايل صاحب الخصب و السلام فقال وما مَنْزِلَتُهُمَا عن الله تعالى قالوا جبريل عن يمينه وميكايل عن يساره و بينهما عداوة فقال كَيْن كان كما تقولون فليسا بعدُوَّيْن و لانتم اكفر من الحمير و من كان عدو احدهما و هو عدو الله تعالى ثم رجع عمر فوجد جبريل قد سبقه بالوهى فقال عليه الصلاة و السلام لقد و افقك ربك يا عمر *

[2] בֵּית מִדְרָשׁ

[3] These are the words referred to above. p. 5.

[4] R. Salomo Ben Adereth on Tract Baba Bathra 74. 2.

חֲכָמִינוּ זִכְרוֹנָם לִבְרָכָה כָּנּוּ בְּכָל מָקוֹם מָרַת הַדִּין

B

nevertheless even the quoted saying is perverted, for
Gabriel is regarded as the messenger of God for the
punishment of sinners only, and in another passage of the
Talmud [1] it is actually said of him that he is called the [2]
one who stops up, because he stops up the sins of Israel *i.e.*,
wipes them away, and therefore he could never be
represented to the Israelites as their enemy.

Further, Muḥammad's intentional misrepresentation [3] is
shown by his changing the order assigned by the Jews to
the Angels. The Jews assert that Michael stands at
God's right hand and Gabriel on His left.[4] This position
is reversed by Muḥammad, in order to give the highest rank
to Gabriel [5] to whom he attributes all his revelations. This

---

לְנַבְרִיאֵל דְּאָמְרָם בָּא גַּבְרִיאֵל וַחֲבָטָן בְּמַרְקַע גַּבְרִיאֵל בָּא לַחֲפוֹד
אתְיסִדוֹם

"Our sages, blessed be their memory, attributed the execution of God's
punitive judgments to Gabriel, as, for instance, Gabriel came and over-
threw them in the earth (Sanhedrin 19. 1), and Gabriel came to destroy
Sodom." Comp. also Sanh. 21. 26. 95, 2. 96.

[1] Sanhedrin 44.

שֶׁאוֹטֵם עֲוֹנֹתֵיהֶם שֶׁל יִשְׂרָאֵל [2]

[3] These words must be taken in the sense explained at the end of the
3rd Section of the 1st Division.

[4] Comp. the evening prayer of the Jews.

מִימִינִי מִיכָאֵל וּמִשְׂמֹאלִי גַּבְרִיאֵל ;

Also the prayer on the Day of Atonement.

מִיכָאֵל מִיָּמִין מְהַלֵּל גַּבְרִיאֵל מִשְׂמֹאל מְמַלֵּל

[5] Comp. also Midrash Tanchuma Sect. וינש f. 21. c. 2. Venetian Ed.
1545, where it is written הַמָּשֵׁל וָפַחַד עִמּוֹ הַמָּשֵׁל זֶה מִיכָאֵל וָפַחַד

זֶה גַּבְרִיאֵל מִיכָאֵל מִן הַמַּיִם וְגַבְרִיאֵל מִן הָאֵשׁ וְאֵינָן מַזִּיקִין זֶה
אֶת זֶה הֲוֵי אוֹמֵר עֹשֶׂה שָׁלוֹם בִּמְרוֹמָיו

"The verse Job, xxv. 2, 'Dominion and fear are with Him,' refers to
Michael and Gabriel, in that the former is made out of water, and the
latter out of fire; still they do not hurt each other, because ' He maketh
peace in His high places.'" Here all the facts which we sought out
separately are given briefly. Michael is the milder, Gabriel the more
terrible, but they are nevertheless in perpetual harmony.

is in spite of the fact that the other view is so fully in accord with the spirit of the doctrine about angels as accepted by the Jews, according to which the positions " on the right" and " on the left " mean only the decision to adopt either merciful or punitive measures. There can of course be no question of enmity between Gabriel and the Jews, or between Gabriel and Michael, and the speech is nothing but a repartee, which however to Muḥammad's thinking justified him in making an accusation against the Jews. This is even more clearly shown in the following narrative related by a commentator on the words " God is poor"[1]: " Thus spoke the Jews when they had heard :—' Who is he that will lend unto God a goodly loan?' Qurán II. 246. It is related that Muḥammad with Abu Bakr had written to the Jews of the Banu Qainuqáʿ calling them to Islâm, to faithful observance of prayer, to offer free will offerings and to give God a good loan. Then Phineas the son of Azariah[2] said : ' Then God is poor, that he desires a loan' ? Abu Bakr boxed his ears and said : ' If there were not a

---

[1] Baidhâwi on Qurán III. 177.

إِنَّ ٱللّٰهَ فَقِيرٌ " God is poor."

قاله اليهود لما سمعوا من ذا الذي يقرض الله قرضا حسنا وروى انه عليه الصلاة والسلام كتب مع ابى بكر رضى الله عنه الى يهود بنى قينقاع يدعونهم الى الاسلام واقام الصلاة وايتاء الزكاة وان يقرضوا الله قرضا حسنا فقال فنحاص بن عازوراء ان الله فقير حين سال القرض فلطمه ابوبكر رضى الله عنه لولا ما بيننا من العهد لضربت عنقك فشكله الى رسول الله صلعم وجحد ما قاله ونزلت *

[2] Phineas the son of Azariah (פנחס בן עזריה), the same to whom the utterance that Ezra is the son of God (ix. 30) is attributed by some.

قال عبيد بن عمير انما قال هذه المقالة رجل واحد من اليهود اسمه فنحاص بن عازورا وهوالذى قال ان الله فقير ونحن الاغنيا *

" ʿAbid ben ʿUmr says : Only one Jew used this expression, and that was Phineas the son of Azariah, the same man who said : God is poor and we are rich." (Elpherar on ix. 30.)

truce between us, I would have broken your neck.' He
then took him bound to Muḥammad, and Phineas denied
having made the speech. Then came this revelation."
The same thing is found in another passage [1] : " The Jews
say the hand of God is tied up." The meaningless character
of the sentence shews in itself that the Jews were not in
earnest ; and if we take into consideration the occasion of
the remark, and the way in which it was made, we shall see
clearly the teasing and scoffing tendency of the Jews in
their dealings with Muḥammad. It was an answer to
an expression, which in its simple meaning " To lend to
God " must have seemed to them ridiculous, and which
might easily give rise to the retort, " if God now needs
money, He must be poor." It was only by a certain amouṇj
of distortion and mutilation that Muḥammad could twist
this speech into an accusation against the Jews. A good
story is preserved for us in Sunna 608 which runs as
follows : " After the conquest of Khaibar the Jews set a
poisoned lamb before Muḥammad. When he discovered
this, he had them called together, and putting them on
oath to tell him the truth, he asked if they had poisoned
the lamb. They confessed, and he then enquired, ' For
what reason ? ' ' To rid ourselves of you, if you are a
deceiver,' was their reply ; ' for if you are a prophet, poison
will do you no harm.' " Who can fail to see in this answer
a desire to free themselves from the importunity of
Muḥammad by biting repartee ?

At other times they changed his words, or used words of
double meaning. In the prescribed salutation they said
indeed " Rá'iná," but not in the sense intended by
Muḥammad, *viz.*, " look on us " ; but either in the sense of
" count us guilty, or with a play on the Hebrew " rạ " in

---

[1] Qurán V. 69. وَقَالَتِ ٱلْيَهُودُ يَدُ ٱللّٰهِ مَغْلُولَةٌ

the sense of the evil one." [1] So that he was obliged to substitute " andhurna," which also means " look on us." [2] Further instead of hittat [3], " forgiveness", they said probably " Khatiat" [4], " Sin." Jalálu'd-dín [5] gives another variation and says that instead of the required word " hubbat", love, the Jews said " habbat fi sh'aírat" i.e., " A grain in an ear of barley." Then they changed the salutation "As-salám 'alaika" [6] i.e., " Peace be upon thee", into " As-sám 'alaika" [7] which means " Mischief on thee," [8] and this is the ground of Muhammad's complaint in Súrah lviii. 9. Such occurrences, though they led later to a great hatred on his part towards the Jews, must at first, while he still had a hope of converting them, have induced him to try all possible means to conciliate them ; for they

---

[1] רַע " ra."

Jalálu'd-dín says (Maracci in loco) :

و هو بلغة اليهود سبّ من الرعونة " And this is among the Jews a word of reproach meaning folly."

[2] اَنْظُرْنَا Qurán II. 98, IV. 48. 49.

[3] حِطَّة VII. 161, 162, II. 55, 56.

[4] خَطِيَّة

[5] Jalálu'd-dín (Maracci.)

حِبَّة " hubbat" i.e. love.

حبّة فى شعيرة " habbat fi sh'aírat" i.e. a grain in an ear of barley.

[6] اَلسَّلَامُ عَلَيْكَ

[7] اَلسَّامُ عَلَيْكَ

[8] On this Elpherar comments as follows :

و ذلك ان اليهود كان يدخلون على النبى صلعم و يقولون السام عليك والسام هوالموت يوهمونه انهم يقولون السلام عليك *

The meaning " death" which Elpherar here assigns to the word سام is quite foreign to it, as is also " contempt", which is more appropriate for سوم. The commentators appear, therefore, to have had in mind the Hebrew word סם, which with הַמָּוֶת understood would mean " poison."

were not only important politically, but were also able
to hold him up to derision by their intellect and wit.
He was anxious therefore to persuade them that his views
were on the whole the same as theirs with some few
differences.

We have given sufficient reasons for Muḥammad's
treating the Jews with consideration, and we shall now
give proofs that he actually made great efforts to win them
over to his way of thinking. Besides the frequent religious
controversies already alluded to, there are many passages
in the Qurán specially addressed to the Jews, in all of
which they are admonished in a very friendly way that the
Qurán would serve as an arbitrator in their own disputes.
Not only did he address them with gentleness and
consideration, he actually did many things on purpose to
please them. At first simply and solely on account of the
Jews the Qibla, or place towards which prayer was to be
made, was changed by Muḥammad to Jerusalem, from
Mecca the spot which the ancient Arabs had always
regarded as holy; and it was only when he recognised the
fruitlessness of attempting to conciliate the Israelites that
he changed back to the former direction.

The first change is not, it is true, stated in so many words
in the Qurán, only a complaint about the second alteration
is given, but some commentators maintain that the allusion
is to the former change.[1] In disputes between Muslims
and Jews he shewed himself at times perhaps too lenient.
This is said to have given occasion to some believers to

---

[1] Qurán II. 136. مَا وَلَّيهُمْ عَنْ قِبْلَتِهِمُ ٱلَّتِى كَانُوا عَلَيهَا

Jalálu'd-dín (Maracci in loco) has as follows:

لما هاجر امر باستقبال بيت المقدس تألفًا لليهود ستة او سبعة شهرا

ثم حول

"After his Flight he ordered his followers to turn to the Temple at
Jerusalem (בֵּית הַמִּקְדָּשׁ) ; this however, which was done to conciliate
the Jews, held good for six or seven months only, and then he changed it
again."

refuse to submit to his judgment, of which he complains in
Súrah IV. 63. In another passage[1] he guards himself
against the accusation of giving wrong judgment by saying
that he judges only according to the right; and again in
another passage[2] he asks, if they are afraid that God and
His apostle will do them wrong, though the commentators
relate another event as the occasion for this utterance.
He advises his Muslims also to go gently in disputes with
the Jews,[3] as e.g. in the following passage: "Dispute not
against those who have received the Scriptures, unless in
the mildest manner; except against such of them as
behave injuriously towards you: and say, 'We believe in the
revelation which hath been sent down unto us, and unto
you; our God and your God is one, and unto Him are we
resigned'".[4] A strong proof that Muḥammad held the Jews

---

[1] Súrah IV. 106. وَلَا تَكُنْ لِلْخَائِنِينَ خَصِيمًا

"Dispute not for those who deceive one another."

[2] Súrah XXIV. 49. أَمْ يَخَافُونَ أَنْ يَحِيفَ اللَّهُ عَلَيْهِمْ وَرَسُولُهُ

"Or do they fear lest God and His Apostle act unjustly towards them?"

[3] Súrah XXIX. 45. وَلَا تُجَادِلُوا أَهْلَ ٱلْكِتَابِ إِلَّا بِالَّتِي هِيَ أَحْسَنُ

إِلَّا ٱلَّذِينَ ظَلَمُوا مِنْهُمْ وَقُولُوا آمَنَّا بِٱلَّذِي أُنْزِلَ إِلَيْنَا وَأُنْزِلَ إِلَيْكُمْ وَإِلَٰهُنَا

وَإِلَٰهُكُمْ وَاحِدٌ وَنَحْنُ لَهُ مُسْلِمُونَ *

[4] In the opinion of Arabic commentators this passage is more a proof
of fear of the Jews than a recommendation to mild dealing. Elpherar in
a long chain of traditions beginning with عبد الواحد المليمى and ending
with ابو هريرة says:

كان اهل الكتاب يقرون التوراة بالعبرانية ويفسرونها بالعربية لاهل الاسلام
فقال رسول الله صلعم لا تصدقوا اهل الكتاب ولا تكذبوهم وقولوا امنا
بالله وما انزل *

"The possessors of the Scriptures (the Jews) read the Law in Hebrew
and explained it to the Muslims in Arabic; so Muḥammad said: 'Neither
agree with the possessors of the Scriptures, nor call them liars, and say
we believe, etc.'" Further, there is another similar narrative first related
by AbúSa'íd, ابو سعيد عبد الله بن احمد الظاهرى but which can be traced
back to Abú Namlatu'l-Ansári ابو نملة الانصارى, which reads as follows:

in great respect lies in the fact that in passages enumerating the different creeds [1], he mentions the Jews immediately after the Muslims.

In two of these passages he even promises Godfearing Jews absolute equality with Muslims; and though in the third and last he is not so lenient, and threatens that a distinction between them will be made, yet even in this passage it is very plain that precedence over other religious bodies is given to the Jews. In Muslim traditions it is said that the sinful among the Muslims will go into the first, the mildest of the seven hells,[2] the Jews into the second, Christians [3] into the third, and so on.[4]

In addition to all this, which produced in Muḥammad the wish to adopt much from Judaism into his religious system, we must consider the fantastic development which the

---

انه بينما هو جالس عند رسول الله صلعم جاءه رجل من اليهود و مر
بجنازة فقال يا محمد هل تتكلم هذه الجنازة فقال رسول الله صلعم
احدثكم (؟) اهل الكتاب فلا تصدقوهم ولا تكذبوهم ولكن قولوا امنا
بالله وملائكته وكتبه ورسله فان كان باطلا لم تصدقوهم وان كان حقا لم
تكذبوهم *

"While he was sitting by Muḥammad, a Jew who had just passed by a corpse came up and said : ' O Muḥammad, does this corpse speak ? ' He said : ' Neither agree with the possessors of the Scriptures, nor call them liars, but say : We believe in God, His angels, His word and His Apostles. If what the Jews say is vain, do not confirm them; if it is true, do not give them the lie,' " *i.e.* preserve a strictly negative attitude, so as on no account to expose yourselves; thus the meaning here seems to be almost identical with that of the word لَا تَتَوَلَّوْا referred to above.

[1] Súrahs II. 59, V. 73, XXII. 17.

الَّذِينَ آمَنُوا the Muslims.

الَّذِينَ هَادُوا the Jews.

[2] See Division I. Section II. Chap. i. Part II A.

[3] D'Herbelot in his Bibliotheque orientale (under "Jahond" page 441.) asserts on the contrary that the Muslims give the Jews a lower place in hell than the Christians, but this is probably the opinion of a later age.

[4] Pococke notæ miscellaneæ, Cap. 7 p. 289.

Jewish traditions and history had reached in the mouth
of the people, as certain to appeal powerfully to the poetic
genius of the prophet; and so we cannot doubt that, in so
far as he had the means to borrow from Judaism, and so
long as the Jewish views were not in direct opposition to
his own, Muḥammad was anxious to incorporate much
borrowed from Judaism into his Qurán. Whether he had
any such means will be discussed in the second section.

SECOND SECTION.

*Could Muḥammad borrow from Judaism? and if so, how was
such borrowing possible for him?*

The possibility of borrowing from Judaism lay for
Muḥammad, partly in the knowledge which might be
imparted to him by word of mouth through intercourse
with the Jews, and partly in personal knowledge of
their Scriptures; while allowing him the first source of
information, we must deny him the second.

From passages already quoted—to which we might add
many others—we gather that there must have been great
intimacy between Muḥammad and the Jews, leading at
times even to mutual discussion of views; but this is still
more clearly shown in a passage in the second Súra,[1]
where the Jews are represented as double faced, professing
belief when they were with him and his followers, and then
when they were alone saying: "Will ye acquaint them
with what God has revealed unto you, that they may
dispute with you?" This shows that the Muslims learned
the Jewish views from conversation only. We shall speak
later of Muḥammad's intimacy with 'Abdu'lláh ibn Salám,
and with Waraka, the cousin of Khadíja, who was for some
time a Jew, a learned man and acquainted with the Hebrew

---

[1] Súra II. 71.   اَتُحَدِّثُوْنَهُمْ بِمَا فَتَحَ اللّٰهُ عَلَيْكُمْ لِيُحَاجُّوْكُمْ هٖ

C

language and scriptures ;[1] so also was Ḥabíb ben Málik, a powerful Arabian prince,[2] who for some time professed the Jewish religion. These all afterwards became followers of the Prophet. Thus Muḥammad had ample opportunity of becoming acquainted with Judaism. That his knowledge thereof was not obtained from the Scriptures is clear, from the matter actually adopted, since there are mistakes, which cannot be regarded as intentional alterations, and which would certainly have been avoided by anyone who had the very slightest acquaintance with the sources.[3] It is evident also from the low level of culture to which Muḥammad himself and the Jews of his time and country had attained. The contempt in which the compilers of the Talmud held the Arabian Jews, in spite of their political power, can be attributed only to the ignorance of the latter.

Though we must not conclude from this that the Jews knew nothing of the Scriptures and, though we hear of schools among them [4] and even of their reading the sacred writings in the original,[5] still we must doubt, if there was any widely diffused critical knowledge of the Scriptures, and we may be quite certain that Muḥammad himself possessed none. Many passages testify to this. First, we may take a passage already quoted,[6] where he says he had formerly no knowledge of reading and writing, and then Súra XLII. 52,[7] where he denies any previous acquaintance with " the Book" or the " Faith." Even if these are mere figures of speech to prove the divine character of his mission, still it

---

[1] Vid. Elbecar in Maracc. Prodomi I. p. 44 ; and Wahl, Einleitung zur Uebersetzung des Koran XXX.

[2] Wahl, Einleitung XXXV.

[3] This will be explained in detail later.

[4] Comp. the passage quoted above from Baidháwi in the 1st Section.

[5] Comp. the passage quoted above from Elpherar in the First Section (foot note).

[6] Súra XXIX. 47.

[7] " Thou didst not understand before this what the book of the Qurán was, nor what the faith was, etc."—(Sale).

is evident from them that he never enjoyed any reputation for learning, such as would necessarily have been accorded to him, had he really known anything of the Jewish writings, and possessing which knowledge he would have lived in fear of being proved to be an impostor.

The order in which he gives the prophets is interesting, for immediately after the patriarchs he places first Jesus, then Job, Jonah, Aaron, Solomon, and last of all David.[1] In another passage[2] the order is still more ridiculous, for here we have David, Solomon, Job, Joseph, Moses, Aaron, Zacharias, John, Jesus, Elijah, Ismael, Elisha, Jonah, and Lot! The incorrect spelling of the names of these prophets, as well as the parts which he assigns to them in history, proves that he had never even looked into the Hebrew Scriptures. He actually asserts that before John the Baptist no one had borne the name of John. Had he known anything of Jewish history he would have been aware that, apart from some historically unimportant people of the name mentioned in Chronicles, the father and the son of the celebrated Maccabean high priest, Mattathias, were both called John. This mistake must have been obvious to the Arabic commentators, for they try to give another meaning to the clear and unmistakable words. Muḥammad himself was aware of his ignorance, and defends himself very neatly against the possible charge. For instance in two passages [3] he asserts that God said to him: "We have not spoken to thee about all the former prophets, only about some of them, of others we said nothing to thee;" thus cleverly defending himself against the accusation of having over-looked some of the prophets. We have quite enough proofs in these passages, apart from those which will come before us fully in the second part, that Muḥammad was singularly ignorant of the Jewish writings, and so we

---

[1] Qurán IV. 161. [2] Qurán VI. 84 ff.

[3] Súra IV. 162; XL. 78.

can afford to give up one thing which is generally
brought forward as specially proving our point. This is
the fact that in certain passages Muḥammad calls himself
an " *ummiyun*," [1] a word which is usually translated
"unlearned " " ignorant." Wahl takes it so, and mentions
it as a proof of Muḥammad's ignorance. But this word has
here the same meaning that is expressed by it in other
passages, viz., belonging to the Arabs. It is used, like the
word " jáhiliyat," [2] of the Arabs in their former ignorance
of Islám, and Muḥammad, having risen from among them,
thus designates himself [3] without reference to his own
individual knowledge. [4] But, as already stated, even
without this proof our conclusion holds good, viz., that
because of his own ignorance especially, but also on
account of that of the Jews around him, Muḥammad could

---

[1] Súra XII. 156.

[2] جَاهِلِيَّة Súra III. 148, III. 69.

[3] مِنَ الأُمِّيِّينَ mina'l-ummíyína or أُمِّيٌّ ummiyun.

[4] The derivation of the word seems to me to support this view. Many
different derivations have been suggested, but all are unsatisfactory. Some
commentators, quoted by Elpherar, derive it from أُمَّة ummat, and give
as examples of a similar formation مَكِّيٌّ makiyun, and مَدَنِيٌّ madaniyun
from مَكَّة makka and مَدِينَة madína (see Ewald's Critical Grammar
of the Arabic language, I. § 261. 2); but then they do not explain the
connection between the meanings of two words. This becomes clear,
however, when we consider the development in the meaning of the
similar Rabbinical word גּוֹי goi. This word, meaning in the Hebrew
" people," later on came to mean a " non-Jew; " because the Jews became
conscious that they themselves were a little community among the other
inhabitants of the land, who were the " people " proper (compare the
expression עַם הָאָרֶץ). So at first the Muslims also must have looked
upon themselves as a small community in the midst of the populace,
the أُمَّة, each man who was not counted among themselves, being
to them one of the أُمَّة, or an أُمِّيّ, and so the word came to be used of
all those who did not believe in revealed religion past and present.

attain to no knowledge of the Hebrew Scriptures, though on the other hand he had abundant opportunity to study Judaism with its wealth of tradition and legend as it lived in the mouth of the people.

In the first section we have shown that Muḥammad had good reasons for incorporating much taken from Judaism in his Qurán. By so doing he hoped to strengthen the opinion that he was taught by direct revelation from God; he had also a strong wish to win over the Jews to his kingdom of the faithful upon earth, and then, too, the legends and fanciful sayings of the Jews harmonised with his poetic nature. In the second section we have shown that he had abundant opportunities of acquainting himself with Judaism; and now in the third section, before finally determining that a borrowing from Judaism really took place, we have to consider and answer the question: Would such a borrowing have been consistent with the other views and opinions held by Muḥammad?

THIRD SECTION.

Was it compatible with Muḥammad's plan to borrow from Judaism?

We must consider this question from two sides.

First, it might have appeared to Muḥammad as inadvisable to borrow from the system of any other religious body lest he should be accused of want of individuality; and secondly, there might have been something in the very fact of adopting from Judaism which would militate against his other plans. On closer examination, however, we find that neither was the case. In general he was in favour of borrowing from earlier religions. He desired no peculiarity, no new religion which should oppose all that had gone before; he sought rather to establish one founded on the ancient creeds purified from later changes and additions, one which should adopt this or that new idea, and which

should above all things acknowledge him as a divinely
commissioned prophet. He let all that was already established stand good, as is seen from the lists of the prophets
quoted above ; and he counts it as a point in favour of his
Qurán that it is [1] in accord with the earlier writings
recognised by him as revelations. Another time he even
says that the Qurán is similar to the earlier religious
writings, that it is only a repetition of them, *i.e.*, if I am
not mistaken in forsaking the general interpretation and
translating the passage Súra XXXIX. 24 [2] as follows :
" God hath sent down the most excellent tidings, [3] a
writing like unto others, a repetition." If- this is not the
meaning, it is incomprehensible how Muḥammad could try to
prove the superiority of his Qurán by pointing to its continual
and almost wearisome repetitions. But if his assertion were
true, he might gain some advantage by being in accord
with earlier revealed writings, and by restoring to their
proper position those of them which had been spoiled by
additions and perversions, and those which had been too
little accounted of. He claims for himself only the same
honour which is paid to the other givers of revealed law ; [4]
with this distinction however that he, as the last of the

---

[1] Súra XLVI. 11.   مُصَدِّقٌ لِمَا مَعَهُم

أَللَّهُ نَزَّلَ أَحْسَنَ ٱلْحَدِيثِ كِتَابًا مُتَشَابِهًا مَثَانِيَ [2]

[3] On the word مَثَانِيَ masáni which is omitted by Elpherar see below
Second Division, Third Section, First Chapter, First Part.

[4] He seems to distinguish between lawgivers and prophets ; for while
he gives the names of the latter in utter confusion, he mentions the
former in their right order, viz., Noah, Abraham, Moses and Jesus (Súras
XXXIII. 7. XLII. 11.) Arabic commentators recognise this difference ; thus
Elpherar on Súra XXXIII. 7 : خص هولا الخمسة بالذكر من النبيين لانهم
اصحاب الكتب والشرائع و اولوا العزم من الرسل
He distinguishes these five viz., the four given above and Muḥammad,
naming them alone of the prophets, because they were the compilers of
writings and laws revealed to them, and were men of strong character
among the apostles.

prophets, is to be considered as the seal of the prophets,[1] and therefore as the most perfect among them, because his book is so clear [2] that no disputes or misunderstandings can arise about it, and, therefore, no apostle would be needed after himself. Thus it is clear that a borrowing from other religions was quite compatible with Muḥammad's general aim. Consideration for his Arab followers, i.e., the fear of being called a mere compiler, a reproach which he did not altogether escape, did not hinder him, from such borrowing, partly, because he believed that he might rely on their ignorance; partly, because he had only to prove the harmony which must necessarily exist between the various revelations of the same God. Muḥammad maintained that it was all revelation, that he derived nothing from Jew or Christian, but that God Himself revealed to him the contents of earlier Scriptures, and the historical facts concerning them. With regard to Judaism in particular Muḥammad found no special difficulty. We have already observed that much in it accorded with the Prophet's poetic spirit, and who can now assert that any objection to an agreement with Judaism would have been raised by Muḥammad's contemporaries? In those days people had not reached such a pitch of so-called enlightenment, as to consider the followers of one creed only as in the right, and to regard everything belonging to another belief as worthless; to restrict to Christians the elements common to humanity, and to condemn Judaism as crafty and lifeless. Thus it was possible for Muḥammad to lay before the Jews the points of union between his religion and their own, carefully avoiding the while those points in his doctrine which would be unacceptable to them.

It is clear in itself that he could not adopt the whole of

---

[1] خَاتَمُ ٱلنَّبِيِّينَ Súra XXXIII. 40.

[2] كِتَابٌ مُبِينٌ

Judaism into his system, but parts only and even these he was obliged to alter and rearrange. In bringing the Jews to his opinion he had to be careful not to alienate others; he could not, therefore, adopt from them such points as stood in complete contradiction to the views of other religious bodies; and so, while he totally excluded some things, he was obliged to elaborate and alter other things with which he could not dispense, in order that they might still more strengthen his own position. Of this he either became aware himself, or others reproached him with it, so that he was forced to assert [1] that the Qurán is not a new invented fiction. He could not maintain with the Jews that their Law was immutable, for that would have been fatal to his system of religious syncretism; nor could he with them expect a Messiah, because if there were another prophet yet to come, he Muḥammad could no longer claim to be the seal of the prophets. This last point was carried so far that the Arabs later on confounded the doctrine of a Dajjál, or deceiver, which they had borrowed from the Christians, with the doctrine of the expected Messiah of the later Jews; and the saying existed :[2] " The name of Dajjál among the Jews is Messiah the son of David." Much in confirmation of what has been stated above will be brought forward in the Second Section of the Second Division, and also in the Appendix.

While this investigation has for the most part consisted in enquiring into what was, or might well have been, in Muḥammad's mind, it is by no means to be imagined that we regard him as a deceiver who deceived intentionally, and with a well-weighed consideration of each step as to whether or no it would help him towards his aim of deluding others. Wahl regards him in this light. On the

---

[1] Súra XII. iii.   ما كان حديثًا يفترى

[2] اسم الدجال عند اليهود مسيح بن داود   Pococke Notæ Miscellaneæ, appendix to Porta Mosis, cap. 7, page 260.

contrary, we must guard ourselves carefully against such an opinion, and look upon it as a sign of persistent prejudice and total misunderstanding of the human heart. Muḥammad seems rather to have been a genuine enthusiast, who was himself convinced of his divine mission, and to whom the union of all religions appeared necessary to the welfare of mankind. He so fully worked himself into this idea in thought, in feeling and in action, that every event seemed to him a divine inspiration. Every thing necessary to the attainment of his aim stood out clearly before him, just because this one idea ruled him. He could think of nothing but what fitted in with it, could feel nothing but what harmonised with it, could do nothing but what was demanded by it. There is no question here of design, for this one idea so possessed his spirit, heart and will as to become the sole thought of his mind, so that every thing which entered his mind was shaped by this idea. Of course, in the most fanatical minds there are occasional lucid intervals, and during these Muḥammad certainly deceived himself and others; it is also undeniable that at times ambition and love of power were the incentives to his actions, but even so the harsh judgment generally passed upon him is unjustifiable.

We may say, as a result of this investigation, that it would be very remarkable if there were not much to be found in the Qurán which is clearly in harmony with Judaism. It is evident that Muḥammad sought to gain the Jews to his side, and this could best be done by approximating to their religious views; it is also evident that he had ample means of acquainting himself with these views; and lastly, that other considerations favoured rather than hindered such a borrowing from Judaism. And now the chief work remains to be done, and that is, to demonstrate by careful reference to the Qurán that borrowing from Judaism has actually taken place.

SECOND DIVISION.

Did Muḥammad borrow from Judaism? If so, what did he borrow?

Before we pass to the consideration of individual passages as instances of borrowing from Judaism, we must show some general historical grounds for the opinion that a borrowing from that source has taken place; and thus this division falls again into two sections, a general and a particular.

FIRST SECTION.

Did Muḥammad borrow from Judaism?

For the answer to this question we are thrown back entirely on the Qurán,[1] as we have no other literature

---

[1] The following story, is related by Kazuin—(Poc. Spec. p. 309):

روى ان رسول الله لما قدم المدينة وجد يهوديا يصومون عاشورا فسالهم عن ذلك فقالوا انه الذى غرق فيه فرعون وقومه ونجى موسى ومن معه فقال انا احق بموسى منهم فامر بصوم عاشورا *

"It is said that when the Apostle of God came to Madína, he found the Jews fasting on 'Áshúra. He asked them their reason for so doing, and they answered: 'Because on this day Pharaoh and his people were drowned, but Moses and his followers were saved'; on which Muḥammad said: 'I stand in closer connection with Moses than they do', and then he commanded the fast day 'Áshúra. The cause of the institution of the fast day 'Áshúra, which like עָשׂוֹר, the tenth day of the seventh month, (Leviticus XXIII, 27) clearly means the day of atonement, is very uncertain. Elpherar is not more exact, for he assigns an equally erroneous cause. On Súra XI. 46 he says:

و هبطوا يوم عاشورا فصام نوح و امر جميع من معه بالصوم شكر الله عزّ وجلّ

"And they went out (of the ark) on the day 'Áshúra, and Noah fasted and commanded all with him to fast out of gratitude to God." In any case, however, the important fact remains, that Muḥammad adopted one of the fast days of the Jews, which was afterwards abolished like the Jewish Qibla. See also D'Herbelot, Bibliotheque Orientale, under the word Aschour, page 127.

of the same date which treats of the matter in question.
Still there are plenty of passages there preserved to us,
which in a general way sufficiently prove our point; and
indeed they all contain either the blame expressed by
Muhammad's contemporaries at his borrowing from
Judaism, or else an appeal from him to the Jews, as
witnesses of the truth of his assertions. He complains
bitterly in many passages that the Arabs said his words
were not original,[1] and even called them antiquated lies.[2]
Sometimes they said still more definitely that a certain
man taught him,[3] and the addition of the words:[4]
"The tongue of the person unto whom they incline
is a foreign tongue, but this is the perspicuous Arabic
tongue," shows plainly that this man was a Jew.
Commentators take this view, and indeed think that it
was 'Abdu'lláh Ibn Salám, a learned Rabbi, with whom
Muhammad was in constant and close intercourse, and who
is frequently mentioned in the commentaries.[5] Another
rather more general statement is as follows:[6] "Other
people have assisted him therein;" on which Elpherar
remarks[7]: "Mujáhid says, by this he means the Jews."
Could any one desire a clearer historical witness than this
accusation, which was so often brought against Muhammad,

---

[1] أَسَاطِيرُ ٱلْأَوَّلِينَ Comp. Súras VIII. 31, XVI. 26, XXIII. 85, XXV. 6,
XXVII. 70, XLVI. 16, LXVIII. 15, LXXXIII. 13.

[2] إِنَّكَ قَدِيمٌ Súra XLVI. 10.

[3] إِنَّمَا يُعَلِّمُهُ بَشَرٌ Súra XVI. 105.

[4] لِسَانُ ٱلَّذِى يُلْحِدُونَ إِلَيْهِ أَعْجَمِىٌّ وَهَذَا لِسَانٌ عَرَبِىٌّ مُبِينٌ

[5] Abulfeda annales Moslemitici I. 283.

[6] Súra XXV. 5. أَعَانَهُ عَلَيْهِ قَوْمٌ آخَرُونَ

[7] قال مجاهد يعنى اليهود

and which appeared to him so important that he constantly referred to it in the hope of refuting the charge? He himself confesses, however, that much related by him is to be found in the earlier Scriptures. To the embarrassing question, as to why he never worked a miracle, he constantly answered that he who was called to be a preacher only, not a wonder-worker, had yet told them plainly of the miracles which are mentioned in the earlier writings,[1] and which the learned Jews knew well.[2] They could testify to the truth of these narratives,[3] and among them one man[4] especially, the aforesaid 'Abdu'lláh Ibn Salám,[5] to whom the laudatory passage in Súra III. 68 is said to refer. Not only were they to corroborate his words to others, but also to remove any doubt from Muḥammad's own mind as to the truth of his Mission. Thus we have in one place the injunction given to him:[6] " If thou art in doubt concerning that which we have sent down unto thee,

---

[1] Súras XX. 133. فِى ٱلصُّحُفِ ٱلْأُولَى XXVI. 196. فِى زُبُرِ ٱلْأَوَّلِينَ

[2] Súra XXVI, 197. يَعْلَمُهُ عُلَمَاءُ بَنِى إِسْرَآئِلَ

On which Elpherar: قال ابن عطية كانوا خمسة عبد الله بن سلام و
ابن ياسين وثعلبة واسد واسيد

[3] Súra XVII. 103. فَٱسْأَلْ بَنِى إِسْرَآئِلَ

[4] Súra XLVI. 9. شَهِدَ شَاهِدٌ مِنْ بَنِى إِسْرَآئِلَ

[5] Elpherar in the name of several commentators, says:

هو مسلام عبد الله بن سلام شهد على نبوة المصطفى محمد صلعم
امن به واستكبر اليهود فلم يومنوا

" This is . . . . , who testified to the prophetic mission of Muḥammad, the chosen one, and believed in him; but the Jews were arrogant and would not believe in him."

[6] Súra X. 94. فَإِنْ كُنْتَ فِى شَكٍّ مِمَّا أَنْزَلْنَا إِلَيْكَ فَٱسْأَلِ ٱلَّذِينَ يَقْرَءُونَ ٱلْكِتَابَ
مِنْ قَبْلِكَ

ask them who have read the book before thee."[7] If he then, however cunningly, acknowledges the Jews as to a certain extent witnesses to his revelations, we are justified in expressing our opinion that Judaism was one source of the utterances in the Qurán, and in this certainty we may proceed at once to discuss the actually borrowed passages.

SECOND SECTION.

What did Muḥammad borrow from Judaism ?

In the case of any single instance of borrowing, the proof that the passage is really of Jewish origin must rest on two grounds. First, it must be shown to exist in Judaism, and to prove this we have every facility. Secondly, in order to attain to certainty we must prove that it is really borrowed, i.e., that it is not founded on anything in old Arabian tradition, which Muḥammad used largely as a foundation though he disputed some points. Then again we must shew that it had its origin in Judaism and not in Christianity. For the complete discussion of the last two points it would be necessary to write two treatises similar to the one on which I am now engaged, of which the respective subjects would be—(1) the points of contact between Islám and the ancient tradition of the Arabs, and (2) the points of contact between Islám and Christianity ; and only in this way could certainty on these points be attained. But these investigations would, on the one hand, lead us too far away from our particular subject,

---

[7] On this Elpherar says : .... قَإِن ...... يعنى القران تاسأل

يخبرونك انك مكتوب عندهم فى التوراة

" By that which we have sent down to thee, the Qurán is meant ; those who have read before thee may instruct thee, that thou art foretold in the Law which they have ; " and again : يعنى من امن من اهل الكتاب

كعبد الله بن سلام و اصحابه " He means the believers among the possessors of the Scriptures, e.g., 'Abdu'lláh ben Salám and his fellows."

and, on the other, they would require a much more exact treatment than could be given while handling our main subject. Then, too, they are made unnecessary by the means which we use in each individual case, and which will be shown in the different divisions of the work; so that on most points we can without them attain to a high degree of probability, practically sufficient for all scientific purposes. For the sake of clearness, it may be well to divide the material borrowed from Judaism into thoughts belonging to it, and narratives taken from it, and later we shall have to subdivide again.

———

SECOND SECTION.
Chapter I.

Thoughts belonging to Judaism which have passed over into the Qurán ?

The new thoughts borrowed by one religion from another are of a twofold nature. Either they are radically new, there being hitherto in the borrowing religion not even a foreshadowing of them, so that the very conceptions are new, and require accordingly new words for their expression; or else the component parts of these thoughts have long been in existence but not in this combination, the form in which these conceptions are blended being a novel one, and the view, therefore, which arises from this unusual presentation being new. We must therefore divide this chapter according to these distinctions.

———

FIRST CHAPTER.
First Part.

Conceptions borrowed from Judaism ?

As the ushering in of hitherto unknown religious conceptions is always marked by the introduction of new words for their expression, and as the Jews in Arabia, even when able to speak Arabic, kept to the Rabbinical Hebrew names for their religious conceptions; so words which from their derivation are shown to be not Arabic but Hebrew, or better still Rabbinic, must be held to prove the Jewish origin of the conceptions expressed. The passage already quoted about the foreign language spoken by those who were accused of helping Muḥammad in writing the Qurán seems to point to the use among the Jews of a language other than Arabic. The object of this chapter is to enumerate the words which have passed from Rabbinical Hebrew into the Qurán, and so into the Arabic language.

Tábút, [1] Ark. The termination *út* is a fairly certain evidence that the word is not of Arabic but of Rabbinical Hebrew origin; [2] for this dialect of Hebrew has adopted in the place of other endings this termination, which is very common also in Chaldaic and Syriac; and I venture to assert that no pure Arabic word ends in this way.[3] Our word appears in two different passages with two different meanings: first, where the mother of Moses is told to put her son into an ark,[4] the signification being here purely Hebrew; but from this it arose that the ark of the covenant [5] was also called by this name. It is used thus especially [6] in the sense of coming before the ark in prayer. In the second Súra[7] we find it mentioned as a sign of the

---

[1] תֵּיבָה. تَابُوت

[2] Rabbinical Hebrew תֵּיבוּתָא.

[3] Comp. مَلَكُوت and طَاغُوت

[4] Súra XX. 39. Comp. תֵּבַת גֹּמֶא Ex. II. 3.

[5] אָרוֹן in the Bible.

[6] עָבַר לִפְנֵי הַתֵּיבָה. Comp. Mishna Berachoth V. 4.

[7] The Arabians sometimes use تبوت السكينة also in the meaning of "ark of the covenant" (D'Herbelot Bibliotheque Orientale under "Aschmouil.")

rightful ruler that through him the ark of the covenant [1] should return. [2]

Taurát, the Law. [3] This word like the Greek equivalent in the New Testament is used only for the Jewish revelation; and although Muḥammad, having only oral tradition, was not able to distinguish so exactly, yet it is obvious that he comprehended the Pentateuch alone under this name; [4] for among the Jewish prophets after the patriarchs he counts Moses alone as a lawgiver. For the most part the Law is mentioned in connection with the Gospel. [5]

Jannátu 'Adn, Paradise. [6] The word "'Adn" is not

---

[1] Súra II. 249.

[2] The masculine gender here given to this word, as indicated by the fact that فِيهِ refers to it, would appear strange, were it not that perhaps the old word אֲרוֹן was in mind; and the termination وَتْ being foreign to Arabic is in that language no sure indication of gender.

[3] תּוֹרָה תּוֹרָאة ὁ νόμος.

[4] Later Arabians maintained just the opposite. Ahmad ben 'Abdu'l-Halím (Maracc. Prod. I. p. 5.) says:

فقوله أخبرني بصفة رسول الله فى التوراة قد يراد فيه نفس الكتب كلها
وكلها تسمى توراة *

"If one says: Instruct me about the allusions to the Apostle of God in the Toráh, one understands by that expression all revealed scriptures, since they are all called Toráh; and further:

ولفظ التوراة قد عرف انه الكتب يراد جنس الشى يقراها اهل الكتاب
فيدخل فى ذلك الزبور ونبوة اشعيا وسائر النبوات خلا الانجيل *

"It is acknowledged that by the word Toráh are meant revealed writings, particularly those which the possessors of the scriptures (Jews and Christians) alike read; therefore it includes the Psalms, the prophecy of Isaiah and other prophecies, but not the Gospel."

However this does not alter the conviction which we have already expressed.

[5] اَلْأَنْجِيلُ Comp. Súras III. 2, 43, 58, 86, V. 70, VII. 157, IX. 112, LXI. 6, LXII. 5.

[6] גַּן עֵדֶן جَنَّات عَدْنٍ

known in the Arabic language in the sense of pleasure or
happiness, but this is the meaning which suits the word in
this connection.[1] In Hebrew this is the radical meaning ;
still this expression, viz., Garden of Eden, which occurs
often in the Bible, is never to be explained out and out as
Paradise ; but rather Eden[2] is there the proper name of
a region which was inhabited by our first parents in their
innocence, and the part in which they actually lived was a
garden of trees. It is only natural that this earthly region
of the golden age should by degrees have come to be
regarded as Paradise, in that the word itself[3] no longer
stands for the name of a place but is applied to a state of
bliss ;[4] though the Jews still held to Eden as a locality
also. It is clear from the translation "gardens of
pleasure" that the Jews of that time not merely transferred
the name Eden into Arabic, but carried over its supposed
etymology as well. The more distinctively Christian name[5]
occurs seldom in the Qurán, though it also is not quite

---

[1] The Arabic commentators give widely different meanings to the word,
but they know nothing of that given by us just because it is foreign to the
Arabic language. Elpherar seems to decide for the view that اَلاَمَة
as well as عَدَن, means permanence, as the pious will remain there
for ever.

[2] עֵדֶן

[3] i. e. עֵדֶן

[4] Muḥammad uses it thus in Súras IX. 73, XIII. 23, XVI. 33,
XVIII. 30, XIX. 62, XX. 78, XXXV. 30, XXXVIII. 50, XL. 8, LXI. 12, and
in other places he translates it جَنَّاتُ ٱلنَّعِيم e. g. V. 70, X. 9, XXII. 55.
XXXI. 7, XXXVII. 42, LXVIII. 34. Sometimes also he uses it in the
singular جَنَّةُ ٱلنَّعِيم XXVI. 85; and even without the article, جَنَّةُ نَعِيم
LVI. 88, LXX. 38.

[5] جَنَّاتُ ٱلْفِرْدَوْس ὁ παράδεισος.

E

strange to later Judaism, as is shown by the story of the four who went alive to Paradise. [1]

Jahannam, Hell. [2] This word also, like its opposite Paradise, is of Jewish origin. According to its primary meaning and Biblical usage it too is the name of a place, though of a locality far less important than that which gave its name to Paradise. The vale of Hinnom was nothing more than a spot dedicated to idol worship; and it is remarkable that the horror of idolatry led to the use of its name to designate hell. That this is the ordinary name for it in the Talmud needs no proof, and from it is derived the New Testament name Gehenna. Now, it might be asserted that Muḥammad got this word from the Christians; but, even setting aside the argument that, as the name for Paradise is Jewish the probabilities are in favour of a Jewish origin for the word for hell also, the form of the word itself speaks for its derivation from Judaism. We lay no stress on the fact that the aspirate *he*, which is not expressed in the Greek, reappears in the Arabic, because this aspirate though not always indicated by grammarians in writing, appears to have been always sounded in speech. This holds good of other Greek words which have passed into Syriac. [3] The letter mím which stands at the end of the Arabic (Jahannam), not being found in the Syriac word, proves the derivation from the

---

[1] פַּרְדֵּס Paradise, Chagiga fol. 14. Compare Súra, XVIII. 107. XXIII. 11.

Among many wrong explanations Elpherar gives the following correct one: قال مجاهد هو البستان بالرومية و قال الزجاج هو منقول الى لفظ العربية

" Mujáhid says it means a garden in Greek, and Zajáj says it has passed into Arabic."

[2] גֵּיהִנֹּם   جَهَنَّم

[3] *E.g.* σύνοδος, *i.e.*, Sunhadus and especially γέεννα, which is pronounced in Syriac, as Gíhano.

Hebrew word, (Gehinnom). The word is found in many places in the Qurán. [1]

Ahbár [2]. This word is found in several places in the Qurán in the sense of teacher. Now the real Hebrew word [3] " hábher, " companion, has acquired in the Mishna a meaning similar to that of " párúsh; " [4] only that the latter was the name of a sect, and the former the name of a party within a sect. The word párúsh means, properly speaking, one separated, *i.e.*, one who withdraws himself out of motives of piety, a Pharisee, as distinguished from one who grasps without scruple all the pleasures of this life, a Sadducee. Among those who were thus separated there grew up a difference from others not only in social customs, but especially in that they adopted a different doctrinal view, viz., a belief in oral tradition. They had also some very strict principles for the guidance of their lives. But the matter was no longer merely one of great carefulness in life and conduct, it became one of special learning and knowledge, which naturally could not be imparted in equal measure to all members of this sect. Hence these learned men, each of whom possessed some special knowledge, became greatly reverenced; and in this way again a community was formed in contra-distinction to which the remaining people of the country were called the laity. [5] The individual members of this community however were called habhérím, [6] " fellows;" and thus, though the meaning ' teacher' is not, properly speaking, in the

---

[1] Súras II. 201, III. 10, 196, IV. 58, 95, 99, 115, 120, etc.

[2] חֲבֵרִים أَحْبَار   V. 48, 68, IX. 31, 34.

[3] חָבֵר

[4] פָּרוּשׁ

[5] עַם הָאָרֶץ, λαϊκος from λαος.

[6] חֲבֵרִים

word itself, yet the peculiar development of this community is the cause of the new meaning of the word.

The excessive veneration paid to these "fellows" by
the Jews gives rise to Muḥammad's reproof in the two
passages last alluded to. He reproaches the Christians
too in both places [1] on account of the esteem in which
they held the ruhbán. This word ruhbán is probably not
derived from rahiba,[2] to fear (thus god-fearing) ; but, like
qissísún [3] the word which accompanies it in Súra V. 85, is
to be derived from the Syriac, which language maintained
its preeminence among the Christians in those regions ;
thus ruhbán is derived from the Syriac word rábhóyé, and
qissísún from the Syriac qáshishóyé.

So then ruhbán does not really mean the ordinary
monks, who are called dáiré, but the clergy ; whereas
qissís stands for the presbyter, the elder, who is called
qáshishó in Syríac.

Darasa [4] = to reach the deep meaning of the Scripture
by exact and careful research. Such a diligent enquiry
is mentioned in several passages.[5] But this kind of
interpretation, which is not content to accept the obvious
and generally accepted meaning of a passage, but which
seeks out remote allusions—this (though it may bring much
of importance and value to light, if used with tact and
knowledge of the limits of the profitable in such study)

---

[1] Súra IX. 31. 34, رُهْبَان ruhbán.

[2] رَهِبَ

[3] قَسِّيسُونَ

[4] דָּרַשׁ دَرَس

[5] Súras III. 73, XXXIV. 43, LXVIII. 37, VII. 168. On the last passage
Elpherar says : ودرس الكتاب قراته و تدبيرة مرة بعد اخرى
The دَرَس of a writing means, to read it and arrange it over and
over again.

is very apt to degenerate and to become a mere laying
of stress on the unimportant, a searching for meanings
where there are none, and for allusions which are purely
accidental. And so the word acquired a secondary meaning, viz., to trifle, to invent a meaning and force it into
a passage. Compare the standing expression [1] current
among many who seek [2] the simple primary meaning.
The word in this usage occurs in the Qurán, particularly
in the mouth of Muhammad's opponents; though until now
this fact has not been recognised. The obviously misunderstood passage in Súra VI. 105 [3] is thus explained, also that
in VI. 157. [4] The former may be thus translated: "And
when we variously explain our signs, they may say if they
like: Thy explanations are far fetched, we will expound it
to people of understanding"; and the latter as follows:
"Lest ye should say: the Scriptures were only sent down
unto two peoples before us, but we turn away from their
system of forced explanation"; i.e., they have left the
Scriptures to us so overlaid and distorted that we cannot
follow them. It is remarkable that this word, which is not
a usual one in the Qurán, appears in this sense only in the
sixth Súra where it occurs twice; and this is evidence that
just at the time of the composition of this Súra the word
in its secondary meaning was used by some persons as
a reproach to Muhammad. This observation furthermore
might well serve to indicate the unity of this Súra.

Rabbáni [5] teacher. This Rabbinical word is probably

---

[1] וְהַדְּרָשָׁה תִדְרַשׁ

[2] פְּשָׁטָנִים

[3] وَلِيَقُولُوا دَرَسْتَ

[4] عَنْ دِرَاسَتِهِمْ

[5] רַבָּן רַבָּנִי

formed by the addition of the suffix án [1] (like nú) to the
word "rab," thus, our lord or teacher. For though the
termination "án" is common in later Hebrew,[2] yet the
weaker word "rabbi" shows that people did not hesitate
to append a suffix to the word rab, and then to treat the
whole as a new word. However that may be, rabbán is a
word of itself now, and is only conferred as a title on the
most distinguished teachers. The Rabbinical rule runs
thus [3] "Greater than rabbi is rabbán." It appears as a
title of honour in Súras III. 73, V. 48, 68. Rabbáni is
evidently a word of narrower meaning than the word
aḥbár explained above; and this explains why rabbáni is
put before aḥbár in the two passages last mentioned,
where they both appear, and also the striking omission of
our word in the other two places where aḥbár occurs, and
where Muḥammad finds fault with the divine reverence
paid to teachers, describing them with the more general
word. The case is the same with qissís and ruhbán. Both
classes are mentioned with praise in Súra V. 85, and with
blame in Súra IX. 31, 34, the latter class however only in
connection with, aḥbár, in that ruhbán (like aḥbár) is
of wider meaning: and further, on account of the combination in one passage of two different classes among the
Jews and Christians, viz., the aḥbár and the ruhbán,
(Cf. other similar combinations) no special differentiation
was to be attempted.

Sabt [4] day of rest, Saturday. This name continued to
be applied to Saturday throughout the East by Christians
as well as Muslims, though it had ceased to be a day of

---

[1] Suffix וֹן‎ ־ָ like וֹ

[2] Suffix ־ָן‎ Syriac. ono. Arabic أَنْ

[3] גָּדוֹל מֵרַבִּי רַבָּן

[4] שַׁבָּת‎ سَبْت‎

rest. [1] In one place [2] Muḥammad seems rather to protest against its being kept holy. The well-known Ben Ezra remarks on this in his commentary on Exodus xvi. 1,[3] where he says: "In Arabic five days are named according to number, first day, second day, etc. But the sixth day is called the day of assembly,[4] for it is the holy day of the week; the Sabbath however is called by the Arabs *sabt*, because the Shin [5] and the Sámech, (*i.e.*, the Arabic *sin* which is pronounced like the Hebrew Sámech) interchange in their writings. They have taken the word from Israel."

Sakínat [6] the Presence of God. In the development of Judaism in order to guard against forming too human an idea of the Godhead, it was customary to attribute the speaking of God, when it is mentioned in the Scripture, to a personified word of God,[7] as it were embodying that emanation from the Deity which came in Christianity to a veritable Incarnation. In like manner also when in the Scriptures the remaining stationary, or the resting of God is mentioned, something sensible proceeding from Him is to be thought of. This is especially so in the case of God's dwelling in the Temple; [8] and this 'emanation of the

---

[1] Súras II. 61, VII. 163.

[2] Súra XVI. 125.

[3] בְּלָשׁוֹן עֲרָבִי קָרְאוּ חֲמִשָּׁה יָמִים עַל דֶּרֶךְ הַמִּסְפָּר וְיוֹם שִׁשִּׁי אלגומע עַל שֵׁם חִבּוּרָם כִּי הוּא לָהֶם הַיּוֹם הַנִּכְבָּד בַּשָּׁבוּעַ וְיוֹם שַׁבָּת קָרְאוּ אוֹתוֹ סבת כִּי הַשִּׁין וְהַסָּמֶךְ מִתְחַלְּפִים בִּכְתִיבָתָם וְאֵלֶּה מִיִּשְׂרָאֵל לָמָדוּ

[4] اَلْجُمْعَة

[5] שׁ Shin.

[6] שְׁכִינָה سَكِينَة

[7] מֵימְרָא דַיְיָ λόγος τοῦ θεοῦ.

[8] וְשָׁכַנְתִּי בְּתוֹכָם Ex. XXV. 8, Cf. Deut. XXXIII. 12, 16.

Godhead' to adopt the speech of the Gnostics, was called on this account the Shekinah, the resting. From this derivation Shekinah came to be the word for that side of Divine Providence which, as it were, dwells among men and exerts an unseen influence among them. In the original meaning, viz. that of the Presence in the Temple over the Ark of the Covenant between the Cherubim,[1] the word is found in Súra II. 249. In the sense of active interposition and visible effectual rendering of aid it occurs in Súra IX. 26, 40 ;[2] in the sense of supplying peace of mind and at the same time giving spiritual aid it is found in Súra XLVIII. 4, 18, 26.[3] It is remarkable that the word appears in three Súras only, (but several times in the two last mentioned,) and with a somewhat different meaning in each ; and it seems here again, as we remarked above on the word *darasa*, as though outside influence had been at work, *i.e.*, that the use of this word by other people seems to have influenced Muḥammad at the time of the composition of these Súras.

Tághút[4] error. Though this mild word for idolatry is

---

[1] Ex. XXV. 22.

[2] Arabic commentators do not seem willing to recognise this meaning. Elpherar on Súra IX. 26 says the word means الامن و الطمانينة, security and rest ; and on Súra XLVIII. 4 he says distinctly ;

قال بن عباس كل سكينة فى القرآن فهى طمانينة الا التى فى سورة البقرة

" Ben 'Abbás says this word Sakínat in the Qurán always means rest except in the second Súra." But even if طمانينة does mean inward peace of mind, still the meaning of outward security need not be excluded.

[3] Elpherar uses the expression الطمانينة والوقار to explain verse 4, and الطمانينة والرضا to explain verse 18. In the same way D'Herbelot (Bibliotheque Orientale under Thalout, page 862) gives in the name of the commentators the explanation تسكين الخاطر *i.e.*, tranquillity of the mind.

[4] שעות, طَاغُوت

not found in the Rabbinical Writings,[1] still the Jews in Arabia seem to have used it to denote the worship of false gods, for it appears in the Qurán [2] in this sense. [3]

Furqán, [4] deliverance, [5] redemption. This is a very important word, and it is one which in my opinion has till now been quite misunderstood. In the primary meaning it occurs in the 8th Súra : " O true believers! if ye fear God, He will grant you a deliverance [6] and will expiate your sins, etc." Elpherar gives five different explanations to this verse, each as unsuitable as Wahl's translation, and the passage seems to me truly classical for the primary meaning of the word. This meaning appears also in Súra VIII. 42, where the day of the Victory of Badr is called the day of deliverance, [7] and in Súra II. 181 where this name is given to the month Ramadhan as the month of redemption and deliverance from sin. Muḥammad entirely diverging from Jewish ideas, intended to establish his religion as that of the world in general ; further he condemned the earlier times altogether calling them times of ignorance. [8] He declared his creed to have been revealed through God's Apostles from the earliest times, and to have been only renewed and put into a clearer and

---

[1] It is to be observed however that the Targums frequently use this word in the plural מַעֲרָא for the idols themselves, but not for idolatry.

[2] Súras II. 257, 259, IV. 63, XVI. 38, XXXIX. 19.

[3] الاوثان as Elpherar explains it.

[4] פֻּרְקָן فُرْقَان

[5] Ibn Said according to Elpherar explains this word as follows :

الفرقان النصر على الاعدا

" Furqán is help against the enemy." Súra XXI. 49.

[6] Súra VIII. 29. نَجْعَلْ لَكُمْ فُرْقَانًا

[7] يَوْم الْفُرْقَان

[8] جَاهِلِيَّة

more convincing form by himself. Hence the condition
of any one outside his belief must have seemed to him
a sinful one, and the divine revelation granted to himself
and his predecessors appeared to him in the light of
deliverance from that sinful life which could only lead to
punishment; and therefore he calls revelation itself in
many places Furqán, as in many he calls it raḥmat, [1] mercy.
In some passages he applies the term to the Qurán, [2] and
in others to the Mosaic revelation. [3]

In this way all the passages fit in under the primary
signification of the word, and there is no need to guess at a
different meaning for each.

Má'ún, [4] refuge. This word bears a very foreign impress,
and is explained by the Arabic Commentators in a variety
of ways. Golius following them, forces the most diverse
meanings into it. It appears in Súra CVII. 7, and seems
to me to mean a refuge—" they refuse refuge," *i.e.*, they
give no shelter to those asking for help. Later on the word
seems to have been regarded as derived from ' ána [5]
(certainly not from ma'ana to which Golius refers it),
and thence it acquired the meaning of support, alms.

Masáni, [6] repetition. There has been much perplexity
about this word, mainly because it has been considered as
an Arabic word and has not been traced back to its source.
As by degrees other teaching viz., tradition, [7] grew up by
the side of that contained in Holy Writ, the whole law

---

[1] رَحْمَة

[2] Súras III. 2, XXV. title and verse 1.

[3] Súras II. 50, XXI. 49.

[4] מָעוֹן‎, مَاعُون

[5] From عَانَ not from مَعَنَ

[6] מִשְׁנֶה‎, مَثَانِى

[7] Compare under أَحْبَار

was divided into two parts, [1] the written teaching, that is
the Bible, and the teaching by word of mouth or tradition.
To occupy oneself with the former was called " to read ;" [2]
to occupy oneself with the latter was called " to say." [3]
In the Chaldaic Gemara the latter word means to speak
after, to repeat the teacher's words after him. In like
manner the word tinnah [4] was used almost exclusively of
choral music, in which the choir repeated verses after the
precentor. Thus teaching by word of mouth was called
mishnah, [5] and so also the collection of oral teaching—the
whole tradition ; and afterwards when this was all written
down the book received the same name. Now, however, an
etymological error crept in and derived this word from
shánáh in its true Hebrew meaning " to repeat," and then
applied it to the repetition of the written teaching.[6] The
error of this explanation is shown both in the use of the
word and in its inflection.[7] Still it seems to have been
accepted by the Roman Jews, and thus it came about that
in Justinian's Novels the Mishna is called secunda editio. [8]
The same thing happened in the case of the Arabian Jews,
and so we get our word masáni. Muḥammad putting his
book in the place of the whole Jewish teaching calls it not
only Qurán (miqrá) but also masáni. [9]

---

[1] תּוֹרָה שֶׁבְּעַל פֶּה and תּוֹרָה שֶׁבִּכְתָב

[2] קָרָא

[3] שָׁנָה connected with the poetic תִּנָּה and the Syriac tano.

[4] תִּנָּה

[5] מִשְׁנָה

[6] מִשְׁנֵה תּוֹרָה

[7] מִשְׁנַת in construct, not מִשְׁנֶה

[8] δευτέρωσις.

[9] Súras XV. 87, XXXIX. 24.

The Arabian commentators on Súra XV. 87 differ much in their
explanation of this word, but one among them gives what seems to us

Malakút, [1] government. This word is used only of God's
rule, in which connexion it invariably appears also in
Rabbinical writings. [2] It occurs in several passages in the
Qurán. [3] From this narrow use of the word, and from a
false derivation from malá,k or malak [4] (a word which
comes from quite a different root, and which in Arabic has
only the meaning of a messenger of God) it came to be
used for the realm of spirits. [5]

These fourteen words, which are clearly derived from the
later, or Rabbinical Hebrew, shew what very important
religious conceptions passed from Judaism into Islám,—
namely, the idea of the Divine guidance, sakínat, malakút ; [6]

---

the true meaning. Elpherar has : وقال الطاوس القران كله مثانى "Tavus
says the whole Qurán is called Masáni." At the same time also a
reference is made to the other passage cited by us, viz., Súra XXXIX. 24.

The word سبعا in Súra XV. 87, seems to me to mean either that this
Súra was really the seventh (the order of the Súras was afterwards much
changed, and we may safely assert that Súra II is of later date than those
following it), or else سبع bears the meaning سبع and مسبع the
seventh part, as fifteen Súras make up about one-seventh of the Qurán.
Elpherar omits the word مثانى in the latter passage, a fact not satis-
factorily accounted for by the supposition that he relied on an earlier
explanation, for the Arabic writers always give the unexplained passages
in full in their commentaries ; and thus it seems that this word must
have been altogether missing from Elpherar's text.

[1] מַלְכוּת , مَلَكُوت

[2] מַלְכוּת שָׁמַיִם ἡ βασιλεία τῶν οὐρανῶν.

[3] Súra VI. 75, VII. 184, XXIII. 90, XXXVI. 83.

[4] (מַלְאָךְ) مَلَك or مَلَاك

[5] Compare the words عالم الملكوت in Professor Freitag's work, Fakiha
Elcholafa 85. 3.

[6] مَلَكُوت , مَكِينَةٌ   God's guiding Presence.

   مَثَانى , فُرْقَانٌ   Revelation.

   جَهَنَّم , جَنَّاتُ عَدْنٍ   Judgment after death.

of revelation, furqán, masáni; of judgment after death, jannátu 'adn and jahannam, besides others which will be brought forward as peculiar to Judaism.

Second Part.
Views borrowed from Judaism.

While in the foregoing section we were content to consider it certain that a conception was derived from Judaism, if the word expressing that conception could be shown to be of Jewish origin, we must now pass on from this method of judging and adopt a new test. We must prove first in detail that the idea in question springs from a Jewish root; then to attain to greater certainty we must further shew that the idea is in harmony with the spirit of Judaism, that apart from Judaism the conception would lose in importance and value, that it is in fact only an off-shoot of a great tree. To this argument may be added the opposition, alluded to in the Qurán itself, which this foreign graft met with from both Arabs and Christians. For the better arrangement of these views we must divide them into three groups: *A.* Matters of Creed or Doctrinal views, *B.* Moral and legal rules, and *C.* Views of Life.

A. Doctrinal Views.

We must here set a distinct limit for ourselves, in order on the one hand that we may not drift away into an endless undertaking and attempt to expound the whole Qurán; and on the other that we may not go off into another subject altogether and try to set forth the theology of the Qurán; an undertaking which was begun with considerable success in the Tübingen Zeitschrift für Evang. Theol. 1831, 3tes Heft. Furthermore, certain general points of belief are so common to all mankind that the existence of any one of them in one religion must not be considered as

proving a borrowing from another. Other views again
are so well-known and so fully worked out that we need
not discuss them in detail, but shall find a mere mention
of them sufficient. Of this kind is that of the idea of the
unity of God, the fundamental doctrine of Israel and Islám.
At the time of the rise of the latter, this view was to be
found in Judaism alone, [1] and therefore Muḥammad must
have borrowed it from that religion. This may be considered as proved without any unnecessary display of learning
on the point. The idea of future reward and punishment
is common to all religions, but it is held in so many
different ways that we shall be obliged to consider it in
our argument. Cardinal points of faith have also passed
from Judaism into Christianity. To decide whether these
points as adopted in the Qurán have come from the Jews
or from the Christians, we must direct our special attention
to a comparison between the forms in which the beliefs are
held in both those religions, and the form in which they
are presented to us by Muḥammad. This is to answer the
objection, that in the following discussion so little is to be
found about the cardinal dogmas, for even the enumeration
of them is foreign to our purpose.

Every religion which conceives God as an active working providence must have some distinct teaching on the
creation, and this Muḥammad gives in accordance with the
Bible, viz., that God created heaven and earth and all that
therein is in six days; [2] although in another place he
diverges somewhat and says that the earth was created in
two days, the mountains and the green herbs in four days,
and the heavens with all their divisions in two days more.[3]
Though this passage is nothing but a flight of poetic fancy,
still it shews how little Muḥammad knew of the Bible,
inasmuch as he is aware of nothing but the general fact

---

[1] Christianity also teaches the Unity of God. *Ed.*
[2] Súras X. 3, XI. 9, L. 37, LVII. 4.　　　[3] Súra XLI. 8—11.

that the creation took place in six days, and that he has not
any knowledge of each day's separate work. We have
already remarked that he calls the seventh day *sabt*, but
does not recognise its sanctity. It remains here to be
added that Muḥammad appears to allude to and reject the
Jewish belief that God rested on the seventh day. [1] He
evidently thought that a necessity for rest after hard
labour was implied, for after mentioning the creation as
having taken place in six days, he adds " and no weariness
affected Us." On this Jalálu'd-dín comments as follows :[2]
" This was revealed as an answer to the Jews who said
that God had rested thoroughly on the sabbath and therefore weariness left Him." The same thing is to be found
in Elpherar's commentary but not so clearly expressed.

The idea of several heavens, which is indicated by the
Biblical expression " heaven of heavens, " [3] came to Muḥammad probably from the Jews, also the notion that they
were seven in number, a notion due to the different
names applied to heaven. In Chagiga [4] we find the assertion
that there are seven heavens, and then the names are
given. All these names occur in the Scripture except the
first, viz. vílón, from the Latin velum.[5] This name in which
heaven is compared to a curtain, which veils the glory of [6]
God, is a very important one in the Talmud. Muḥammad
speaks often of the seven heavens, [7] and in one passage he

---

[1] Súra L. 37.

[2] Maracci. نزل ردّا على اليهود فى قولهم ان الله استراح يوم السبت
وانتفاه التعب عنه

[3] שְׁמֵי שָׁמַיִם

[4] Chagiga 9. 2. שִׁבְעָה רְקִיעִין הֵן וִילוֹן רָקִיעַ שְׁחָקִים זְבוּל
מָעוֹן מָכוֹן עֲרָבוֹת

[5] וִילוֹן

[6] Cf. Midrash on the Psalms at the end of Psalm xi.

[7] ٱلسَّمَوَاتُ ٱلسَّبْعُ or سَبْعَ ٱلسَّمَوَاتِ
Súras II. 27, XVII. 46, XXIII. 88, XLI. 11, LXV. 12, LXVII. 3, LXXI. 14.

calls the heavens the seven strongholds [1] and in another
the seven paths. [2] This last expression occurs also in the
Talmud. [3] During the creation, however, His throne was
upon the waters. [4] This idea also is borrowed from the
Jews, who say: [5] "The throne of glory then stood in the
air, and hovered over the waters by the command of God."
This is somewhat more clearly expressed by Elpherar who
says: "And this water was in the middle of the air." [6]

A second pivot of every revealed religion is the belief
in a judgment after death; for while the fact of the
creation sets forth the omnipotence of the Creator, the
doctrine of a final account teaches that it is God's will that
His revealed laws shall be obeyed. This, then, in Judaism
developed into a local Paradise and Hell, and both conceptions have passed, as we have already shown, into Islám.
These localities, although at first mere symbols, mere
embodiments of the spiritual idea of a state, afterwards
became crystallised, and suffered the fate of every symbol,
i.e., they were taken for the thing symbolised, and the
places were more definitely indicated. Thus the Jews

---

[1] سَبْع شِدَاد Súra LXXVIII. 12.

[2] سَبْع طَرَائِق Súra XXIII. 17.

[3] שְׁבִילֵי דִרְקִיעַ

[4] Súra XI. 9. كَانَ عَرْشُهُ عَلَى ٱلْمَاء

[5] Rashi on Gen. I. 2. כְּסֵא כָבוֹד עוֹמֵד בָּאֲוִיר וּמְרַחֵף עַל
פְּנֵי הַמַּיִם בְּרוּחַ פִּיו שֶׁל הַקָּדוֹשׁ בָּרוּךְ הוּא
Cf. ٱلْعَرْشُ ٱلْعَظِيمُ Súra XXIII. 88, XXVII. 26.

LXXXV. 15, ٱلْعَرْشُ ٱلْمَجِيدُ XXIII. 117, ٱلْعَرْشُ ٱلْكَرِيمُ

כְּסֵא כָבוֹד with

[6] وكان ذلك الماء على متن الريح

have a saying :[1] " The world is the sixtieth part of the garden, the garden is the sixtieth part of Eden ; "[2] and in the Qurán we find a similar expression, viz., " paradise whose breadth equalleth the heavens and the earth :[3] Generally speaking, fear is stronger than hope, and the dread of a terrible condemnation appeals far more powerfully than the hope of eternal happiness to a nature which pure religious feeling does not impel to piety of life. This is probably the reason for describing hell in a more detailed and particular manner than Paradise.

Seven hells are pictured as forming different grades of punishment, and these have been developed out of the seven different names mentioned in the Talmud. [4] These names with one exception [5] (Erets tahtith, subterranean realm, which is clearly adopted from the Roman ideas at the time of their ascendancy) are Biblical. Later on these names came to be construed as seven hells, e. g. in the Midrash on the Psalms at the end of the eleventh Psalm where [6] it is said, " there are seven abodes of the wicked in hell, " after which the above mentioned names are cited with a few variations. It is also said that David by a sevenfold reiterated cry of " my son " (בְּנִי) rescued Absalom from the seven habitations of hell ; [7] furthermore hell is said to have seven portals. [8] Muḥammad is not

---

[1] עוֹלָם אֶחָד מִשִּׁשִּׁים בְּגַן גַּן אֶחָד מִשִּׁשִּׁים בְּעֵדֶן

[2] Taanith 10. Pesachim 94.

[3] Súra III. 127. عَرْضُهَا السَّمٰوَاتُ وَآلْاَرْضُ

[4] שְׁאוֹל וַאֲבַדּוֹן וּבְאֵר שַׁחַת וּבוֹר שָׁאוֹן וְטִיט הַיָּוֵן וְצַלְמָוֶת
וְאֶרֶץ תַּחְתִּית See Erubin 19. 1.

[5] אֶרֶץ תַּחְתִּית

[6] שִׁבְעָה בָּתֵּי דִירוֹת לָרְשָׁעִים בַּגֵּיהִנֹּם

[7] 2 Sam, xix. 1-5. (Sota 10.) שִׁבְעָה מְדוֹרֵי גֵּיהִנֹּם

[8] שִׁבְעָה פְּתָחִין אִנּוּן לְגֵּיהִנֹּם Zohar II. 150.

G

behind hand, for we read in one passage that [1] " it (hell)
hath seven gates, unto every gate a distinct company
of them shall be assigned." According to the Jews,
a tree stands at the entrance to hell: [2] " Two date palms
grow in the valley of Ben Hinnom, smoke issues from
between them and this is the entrance to hell"; but
Muḥammad knows a tree of hell called Al Zaqqúm [3] which
serves sinners for food, about which he has much to relate.
The step from such a definite idea of hell to the notion of a
personality connected with it is an easy one, and we find
such an individual mentioned by the Rabbis as the " prince
of Gehinnom ; " [4] he is called however in the Qurán simply
Jahannam. In one Rabbinical book [5] we find the following :
" That the prince of hell says daily, Give me food to satisfy
me, comes from Isaiah, v. 14." Muḥammad says similarly: [6]
" On that day We will say unto hell, ' Art thou full ?' and
it shall say ' Are there more'?"

When the conceptions of Paradise and hell became so
definite, and their names were no longer general terms for
reward and punishment, a third destination had to be
provided for those whose conduct had not been such as to

---

[1] Súra XV. 44. لَهَا سَبْعَةُ أَبْوَابٍ لِكُلِّ بَابٍ مِنْهُمْ جُزْءٌ مَقْسُومٌ

[2] Sukkah 32. שְׁתֵּי תְמָרוֹת יֵשׁ בְּנֵי בֶן הִנֹּם וְעָלֶה עָשָׁן
מִבֵּינֵיהֶם וְזוֹ הִיא פְּתָחָהּ שֶׁל גֵּיהִנֹּם

[3] شَجَرَة الزَّقُّوم Súras XXXVII. 60, XLIV. 43.

[4] שַׂר שֶׁל גֵּיהִנֹּם

[5] Othioth Derabbi Akiba, 8. 1. מִנַּיִן שֶׁשָּׂרָהּ שֶׁל גֵּיהִנֹּם
אָמַר בְּכָל יוֹם וָיוֹם תֶּן לִי מַאֲכָל כְּדֵי סְפוּק כְּדֵי שֶׁנֶּאֱמַר לָכֵן
הִרְחִיבָה שְׁאוֹל נַפְשָׁהּ וּפָעֲרָה פִּיהָ לִבְלִי חֹק וְיָרַד הֲדָרָהּ
וַהֲמוֹנָהּ וּשְׁאוֹנָהּ וְעָלֵז בָּהּ

[6] Súra L. 29. يَوْمَ نَقُولُ لِجَهَنَّمَ هَلِ امْتَلَأْتِ وَتَقُولُ هَلْ مِنْ مَزِيدٍ

entitle them to the former nor condemn them to the latter place. Thus while the righteous [1] found their place in Paradise, and the sinners had their portion in hell, those who belonged to neither class were placed in a space between Paradise and Hell, of which it is said in the Midrash on Ecclesiastes, vii. 14: [2] " How much room is there between them ? Rabbi Jochanan says a wall; R. Acha says a span; other teachers however hold that they are so close together that people can see from one into the other." [3] The idea just touched upon in this passage is most poetically worked out in Súra VII. 44, [4] " And between the blessed and the damned there shall be a veil;

---

[1] צַדִּיקִים righteous, רְשָׁעִים sinners.

בֵּינוֹנִים those who stand between.

[2] כַּמָּה רֶוַח בֵּינֵיהֶם רַבִּי יוֹחָנָן אָמַר כֹּתֶל רַבִּי אַחָא אָמַר

טֶפַח וְרַבָּנָן אָמְרִין שְׁתֵּיהֶן שָׁווֹת כְּדֵי שֶׁיִּהְיוּ מְצִיצוֹת מִזוֹ לְזוֹ

[3] Concerning this intermediate place S'adi cleverly remarks that it seems to the blessed as hell, to the lost as paradise (D'Herbelot Bibliotheque Orientale under A'ráf. page 113).

[4] Elpherar comments on this passage as follows :

هم قوم استوت حسناتهم وسياتهم و قصرت بهم سياتهم عن الجنة
وتجاوزت بهم حسناتهم عن النار فوقفوا هناك حتى يقيض الله فيهم
ما يشاه *

" These are those whose good and evil deeds are so evenly balanced that the latter preclude them from paradise, while the former save them from hell, therefore they remain standing here until God has declared His pleasure concerning them." And later, when he gives our explanation of verse 45 in a long chain of traditions, he says :

ومن استوت حسناته و سيانه كان من اصحاب الاعراف فوقفوا على
الصراط ثم عرفوا اهل الجنة و اهل النار فاذا راوا اهل الجنة نادوا سلام
عليكم و اذا صرفوا ابصارهم الى اصحاب النار ......

" Those whose good and evil deeds are equal are the middle men and stand on the road. Thence they can see at once the inhabitants of paradise and those of hell; if they turn to the former, they cry ' Peace be unto you :' if to the latter " etc.

and men shall stand on Al-Aráf who shall know them by
their marks ; and shall call unto the inhabitants of Paradise
saying, Peace be upon you ; yet they shall not enter therein,
though they earnestly desire it.   And when they[1] shall
turn their eyes towards the companions of hell fire, they
rejoice that they are not among them, and shew them the
folly of their earthly walk and hopes. "

It is interesting to compare this view of a threefold
dealing with the dead with the very similar Platonic idea.[2]

The idea of the bliss of eternal life, as well as the
metaphor which expresses the difficulty of attaining it, is
common to the Qurán and Judaism.   There is a Rabbinical
saying[3] to the effect that "one hour of rapture in that
world is better than a whole life-time in this."   With this
we may compare the Qurán :[4] "And what is this life in
comparison with the life to come except a passing amuse-
ment ? "   Then for the difficulty of attaining Paradise we
may compare the Rabbinical picture[5] of the elephant
entering the needle's eye with the words in Súra VII. 38[6]
"Neither shall they enter into paradise until a camel pass
through the eye of a needle. "   This last metaphor seems
to be borrowed from Christianity, (partly because of the
similarity of the figure, in that " camel " is the metaphor
used in the Gospels, and partly because of the frequent
mention of the same by the Evangelists)[7], and is only

---

[1] " They " i e. the men between, not as Wahl and others explain it.

[2] Phaedon, Chap. 62.

[3] Mishna Aboth, IV. 17.   יָפָה שָׁעָה אַחַת שֶׁל קוֹרַת
רוּחַ בָּעוֹלָם הַבָּא מִכֹּל חַיֵּי הָעוֹלָם הַזֶּה

[4] Súras IX. 38, XIII. 26.   وَمَا ٱلْحَيَوةُ ٱلدُّنْيَا فِى ٱلْآخِرَةِ إِلَّا مَتَاعٌ

[5] כְּמָא דִמְעֵיל פִּילָא בְּקוּפָא דְמַחְטָא

[6] Súra VII. 38.   حَتَّى يَلِجَ ٱلْجَمَلُ فِى سَمِّ ٱلْخِيَاطِ

[7] Matt, xix. 24 ; Mark, x. 25 ; Luke, xviii. 24.

deserving of mention here, because the fact that in the Talmud elephant is used seems to confirm the ordinary translation of the Greek word in the Gospels, and the Arabic word in the Qurán, and to remove the doubt as to whether they might not be better rendered "cable."

Given the pure conception of immortality viz., that the life of the soul never ceases, it becomes unnecessary to fix a time at which the judgment shall take place; and so in most Talmudic passages a future world is pictured[1] in which every thing earthly is stripped away and pious souls enjoy the brightness of God's Presence.[2] Echoes of this teaching are to be found in the Qurán. In one passage[3] we read of a soul gazing on its Lord, and in another[4] the condition of a perfectly peaceful soul is beautifully described. But this entirely spiritual idea was not thoroughly carried out. Rather by the side of the pure conception of a continued life of the soul after the death of the body,[5] there existed that of the quickening of the dead.[6] Thus because the man cannot receive the requital

---

[1] עוֹלָם הַבָּא

[2] נֶהֱנִין מִזִּיו הַשְּׁכִינָה

[3] Súra LXXV. 23. اِلَى رَبِّهَا نَاظِرَةٌ

[4] Súra LXXXIX. 27 ff. مُطْمَئِنَّةٌ

[5] Take e. g. the Rabbinical saying:

צַדִּיקִים אֲפִלּוּ בְּמִיתָתָם קְרוּיִם חַיִּים "Even in their death the righteous are called living;" and in Súras II. 149, III. 163, it is ordered that those who fall in holy war shall not be called أَمْوَاتٌ dead, but أَحْيَاءٌ living.

[6] תְּחִיַּת הַמֵּתִים

The view that by the expression Techiyath Hammethim the future world or the (spiritual) continued life of the (bodily) dead is meant, is given clearly in the explanation which a Baraitha adds to the quoted utterance of the Mishna. To the words: "he who asserts that the belief in Techiyath Hammethim is no part of the Jewish religion has no part in

of his deeds while he is still in a state of death, the time of resurrection must be the time for the judgment.[1]

These two views of the resurrection and the judgment day, though different in themselves, are both closely connected in Judaism and more especially in Islám.[2] In Judaism there is a third period the advent of a Messiah, which it is not easy to separate from the other two. Naturally this time, which is to bring forth two such important events as judgment and resurrection, will be ushered in by terrible signs. In Judaism statements to this effect are to be found only about the third period, which is generally connected with the other two, viz., the earthly period of the Messiah ; in Islám on the contrary everything is attributed to the last day. The utterance most in accord with the Talmud is that in Sunnas 41 and 141, which says that learning shall vanish, ignorance shall take root, drunkenness and immorality shall increase. With this we must compare the passage in Sanhedrin 97 :[3] " At the time when David's son comes the learned diminish, and the place of learned meetings serves for immorality." The descriptions in the Qurán refer more to the last day itself, and remind us of many passages in Holy Scripture, where it is also said of those days that the world will bow itself before God, the heavens will be rolled together [4] and

---

the future world," he adds : " he denies the T. H., therefore he has no more a portion in it." Here the expression תחית המתים and " future, world" are taken as identical in meaning. Compare too the Book Ikkarim, IV. 31.

[1] יֹום הַדִּין

[2] Compare, e.g. Súra XXVI. 87. 88.

[3] דֹור שֶׁבֶּן דָּוִד בָּא תַּלְמִידֵי חֲכָמִים מִתְמַעֲטִים וּבֵית הַנַּעַד יִהְיֶה לִזְנוּת

[4] Súras XXI. 104, XXXIX. 67.

Cf. וְנָגֹלּוּ כַסֵּפֶר הַשָּׁמַיִם   Isaiah XXXIV. 4.

vanish in smoke,[1] all cities will be destroyed,[2] and men will be drunken and yet not drunken.[3]

Another very distinct sign of the advent of a Messiah, which is remotely alluded to in the Bible but which attained to an extraordinary development in the Talmud and especially in later writings, is the battle of Gog, Prince of Magog.[4] Gog and Magog are, however, named by the Rabbis as two princes, and this view has taken root in the Qurán in the Rabbinical form,[5] since two persons, Gog and Magog, are mentioned as dwellers in the uttermost parts of the earth.[6]

In the details of the idea of future retribution many resemblances are to be found, which, by virtue of the unity of the Jewish view and its derivation from the Scriptures, shew themselves as borrowings from Judaism. Thus according to the Talmud, a man's limbs themselves shall give testimony against him ;[7] in one passage we find these words : " The very members of [8] a man bear witness against him, for it is said : ' Ye yourselves are my witnesses saith the Lord.'" With this we may compare Súra XXIV. 24 :[9] " Their own tongues, and hands, and feet, shall one day be witness against them of their own doings.[10] The judgment

---

[1] Súra XLIV. 9 ff.

[2] Súra XVII. 60.

[3] Súra XXII. 2. Comp. Súras XXVII. 89, XXXIX. 68, LXIX. 13 ff.

[4] Ezekiel, xxxviii. and xxxix.

[5] Súra XXI. 96. يَأْجُوجُ وَمَأْجُوجُ

[6] Súra XVIII. 93.

[7] Chagiga 16, Taanith 11.

"אַף אֵיבָרָיו שֶׁל אָדָם מְעִידִים בּוֹ שֶׁנֶּ' וְאַתֶּם עֵדַי נְאֻם ה'

[8] Isaiah, xliii. 12.

[9] يَوْمَ تَشْهَدُ عَلَيْهِمْ أَلْسِنَتُهُمْ وَأَيْدِيهِمْ وَأَرْجُلُهُمْ بِمَا كَانُوا يَعْمَلُونَ

[10] Cf. also Súras XXXVI. 65, XLI. 19.

day gains also a greater importance from the fact that not
only individuals and nations appear at it, but also those
beings who have been honoured as gods by the nations,
and they too receive punishment with their worshippers.
In Sukkah XXIX we find this statement : [1] " As often as a
nation (on account of idolatry) receives its punishment,
those beings honoured by it as gods shall also be punished ;
for, it is written : [2] ' Against all the gods of Egypt I will
execute judgment.' "   That this general sentence admits of
a reference to the punishment of the last day is not expressly
stated, but it is worthy of acceptation.   Muḥammad
expresses himself still more clearly about it : [3] " Verily
both ye and the idols which ye worship besides God shall
be cast as fuel into hell fire."

A view closely interwoven with Judaism and Islám
is that retributive punishment is entirely confined to the
state after death, and that any single merit which a sinner
has gained will be rewarded in this world, to the end that
nothing may impede the course of judgment in the next.
The same view, only reversed, holds good in the case of the
righteous.   It is a view which was thought to explain the
course of destiny upon earth, which so often seems to run
contrary to the merits and demerits of men.

The Rabbinical view is expressed in the following
passage : [4] " Whereunto are the pious in this world to be

אֵין לְךָ כֹּל אֻמָה וְאֻמָה שֶׁהִיא לוֹקָה שֶׁאֵין אֱלֹהֶיהָ לוֹקִין [1]
עִמָּהּ שֶׁנֶּ׳ וּבְכָל אֱלֹהֵי מִצְרַיִם אֶעֱשֶׂה שְׁפָטִים

[2] Exodus, xii. 12.

[3] Súra XXI. 98.   اِنَّكُمْ وَمَا تَعْبُدُونَ مِنْ دُونِ اللّٰهِ حَصَبُ جَهَنَّمَ

לְמָה צַדִּיקִים נִמְשָׁלִים בָּעוֹלָם הַזֶּה לְאִילָן שֶׁכֻּלּוֹ עֹמֵר [4]
בְּמָקוֹם טָהֳרָה וְנוֹפוֹ נֹטֶה לְמָקוֹם טֻמְאָה נִקְצַץ נוֹפוֹ נִמְצָא כֻּלּוֹ
עֹמֵד בְּמָקוֹם טָהוֹר כָּךְ הַקָּ״בָּ׳ ה מֵבִיא יִסּוּרִים עַל צַדִּיקִים
בָּעֹלָם הַזֶּה כְּדֵי שֶׁיִּירְשׁוּ הָעוֹלָם הַבָּא שֶׁנֶּ׳ וְהָיָה רֵאשִׁיתְךָ מִצְעָר

compared? To a tree which stands entirely in a clean place; and when a branch bends to an unclean place, it is cut off and the tree itself stands there quite clean. Thus God sends afflictions in this world to the righteous, that they may possess that which is to come, as it is written: 'Though thy beginning was small, yet thy latter end should greatly increase.'[1] Sinners are like a tree which stands in an altogether unclean place; if a branch bends over to a clean place, it is cut off and the tree itself stands there quite unclean. Thus God allows the ungodly to prosper, in order to plunge them into the lowest depth of hell, as it is written: 'There is a way which seemeth right unto a man, but the end thereof are the ways of death.'"[2] Muḥammad expresses this same view in several passages, but restricts himself to the latter part which refers to the prosperity of sinners, partly because his own ideas were too unspiritual for him to be able to imagine the righteous as truly happy without earthly goods, partly because in so doing his teaching would have lost in acceptability to his very degraded contemporaries. Thus in one passage[3] we read: "We grant them long and prosperous lives only

---

וְאַחֲרִיתְךָ יִשְׂגֶּא מְאֹד וּלְמָה רְשָׁעִים דּוֹמִים בָּעֹהַז לְאִילָן שֶׁכֻּלּוֹ
עֹמֵד בְּמָקוֹם טָמֵא וְנוֹפוֹ נוֹטֶה לְמָקוֹם טָהֳרָה נִקְצַץ נוֹפוֹ כֻּלּוֹ
עֹמֵד בְּמָקוֹם טָמֵא כַּךְ הַקָּ" בָּ"ח מַשְׁפִּיעַ לָהֶם טוֹבָה בָּעֹהַז
כְּדֵי לְטָרְדָן וּלְהוֹרִישָׁן לַמַּדְרֵגָה הַתַּחְתּוֹנָה שֶׁל גֵּיהִנֹּם שֶׁנֶּ' יֵשׁ
דֶּרֶךְ יָשָׁר לִפְנֵי אִישׁ וְאַחֲרִיתָהּ דַּרְכֵי מָוֶת

[1] Job, viii. 7.

[2] Proverbs, xiv. 12. Kiddushin, 40. 2. Compare Derech Erets; Sutta end of Chap. II; Aboth of Rabbi Nathan, end of Chap. IX; Erubin 26. 2; also the Targums and their Commentators on Deuteronomy, vii. 10.

[3] Súra III. 172. اِنَّمَا نُمْلِى لَهُمْ لِيَزْدَادُوا اِثْمًا

H

that their iniquity may be increased," [1] still the second
view is to be found among the Arabians also, *e.g.*, Elpherar
in his comments on Qurán XII. 42 [2] says : " It is said that
the righteous are punished and tried, in order that the day
of resurrection may be perfect in light and power, as the
contumacy of the righteous has been already expiated."
Muḥammad naturally avoided specifying any time at
which the judgment should take place, though he was
much pressed to do so. He excused himself with the
Jewish saying that with God a thousand years are as
one day, [3] which was divested of its poetic adornment
and taken by the Rabbis in a purely literal sense. [4]
Muḥammad says [5] : " Verily one day with thy Lord is as a
thousand years of those which ye compute"; and again [6] :
" On the day whose length shall be a thousand years
of those which ye compute."

As has been already shown, with the establishment of

---

[1] Compare Súra IX. 55, 86, XXXI. 23. In IX. 55, 86, the words
فى (اَلْحَيَوٰةِ) الدُّنْيَا are evidently to be connected with أَوْلَادَهُمْ and not
with what immediately precedes.

Thus Elpherar says on IX. 55 : قال المجاهد وقتادة فى الاية تقديم
وتاخير تقديرها ولا تعجبك اموالهم ولا اولادهم فى الحيوة الدنيا انما
يريدالله ليعذبهم بها فى الاخرة *

Mujáhid and Ketádá say that this verse has been transposed, it should
run : " Let not therefore their riches or their children in this world cause
thee to marvel. Verily God intendeth only to punish them by these
things in that world."

وقيل انهم ابتلاهم بالذنوب لينفرد بالطهارة والعزة يوم القيامة على انكسار [2]
المعصية

[3] Psalm, xc. 4.

[4] Sanhedrin 96. 2. See also Preface to Ben Ezra's Commentary on the
Pentateuch where he opposes this view.

[5] Súra XXII. 46. اِنَّ يَوْمًا عِنْدَ رَبِّكَ كَأَلْفِ سَنَةٍ مِمَّا تَعُدُّونَ

[6] Súra XXXII. 4.

the doctrine of the day of judgment, the view of the resurrection and of the quickening of the dead was also formed; and this the more readily, because it found support in expressions in the Scripture, as *e.g.* those in Ezekiel, xxxvii. [1] : "I have opened your graves, and caused you to come up out of your graves, ... ye shall live," etc.; and those in other passages referring partly to the metaphorical quickening of the dead land of Israel. Of this doctrine it is said that it is such a fundamental teaching of the Jewish faith that the declaration that it did not belong to the law entailed the exclusion of him who thus spoke from eternal life. [2] The Qurán is, so to speak, founded upon this doctrine along with that of the unity of God, and there is scarcely a page in it where this doctrine is not mentioned. To adduce proofs here would be as easy as it would be useless; and indeed it is not required by our purpose, since Christianity also has inherited this view from Judaism, as is shown in the argument of Jesus in refutation of the Sadducees. Only one point deserves particular mention, because on the one hand it contains a detail adopted from Judaism, and on the other it shows the low level of thought at that time.

As soon as it becomes a question not merely of the immortality of the soul, but also of the resurrection of the body, then the soul without its body is no longer regarded as the same person, and the question naturally presents itself to the ordinary understanding: "How can this body which we have seen decay rise again, so that the same personality shall reappear?" Neither the soul alone nor the body alone is the person, but the union of the two. Now one part of this union is dissolved; another body can indeed be given to this soul, but by this means he who died

---

[1] Ezekiel, xxxvii. 13. פִּתְחִי אֶת־קִבְרוֹתֵיכֶם

Súra C. 9. بُعْثِرَ مَا فِى ٱلْقُبُورِ

[2] Mishna Sanhedrin X. 1

does not reappear, but a new man, another personality, another consciousness comes into being. This question dimly anticipated obtrudes itself, and can only be set at rest by proving that the very same personality can appear again. Instead of showing this Muḥammad contents himself with the parable, used also occasionally in the Talmud, of the renewal of the dried up earth by fertilising rain. He found however that he could not silence the common convictions of men thereby,[1] and so he was compelled to come back to it again and again. The Jews also sought to give prominence to this resemblance, and they put the eulogium[2] "Who sendeth down the rain" into the second benediction which treats of the resurrection.[3] The fact that the righteous rise actually in their clothes[4] (which after all is not more wonderful than in their bodies) is explained by the parable of the grain of wheat, which is laid in the earth without covering, but springs up again with many coverings. The passage in Qurán VI. 96 contains a similar statement. This view is not strange to Islám, for a saying which is attributed to Muḥammad runs thus:[5] "The dead man shall be raised in the clothes in which he died."

That from the standpoint of revealed religion the belief in the possibility of revelation is fundamental needs of course no proof, and in this the views of all revealed religions are alike; yet differences can be found in the manner of conceiving of the revelation, and here we recognise again that Muḥammad derived his view of it from Judaism, of course with some modification.

---

[1] Súras VI. 95, XXX. 49, XXXVI. 33, XLI. 39, XLIII. 10, etc.

[2] מוֹרִיד הַגֶּשֶׁם

[3] Taanith at the beginning.

[4] Sanhedrin 90. 2, and Kethúbhoth III. 2.

[5] ان الميت يبعث فى ثيابه التى يموت فيها

(Poc. notœ misc. cap. 7, p. 271.)

The Jews have a saying that "all the prophets saw through a dark glass, but Moses through a clear one," [1] and Muḥammad says : [2] It was not granted to a man that God should speak unto him otherwise than in a vision or from behind a veil ; [3] and then he adds : [4] " or by the sending of a messenger to reveal by His permission that which He pleaseth. " This messenger is the Holy Spirit, [5] or simply the spirit, [6] like the spirit in the story of Micaiah's vision. [7] The Arabic commentators take this holy spirit to mean Gabriel, a view which is not unknown to the Jews, for

---

[1] Jebamoth 49. כָּל הַנְּבִיאִים רָאוּ בְּאִסְפְּקַלָרְיָא שֶׁאֵינָה מְאִירָה
מֹשֶׁה בְּאִסְפְּקַלָרְיָא הַמְּאִירָה

[2] Súra XLII. 50. وَمَا كَانَ لِبَشَرٍ أَنْ يُكَلِّمَهُ ٱللَّهُ إِلَّا وَحْيًا أَوْ مِنْ وَرَآءِ حِجَابٍ

[8] Commentators cite this verse as one in which the superiority of Moses is disputed ; thus Elpherar says :

وذلك ان اليهود قالوا للنبى صلعم الله اتكلم الله و تنظر اليه
ان كنت نبيا كما كلمة موسى و نظر اليه فقال لم ينظر موسى الى الله
عز وجل فانزل الله عز وجل وما كان لبشر ان يكلمه الله الا وحيا اليه فى
المنام او بالالهام او من وراء حجاب يسـمعه كلامة ولا يراه كما كلم موسى
عليه السلام *

" The Jews said to Muḥammad ; ' By God ! if thou art a prophet, dost thou speak with God and see Him as Moses spoke with Him and saw Him ? ' Then he said : ' Moses did not see God ' And then came this verse : ' It was not granted to a man that God should speak to him, except in a vision, in a dream or through supernatural inspiration, or from behind a curtain, so that man hears His Voice, but does not see Him ; He spoke thus to Moses also.' "

[4] أَوْ يُرْسِلَ رَسُولًا فَيُوحِيَ بِإِذْنِهِ مَا يَشَآءُ

[5] رُوحַ הַקֹּדֶשׁ רוּחַ , το πνεῦμα ἅγιον

[6] روح Súras LXXVIII. 38, XCVII. 4.

[7] וַיֵּצֵא הָרוּחַ 1 Kings, xxii. 21.

the Jewish commentators understand the words [1] " the
definitely speaking Spirit " to refer to Gabriel. One of
Muḥammad's own utterances, one which is fully explained
only by the 52nd Sunna, is much more striking : [2] " And
they will ask thee of the spirit, say : the spirit (proceedeth)
at my Lord's command. "

With this the teaching about angels is closely connected,
and it also had its beginning in Scripture, but appears to
have been developed in later days especially through
Parseeism. Muḥammad is unwearied in his descriptions
of angels; so too are the later Jews in their many prayers
on the day of atonement, but these are of rather late
origin. [3] The angel of death [4] is specially mentioned in
Súra XXXII. 11.

While angels were regarded as purely spiritual beings
who execute God's commands, a class of beings was
imagined who stood between man and the purest spirits;
these were mixed spirits, who were made out of fire, [5] who
possessed superior mental powers, but who were mostly
inclined to evil, they were called [6] demons, but there are
numerous other names for them in Arabic. The Talmud
has the following statement about them : [7] " Demons

---

[1] רוּחַ פְּסָקָנִית Sanhedrin 44.

[2] Súra XVII. 87. وَيَسْأَلُونَكَ عَنِ ٱلرُّوحِ قُلِ ٱلرُّوحُ مِنْ أَمْرِ رَبِّى

[3] Compare Súras XXXV. 1, XXXVII. 1, XL. 7, LXXVII. 1 ff.
LXXIX. 11 ff.

[4] Súra XXXII. 11. مَلَكُ ٱلْمَوْتِ, מַלְאַךְ הַמָּוֶת

[5] Súra XV. 27.

[6] גִּן שֵׁדִים

[7] שִׁשָּׁה דְבָרִים נֶאֶמְרִים בַּשֵּׁדִים שְׁלֹשָׁה כְּמַלְאֲכֵי הַשָּׁרֵת
וּשְׁלֹשָׁה כִּבְנֵי אָדָם שְׁלֹשָׁה כְּמַלְאֲכֵי הַשָּׁרֵת יֵשׁ לָהֶם כְּנָפַיִם

are declared to possess six qualities, three of which are
angelic and three human. The three which pertain to
angels are that they have wings, that they can fly from one
end of the earth to the other (*i. e.* they are bound by no
space), and that they know the future beforehand. They
know the future beforehand ? No! but they listen behind
the curtain. The three human qualities are that they eat
and drink, increase and multiply, [1] and die. " [2] Muslim
tradition cannot do enough in their description, but there
is but little about them in the Qurán. The fact that they
listened at the canopy of heaven gained for them in the
Qurán the nickname of the stoned, [3] for, say the commentators, the angels threw stones to drive them away when
they found them listening. [4] Thus it is said expressly : [5]
" We have appointed them (the lamps of heaven) to be
darted at the devils. " The seventy-second Súra treats of
them in detail, and seeks especially to set forth their assent
to the new doctrine. The Talmud also states that they
are present at the giving of instruction. The following

וְרָמְזִין מִסוֹף הָעוֹלָם וְעַד סוֹפוֹ וְיוֹדְעִין מַה שֶׁעָתִיד לִהְיוֹת יוֹדְעִין
סָלְקָא דַעְתֵּךְ אֶלָּא שׁוֹמְעִין מֵאֲחוֹרֵי הַפַּרְגּוֹד וּשְׁלֹשָׁה כִּבְנֵי אָדָם
אוֹכְלִין וְשׁוֹתִין פָּרִין וְרָבִין וּמֵתִין

الجن قيل هم نوع من الملائكة و ابليس ابو الجن فله ذرية ذكرة معه [1]
الملائكة لا ذرية لهم

" The genii are supposed to be a species of angels, and the devil is their
father; he has thus a posterity, which is mentioned with him; the
(remaining) angels however have no posterity." Jalálu'ddin in Maracc
Prodr. II. 15.

[2] Chagiga 16. 1.

[3] Súras XV. 17, 34, XXXVIII. 78, LXXXI. 24. رَجِيمٌ

[4] The Muslim explanation of falling stars.

[5] وَجَعَلْنَاهَا رُجُومًا لِلشَّيَاطِينِ Súra LXVII. 5; compare Súra XXXVII. 7.

passage from the Berachoth shows this : "The press in the school is caused by them, the demons." [1]   With this we may compare the Qurán : " When the servant of God stood up to invoke Him, it wanted little but that the genii had pressed on him in crowds. " [2]   It cannot be maintained that the greater part of the teaching about genii was adopted from Judaism, it must rather be said to have come from the same dark source whence the Jews of those times drew these conceptions, viz., Parseeism.

Still here, as in the case of any point which is of inaccessible origin, a reference to a mere similarity is not without use.

Under these four heads then, viz., (1) Creation, (2) Retribution including the Last Judgment and the Resurrection, (3) Mode of Revelation, and (4) Doctrine of Spirits, details are found, the adoption of which from Judaism we may regard as sufficiently proved.   The precaution against representing, out of love for our theme, that which is common either to the general religious feelings of mankind, or to all revealed religions, or at least that which belonged to other known religious parties in Muḥammad's time as peculiar only to Judaism, compels us to fix these limits.   We have found much of interest especially under the second head, so that the demands of our theme might seem to be fairly well satisfied.

B.   Moral and Legal Rules.

It is obvious that in a revealed religion all individual commands form part of the religion, and therefore one cannot draw any sharp line of distinction between the " religious" and the " moral. " We have accordingly

---

[1] הוּא דְּחָקָא דְּבֵית כַּלָּה מִנַּיְיהוּ הוּא

[2] Súra LXXII. 19, كَادُوا يَكُونُونَ عَلَيْهِ لِبَدًا

considered nothing which has to do with conduct under the heading A, even though it might be immediately connected with the points of belief under discussion and so we are able to bring together here all commands as to conduct. From the fact that every individual command is Divine, a conflict of duties may easily arise, which cannot be readily decided by private judgment, seeing that all the commandments are equal, [1] so far as their Author is concerned. Rules for such cases must therefore be laid down. For instance, we find the following statement in the Rabbinical writings : [2] "If a father saith (to his son if he is a priest), ' defile thyself '; or if he saith, ' Make not restitution (of the thing found to the owner) ', shall he obey him ? Therefore, it is written : [3] ' Let every, man reverence his father and mother, but keep my Sabbaths all of you, ye are all bound to honour me.' " And Muḥammad says : [4] " We have commanded man to show kindness towards his parents, but if they endeavour to prevail with thee to associate with me that concerning which thou hast no knowledge, obey them not. "

---

[1] Fakihat Elcholefa, 94, proves that this is really the Arabic view :

قال بعض أهل الافضان ان معاصى العباد ليس فيها صغيرة و انما كل ما

بخالف الامر كبيرة وذلك بالنظر الى جناب آلامر تعالى و تقدّس *

"A meritorious man says that in the sins of men there is nothing small, but whatever is done contrary to the Commandment is great with respect to Him who commands, who is exalted and holy."

[2] Jebamoth 6.   אָמַר לוֹ אָבִיו הִטַּמֵּא אוֹ אָמַר לוֹ אַל

תַּחֲזִיר יָכוֹל יִשְׁמַע לוֹ תִּלְמָדוּ לֵאמֹר אִישׁ אִמּוֹ וְאָבִיו תִּירָאוּ

וְאֶת־שַׁבְּתֹתַי תִּשְׁמֹרוּ כֻּלְּכֶם חַיָּבִים בִּכְבוֹדִי

[3] Leviticus, xix. 3.

[4] Súra XXIX. 7.   وَوَصَّيْنَا آلْإِنْسَانَ بِوَالِدَيْهِ حُسْنًا وَإِنْ جَاهَدَاكَ لِتُشْرِكَ

بِى مَالَيْسَ لَكَ بِهِ عِلْمٌ فَلَا تُطِعْهُمَا

I

Judaism is known to be very rich in single precepts, and Muḥammad has borrowed from it much that seemed to him suitable.

1. *Prayer.* Muḥammad like the Rabbis prescribes the standing position [1] for prayer. Thus: "Stand obedient to the Lord; but if ye fear any danger, then pray while walking or riding"; [2] and also: "Who standing, and sitting, and reclining, bear God in mind." [3]

These three positions are mentioned again in Súra X. 13 : [4] "When evil befalleth a man he prayeth unto us, lying on his side or sitting or standing," where with a true perception of the right order, the least worthy position is the first spoken of. [5]

Baidháwi comments thus on Súra III. 188, the passage alluded to above: "The meaning is that the man may take any of the three positions according to his strength, as Muḥammad said to Amrán Ibn Husain: 'Pray standing if thou art able; if not, sitting; and if thou canst not sit up, then leaning on the side." [6] The Jews were not so strict in this matter, yet they too have the rule that prayer should be offered standing; [7] and in Rabbinical writings it is also

---

[1] Note the technical expression أَقَامَ ٱلصَّلَوٰةَ

Comp. Rabb. עָמַד בִּתְפִלָּה

[2] Súra II. 240. وَقُومُوا لِلّٰهِ قَانِتِينَ فَاِنْ خِفْتُمْ فَرِجَالاً أَوْ رُكْبَاناً

[3] Súra III. 188. قِيَاماً وَقُعُوداً وَعَلَى جُنُوبِهِمْ

[4] لِجَنْبِهِ أَوْ قَاعِداً أَوْ قَائِماً

[5] Cf. also Súra IV. 46.

[6] معناه يصلون على الهيات الثلاث حسب طاقتهم لقوله عليه الصلاة والسلام لعمران بن حصين صل قائما فان لم تستطع فقاعدا فان لم تستطع فعلى جنب *

[7] תְּפִלָּה מְעֻמָּד Cf. Berachoth X.

said that he who rides on an ass is to dismount, but the addition is made that, if he cannot dismount he is to turn his face (towards Jerusalem). [1] As the bodily position may be altered in urgent cases, so the prayer itself may be shortened on similar occasions. [2] So we find the permission to shorten prayer in time of war: "When ye march to war in the earth, [3] it shall be no crime in you if ye shorten your prayers." The Jews also were permitted to pray a short prayer when in a dangerous place. [4] Muḥammad is quite opposed to senseless chattering, for he counts it a merit in believers to "eschew all vain discourse. [5] Therefore because attention and pious concentration of thought are to be aimed at, he enjoins [6] on believers not to draw near to prayer when they are drunk. This is in accordance with the Talmudic rule: "Prayer is forbidden to the drunken." [7] It is also forbidden to those who have touched women. [8] These persons may not engage in

---

[1] Mishna Berachoth IV. 5.   הָיָה רוֹכֵב עַל הַחֲמוֹר יֵרֵד

וְאִם אֵינוֹ יָכוֹל לֵירֵד יַחֲזִיר פָּנָיו

[2] Súra IV. 102.   وَاِذَا ضَرَبْتُمْ فِى ٱلْاَرْضِ فَلَيْسَ عَلَيْكُمْ جُنَاحٌ اَنْ تَقْصُرُوا مِنَ ٱلصَّلٰوةِ

[3] Compare the similar expression in Hebrew   שׁוּט בָּאָרֶץ

[4] Mishna Berachoth IV. 4.   הַמְהַלֵּךְ בִּמְקוֹם סַכָּנָה מִתְפַּלֵּל תְּפִלָּה קְצָרָה

[5] Súra XXIII. 3.   وَٱلَّذِينَ هُمْ عَنِ ٱللَّغْوِ مُعْرِضُونَ

Compare Ecclesiastes, v. 1.   עָלֵכֵּן יִהְיוּ דְבָרֶיךָ מְעַטִּים

[6] Súra IV. 46.   لَا تَقْرَبُوا ٱلصَّلٰوةَ وَاَنْتُمْ سُكَارَى

[7] שִׁכּוֹר אָסוּר לְהִתְפַּלֵּל   Berachoth 31. 2. Erubin 64.

[8] Súras IV. 46. V. 9.   لَامَسْتُمُ ٱلنِّسَاءَ   Cf. Mishna Berachoth III. 4.

בַּעַל קְרִי

prayer before washing with water, which cleansing is
recommended as a general rule before prayer both in the
Qurán [1] and in the Talmud. Instead of water, purification
with sand may take place. [2] So in the Talmud: "He
cleanses himself with sand and has then done enough."
As concentrated thought is urged as a duty, it follows that
prayer though audible must not be noisy, [3] and so Muhammad says: "Pronounce not thy prayer aloud, neither
pronounce it with too low a voice, but follow a middle way
between these;" and in the Talmud we find: [4] "From the
behaviour of Hannah who in prayer moved her lips we
learn that he who prays must pronounce the words, and
also as her voice was not heard we learn that he must
not raise his voice loudly." But because our mood does
not at all times move us to fervency of prayer, outward
ceremony is necessary, and indeed prayer in a great
congregation, whose devotion will stir up our own. [5]
"The prayer in the congregation" [6] is greatly praised
also by the Jews. Daybreak, which is mentioned in the
Talmud in connection with the Shĕma prayer, as the time
when "one can distinguish between a blue and a white
thread," [7] is not mentioned in this connection in the

---

[1] Súra V. 8. Berachoth 46.

[2] تَيَمَّم   Súras IV. 46, V. 9. Cf. the Talmudic phrase

מְקַנֵּחַ בִּצְרוֹר וְדַיּוֹ

[3] Súra XVII. 110. لَا تَجْهَرْ بِصَلَوتِكَ وَلَا تُخَافِتْ بِهَا وَٱبْتَغِ بَيْنَ ذٰلِكَ سَبِيلًا

[4] 1 Samuel, i. 13. Berachoth 31. 2.

רַק שְׂפָתֶיהָ נָעוֹת מִכַּן לְמִתְפַּלֵּל צָרִיךְ שֶׁיַּחְתֹּךְ בִּשְׂפָתָיו
וְקוֹלָהּ לֹא יִשָּׁמַע מִכַּן לְמִלְפַּלֵּל שֶׁלֹּא יַשְׁמִיעַ קוֹלוֹ

[5] Cf. Sunna 86. 87. 88. 89.

[6] תְּפִלָּה בְּצִבּוּר

[7] Mishua Berachoth I. 2.   מִשֶּׁיַּכִּיר בֵּין תְּכֵלֶת לְלָבָן

Qurán it is true, for the Qurán knows nothing of a Shĕma prayer, but it appears in connection with the beginning of the Fast Day:"[1] Until ye can discern a white thread from a black thread by the daybreak."

2. Some rulings in respect of women tally with Judaism; *e.g.*, the waiting of divorced woman for three months before they may marry again.[2] The time of suckling is given in both as two years:[3] "Mothers shall give suck unto their children two full years." Similarly in Súra XLVI. 14 we find: "His bearing and his weaning is thirty months," which is explained by Elpherar as follows:[4] "He takes the shortest duration of pregnancy, viz., six months, and the shortest of suckling, viz., twenty-four months." Compare the Talmudic saying:[5] "A woman is to suckle her child two years, after that it is as though a worm sucked." That those relatives to whom inter-marriage is forbidden in the Scripture are precisely those whom Muḥammad permits[6] to see their near relations unveiled has been already noticed by Michaelis in the Mosaic system, and he has shewn the connection between these two laws.

---

[1] Súra II. 183. حَتَّى يَتَبَيَّنَ لَكُمُ ٱلْخَيْطُ ٱلْأَبْيَضُ مِنَ ٱلْخَيْطِ ٱلْأَسْوَدِ

Compare the note in the first section (p. 26) for remarks on the Fast Day, ' Áshúra.

[2] Súra II. 228. Cf. Mishna Jabhamoth IV. 10.

גרושות לא ינשאו עד שיהיו להן שלשה חדשים

[3] Súra II. 233. وَٱلْوَالِدَاتُ يُرْضِعْنَ أَوْلَادَهُنَّ حَوْلَيْنِ كَامِلَيْنِ

Cf. XXXI. 13.

[4] يريد اقل مدة الحمل ستة اشهر و اقل مدة الرضاع اربعة وعشرون شهرا

[5] Kethúboth 60. 1.

אשה מיניקה את בנה שתי שנים מכן ואילך כיונק שקץ

Compare Josephus Ant. 2. 9.

[6] Súra XXIV. 31.

As Muḥammad had very little intention of imposing a new code of individual laws, since his aim was much more the spread of new purified religious opinions, and as in the matter of practice he was far too much of an Arab to deviate from inherited usages, unless they came directly into opposition to these higher religious views, it is easily to be explained how so few borrowings are to be found in this part and much even of what is adduced might perhaps be claimed to be general oriental custom. We shall find moreover in the Appendix that Muḥammad mentions many Jewish laws which were known to him; he alludes to these sometimes as binding on the Jews, sometimes merely for the sake of disputing them, and hence we see that it was not want of knowledge of them that kept him back from using them, but his totally different purpose. This remark must apply also to our third heading, under which isolated instances of adaptation only will be found, except in cases where the view is directly connected with the higher articles of Faith adopted from Judaism, which have been already mentioned.

C. Views of Life.

In putting together these single fragmentary utterances, it is scarcely worth while to arrange them according to any new system, and we will therefore follow the order of the Qurán.

Death with the righteous is to be prized, hence the request in the Qurán: "Make us to die with the righteous," [1] which corresponds with that of Balaam, "Let me die the death of the righteous."

---

[1] Súra III. 191. تَوَفَّنَا مَعَ ٱلْأَبْرَارِ

Cf. Numbers, xxiii. 10. תָּמֹת נַפְשִׁי מוֹת יְשָׁרִים

" Say not of any matter, ' I will, surely do this to-
morrow,' unless thou add, ' If God please.' " [1] Full understanding is first imputed to a man when he is forty years
old, [2] and it is said in the Mishna : " At forty years of
age a man comes to intelligence." So the hunting for
some particular persons, to whom this sentence of the
Qurán shall apply, as the Arabic Commentators do, appears
altogether unnecessary ; it is also rendered very dubious
by the wide differences between the various opinions.

In the Qurán a comparison is found between those who
bear a burden without understanding the nature of it and
who thus carry without profit, and an ass carrying books. [3]

" He who intercedeth (between men) with a good intercession shall have a portion thereof." [4] This saying is very
similar to the Hebrew one : " He who asks for mercy for
another while he needs the same thing himself obtains help

---

[1] Súra XVIII. 23. وَلَا تَقُولَنَّ لِشَىْءٍ إِنِّى فَاعِلٌ ذَٰلِكَ غَدًا إِلَّا أَنْ يَشَاءَ ٱللَّهُ

Cf. the Hebrew expression אִם יִרְצֶה הַשֵּׁם

[2] Súra XLVI. 14. بَلَغَ أَرْبَعِينَ سَنَةً   Cf. Aboth V. 21.

בֶּן אַרְבָּעִים לַבִּינָה

That full understanding is not reached until the completion of the
fortieth year is observed also by Philo (ἕκτῃ δὲ (ἑβδομάδι)
συνέσεως ἀκμή), who here takes the forty-second year, only because
he attaches particular virtue to the number 7, in which Solon also agrees
with him (Vid. Philo, de Opificio Mundi, P. 70-72, Ed. Pfeifer I)

[3] Súra LXII. 5. حِمَارٍ يَحْمِلُ أَسْفَارًا

Cf. the Hebrew חֲמוֹר נֹשֵׂא סְפָרִים

[4] Súra IV. 87. مَنْ يَشْفَعْ شَفَاعَةً حَسَنَةً يَكُنْ لَهُ نَصِيبٌ مِنْهَا

Cf. Baba Kamma 92. כָּל הַמְבַקֵּשׁ רַחֲמִים עַל חֲבֵרוֹ הוּא

צָרִיךְ לְאוֹתוֹ דָּבָר הוּא נַעֲנֶה תְּחִלָּה

first." In Sunna 689 it is said : " Three things follow the
dead, but two of them turn back ; his family, his goods,
and his works follow him ; his family and his goods
forsake him again, and only his works remain with him. "
This is also found in great detail in Rabbinical Hebrew : [1]
" Man has three friends in his life time,—his family, his
property, and his good works. At the time of his departure from earth he collects the members of his family, and
says to them, ' I beg you, come and free me from this evil
death. ' They answer : ' Hast thou not heard [2] that no one
has power over the day of death.' It is also written : [3] ' None
of them can by any means redeem his brother, even his

---

[1] Pirke Rabbi Eliezer 34.

שְׁלֹשָׁה אֹהֲבִים יֵשׁ לוֹ לָאָדָם בְּחַיָּיו וְאֵלּוּ הֵן בָּנָיו וּבְנֵי בֵּיתוֹ
וּמָמוֹנוֹ וּמַעֲשָׂיו הַטּוֹבִים וּבְשָׁעַת פְּטִירָתוֹ מִן הָעוֹלָם הוּא מַכְנִיס
לְבָנָיו וְלִבְנֵי בֵיתוֹ וְאֹמֵר לָהֶם בְּבַקָּשָׁה מִכֶּם בָּאוּ וְהַצִּילוּנִי
מִן הַמָּוֶת הָרָע הַזֶּה וְהֵן מְשִׁיבִין אֹתוֹ וְאֹמְרִין לוֹ וְלֹא שָׁמַעְתָּ
שֶׁאֵין שִׁלְטוֹן בְּיוֹם הַמָּוֶת וְלֹא כַּךְ כְּתִיב אָח לֹא פָדֹה יִפְדֶּה
אִישׁ וַאֲפִלּוּ מָמוֹנוֹ שֶׁהוּא אֹהֵב אֵינוֹ יָכוֹל לִפְדּוֹת שֶׁנֶּ' וְלֹא יִתֵּן
לֵאלֹהִים כָּפְרוֹ לָמָּה וְיֵקַר פִּדְיוֹן נַפְשָׁם וְחָדַל מִדְּבָר זֶה לְעוֹלָם
אֶלָּא לֵךְ לְשָׁלוֹם וְתָנוּחַ עַל מִשְׁכָּבְךָ וְתַעֲמֹד לְגוֹרָלְךָ לְקֵץ
הַיָּמִים וִיהֵא חֶלְקוֹ עִם חֲסִידֵי הָעוֹלָם וּכְשֶׁהוּא רֹאֶה כֵּן מַכְנִיס
אֶת מָמוֹנוֹ וְאֹמֵר לוֹ הַרְבֵּה טָרַחְתִּי עָלֶיךָ לַיְלָה וָיוֹם בְּבַקָּשָׁה
מִמְּךָ פְּדֵנִי מִן הַמָּוֶת הַזֶּה וְהַצִּילֵנִי וְהוּא מְשִׁיבוֹ וַהֲלֹא שָׁמַעְתָּ
וְלֹא יוֹעִיל הוֹן בְּיוֹם עֶבְרָה אַחֲרֵי כֵן מַכְנִיס מַעֲשָׂיו הַטּוֹבִים וְאֹמֵר
לָהֶם בֹּאוּ וְהַצִּילוּנִי מִן הַמָּוֶת הַזֶּה וְהִתְחַזְּקוּ עִמִּי וְאַל תַּנִּיחוּנִי
לָצֵאת מִן הָעוֹלָם שֶׁעֲדַיִן יֵשׁ לָכֶם תּוֹחֶלֶת עָלַי אִם אֶנָּצֵל וְהֵן
אֹמְרִין לוֹ לֵךְ לְשָׁלוֹם עַד שֶׁלֹּא תֵלֵךְ תֵּלֵךְ לְשָׁלוֹם אָנוּ מַקְדִּימִן
אֹתְךָ שֶׁנֶּ' וְהָלַךְ לְפָנֶיךָ צִדְקֶךָ וּכְבוֹד ח' יַאַסְפֶךָ

[2] Ecclesiastes, viii. 8.   [3] Psalm, xlix. 8.

wealth which he loves avails not, he cannot give to God a
ransom for him, for the redemption of their soul is costly
and must be let alone for ever ; but enter thou into peace,
rest in thy lot till the end of days.[1] May thy part be
with the righteous.' When the man sees this, he collects
his treasures and says to them : ' I have laboured for you day
and night, and I pray you redeem and deliver me from this
death'; but they answer : ' Hast thou not heard that riches
profit not in the day of wrath ? '[2] So then he collects his
good works and says to them : ' Then you come and deliver
me from this death, support me, let me not go out of this
world, for you still have hope in me if I am delivered.'
They answer : ' Enter into peace! but before thou departest
we will hasten before thee; as it is written, Thy
righteousness shall go before thee, the glory of the Lord
shall be thy rearward.' "[3]

SECOND SECTION.

Chapter II.

Stories borrowed from Judaism.

This division will prove to be the largest, partly, because
these narratives, draped in the most marvellous garb of
fiction, lived mostly in the mouth of the people ; partly,
because this fairy-tale form appealed to the poetic fancy of
Muḥammad, and suited the childish level of his contemporaries. In the case of the Old Testament narratives, which
are seldom related soberly, but are for the most part
embellished, it needs scarcely a question, or the most
cursory enquiry, as to whether or no they have passed from
the Jews to Muḥammad ; for the Christians, the only
other possible source to which they could be attributed,
bestowed very little attention in those days on the Old
Testament, but in their narratives kept to what is strictly

---

[1] Daniel, xii. 13.   [2] Proverbs, xi. 4.   [3] Isaiah, lviii. 8.

K

Christian, viz., the events of the Life of Jesus, of His disciples and His followers, and of the multitude of subsequent Saints and wonder-workers, which afforded them abundant material for manifold embellishments. The Christians, for all that they accepted the Old Testament as a sacred writing, and although in those days no doubt had arisen as to whether or no they were to put the Old Testament on a level with the New in respect of holiness and divine inspiration, a doubt which has been brought forward for example by Schleiermacher in later times,—the Christians of that period, I say, had nevertheless a more lively interest in the New Testament, since it was the expression of their separation and independence. The Old Testament was common to them and the Jews, and indeed they could not deny to the latter a greater right of possession in it, for the Jews possessed it entirely, and were versed in it even to the minutest details, an intimate knowledge with which we cannot credit the Christians. Further, just those points in the Old Testament which were specially suited to the Christian teaching are found to be scarcely touched upon in the Qurán; thus, for instance, the narrative of the transgression of the first human pair is not at all represented as a fall into sin, involving the entire corruption of human nature which must afterwards be redeemed, but rather Muḥammad contents himself with the plain, simple narration of the fact. This may be taken as an instance to prove that the narratives about persons mentioned in the Old Testament are almost all of Jewish origin, and this will be more clearly shewn when we come to details.

As we proceed to the enumeration of the individual borrowed stories, the necessity is forced upon us of arranging them in some order. We have no reason for arranging them according to their sources, (Bible, Mishna, Gemara, Midrash, etc.) as Muḥammad did not gain his knowledge of these narratives from any of these sources, but was taught them all verbally by those round him, and so they were all of the same value for him, and were all called biblical; furthermore we must pay no attention to their contents, for the narratives are not given as supporting any doctrines of Islám, but are merely quoted as records of historical facts; and even in those cases where they are intended to set forth a doctrine, it is almost always either that of the unity of God, or that of the Resurrection of the dead. It appears therefore advisable to arrange them chronologically, by which means it will be most easy to recognize the numerous anachronisms among them. Either Muḥammad did not know the history of the Jewish nation, which is very probable, or the narration of it did not suit his object, for only once is the whole history summed up in brief,[1] and only the events in the lives of a few persons are mentioned. In this chronological arrangement we shall have to pay more attention to the personal importance of individuals than to any changes in the condition and circumstances of the nation, and thus in this arrangement we shall have the following Divisions : 1. Patriarchs; 2. Moses; 3. The three Kings who reigned over the individed Kingdom, viz., Saul, David and Solomon; and 4. Holy men who lived after them.

SECOND CHAPTER.

First Part.

Patriarchs : A.—From Adam to Noah.

The great event of the creation of the first man gave occasion for much poetical embellishment. Before the appearance of Adam, the jealousy of the angels, who had counselled against his creation, was roused, and God shamed them by endowing Adam more richly with knowledge than any of them. In the Qurán we have the following description :[2] " When thy Lord said unto the angels, ' I am

---

[1] Súra XVII. 4-8.   [2] Súra II. 28-32.

going to place a substitute on earth'; they said, 'Wilt thou place there one who will do evil therein and shed blood? but we celebrate thy praise and sanctify thee.' God answered: ' Verily I know that which ye know not'; and He taught Adam the names of all things, and then proposed them to the angels, and said : ' Declare unto me the names of these things, if ye say truth.' They answered : ' Praise be unto thee, we have no knowledge but what thou teachest us, for thou art knowing and wise.' God said : ' O Adam, tell them their names ; ' and when he had told them their names, God said: ' Did I not tell you that I know the secrets of heaven and earth, and know that which ye discover, and that which ye conceal ? ' " The corresponding Hebrew passage may be thus translated : [1] " When the Holy One, blessed be He! would create man, he took counsel with the angels, and said to them : ' We will make man in our image; ' [2] then they said : ' What is man that thou art mindful of him ? [3] What will be his peculiarity ? ' He said: 'His wisdom is greater than yours.' Then He brought beasts, cattle, and birds before them, and asked for their names, but they knew them not. But when He had

---

[1] Midrash Rabbah on Numbers, para. 19.

בְּשָׁעָה שֶׁבָּא הַקָּדוֹשׁ בָּרוּךְ הוּא לִכְרֹאת אֶת הָאָדָם נִמְלַךְ
בְּמַלְאֲכֵי הַשָּׁרֵת אָמַר לָהֶן נַעֲשֶׂה אָדָם בְּצַלְמֵנוּ אָמְרוּ לְפָנָיו
מָה אֱנוֹשׁ כִּי תִזְכְּרֶנּוּ אָדָם זֶה מָה טִבּוֹ אָמַר לָהֶן הָכְמָתוֹ
מְרֻבָּה מִשֶּׁלָּכֶם הֵבִיא לִפְנֵיהֶם אֶת הַבְּהֵמָה וְאֶת הַחַיָּה וְאֶת
הָעוֹף א' ל' זֶה מָה שְׁמוֹ וְלֹא הָיוּ יוֹדְעִין כֵּן שֶׁבָּרָא אָדָם
הֶעֱבִירָן לְפָנָיו אָמַר לוֹ זֶה מָה שְׁמוֹ אָמַר זֶה שׁוֹר זֶה חֲמוֹר
זֶה סוּס וְזֶה גָּמָל וְאַתָּה מָה שְׁמֶךָ אָמַר לוֹ אֲנִי נָאֶה לְהִקָּרֵא
אָדָם שֶׁנִּבְרֵאתִי מִן הָאֲדָמָה וַאֲנִי מַח־שְׁמִי א' ל' לְךָ נָאֶה
לְהִקָּרֵאת אֲדֹנָי שֶׁאַתָּה אָדוֹן לְכָל בְּרִיּוֹתֶיךָ

Compare Midrash Rabbah on Genesis, para. 8 and 17, and also Sanhedrin 38.

[2] Genesis, i. 26.   [3] Psalm, viii. 5.

created man He caused the animals to pass before him and asked him for their names, and he replied: 'This is an ox, that an ass, this a horse and that a camel.' 'But what art thou called?' 'It is fitting that I should be called earthy, for I am formed of the earth.' 'And I?' 'Thou art called LORD, for thou rulest all Thy creatures.'" From this arose the other legend [1] that God, after the creation of man, commanded the angels to fall down before him, which they all did except Iblís,[2] the devil. The legend bears unmistakeable marks of Christian development, in that Adam is represented in the beginning as the God-man, worthy of adoration, which the Jews are far from asserting.[3] It is true that in Jewish writings great honour is spoken of as shewn by the angels to Adam, but this never went so far as adoration; indeed when this was once about to take place in error, God frustrated the action. We find in Sanhedrin 29,[4] "Adam sat in the Garden of Eden, and the angels roasted flesh for him, and prepared cooling wine"; and in another passage it is said,[5] "After God had created man, the angels went astray in regard to him, and wanted to say before him,

---

[1] Súras VII. 10-18, XV. 28-44, XVII. 63-68, XVIII. 48, XX. 115, XXXVIII. 71-86.

[2] أَبْلِيس διάβολος.

[3] The legend of the devil's refusal to worship Adam, given by me as a Christian one, was found by Zunz (" Die Gottesdienstlichen Vor träge der Juden," page 291. Note.) in the MS. Midrash of Rabbi Moses Haddarshan, who however lived in the eleventh century.

[4] אָדָם הָרִאשׁוֹן מֵסֵב בְּגַן עֵדֶן הָיָה וְהָיוּ מַלְאֲכֵי הַשָּׁרֵת צוֹלִין לוֹ בָּשָׂר וּמְצַנְּנִין לוֹ יַיִן

[5] Midrash Rabbah on Genesis, para. 9.

בְּשָׁעָה שֶׁבָּרָא הַקָּדוֹשׁ בָּרוּךְ הוּא אֶת הָאָדָם טָעוּ בּוֹ מַלְאֲכֵי הַשָּׁרֵת וּבִקְּשׁוּ לֵאמֹר לְפָנָיו קָדוֹשׁ מֶה עָשָׂה הַקָּ׳ ב׳ ה׳ הִפִּיל עָלָיו תַּרְדֵּמָה וְיָדְעוּ הַכֹּל שֶׁהוּא אָדָם

O Holy one! then God permitted sleep to fall on him, and all knew that he was of earth." In favour of the Christian origin of this narrative we must count the fact that the name used by Christians for the devil is the one used in all the passages referred to instead of the general Hebrew name.[1]   From this event according to Muḥammad arises the hatred of the Devil against the human race, because on their account he became accursed of God; and so his first work was to counsel man in the Garden of Eden [2] to eat of the tree of knowledge.[3]   In this narrative the Devil is again given his Hebrew name,[4] and yet the first explanation of the temptation through the snake as coming from the Devil seems to be entirely Christian, as no such reference is to be found in the older Jewish writings; the passage quoted below can only be regarded as a slight allusion: [5] "From the beginning of the book up to this point [6] no Samech is to be found; as soon however as woman is created, Satan (with the initial letter Sin ש like Samech ס) is created also." Still we find in a book which, though forged, is undoubtedly old,[7] the following statement:

---

[1] (שָׂטָן) instead of (διάβολος) الشَّيْطَان (إِبْلِيس)

[2] This proper name is never used by Muḥammad in this narrative; he uses throughout simply جَنَّة, which shows that the Jews knew well the distinction between the home of our first parents and Paradise.

[3] Súras VII. 18-25, XX. 115-127.

[4] الشيطان

[5] Midrash Rabbah on Genesis, para. 17.

מִתְּחִלַּת הַסֵּפֶר וְעַד כַּן אֵין כְּתִיב סָמֶךְ כֵּיוָן שֶׁנִּבְרֵאת נִבְרָא שָׂטָן עִמָּהּ

[6] Genesis, ii. 21. וַיִּסְגֹּר

[7] Pirke Rabbi Eliezer, xiii.

הָיָה סַמָּאֵל הַשַּׂר הַגָּדוֹל שֶׁבַּשָּׁמַיִם לָקַח אֶת חַכַּת שֶׁלּוֹ וְיָרַד וְרָאָה כָּל הַבְּרִיּוֹת שֶׁבָּרָא הַקָּדוֹשׁ בָּרוּךְ הוּא וְלֹא מָצָא חָכָם

" Samael, the great prince in heaven, took his companions and went down and inspected all God's creatures; he found none more maliciously wise than the serpent, so he mounted it, and all that it said or did was at the instigation of Samael." [1] Thus this legend, even if not entirely Jewish, appears to have been derived by Muḥammad from the Jews. In the details of this narrative some confusion is found between the tree of knowledge and the tree of life. The former only is mentioned in Scripture as prohibited by God,[2] and to the eating of that alone the serpent incites Eve. After the transgression has taken place, we find the fear mentioned lest men should eat of the tree of life and live for ever.[3] Muḥammad confuses the two. In one passage he puts into the devil's mouth the statement that men through eating of this tree would become " Angels," or " immortal," [4] but in another passage he mentions only the tree of eternity.[5] All the rest of the history of the first human pair is omitted, and

---

לְהָרַע בְּנָחָשׁ עָלָה וְרָכַב עָלָיו וְכָל דְּבָרָיו שֶׁדִּבֵּר לֹא דִבֵּר וְלֹא עָשָׂה אֶלָּא מִדַּעְתּוֹ שֶׁל סַמָּאֵל

[1] To the same effect Muḥammad ben Kais (vide Elpherar on VII. 21):

ناداه ربّه يا ادم لم اكلت منها وقد نهيتك عنها قال يا رب اطعمتنى حوا قاله

لَحَّوا لم اطعمتيه قالت امرتنى الحية قال للحية لم امرتيها قال امرنى ابليس *

" His Lord called to him : ' O Adam, why hast thou eaten of that, when I had forbidden it to thee ?' He replied, ' Lord, Eve gave it to me.' Then said He to Eve : ' Why didst thou give it to him ?' she replied, ' The snake commanded me to do it.' Then said He to the snake : ' Why didst thou command it ?' ' The devil ordered me to do it.' "

See also Abulfedae Historia Anteislamica, Fleischer's edition, page 12.

[2] Genesis, ii. 17, and iii. 5. (וִהְיִיתֶם כֵּאלֹהִים יֹדְעֵי טוֹב וָרָע)

[3] Genesis, iii. 22. וָחַי לְעוֹלָם

[4] Súra VII. 19. مِنَ ٱلْخَالِدِينَ or مَلَكَانِ

[5] Súra XX. 118. شَجَرَةُ ٱلْخُلْد

only one event in the life of Cain and Abel is depicted.
This is depicted for us quite in its Jewish colours. In this
passage, and indeed throughout the Qurán, they are called
sons of Adam, but in later Arabic writings [1] their names
are given as Qábíl and Hábíl, which are clearly chosen out
of love for the rhyming sounds. The one event mentioned is
their sacrifice and the murder which it led to.[2] Muḥammad
makes them hold a conversation before the murder, and
one is likewise given in the Jerusalem Targum [3] on the
strength of the words in Genesis, " Cain said unto Abel
his brother." Still, the matter of the conversation is
given so differently in each case that we do not consider
it worth while to compare the two passages more closely.
After the murder, according to the Qurán, God sent a
raven which scratched the earth to shew Cain how to bury
Abel. What is here attributed to Cain is ascribed by the
Jews to his parents, and in a Rabbinical writing we find
the following passage: [4] " Adam and his companion sat
weeping and mourning for him (Abel) and did not know
what to do with him, as burial was unknown to them.
Then came a raven, whose companion was dead, took its

---

[1] See Abulfeda Historia Anteislámica, Fleischer's Edition, page 12, for
قَابِيل وَهَابِيل. D'Herbelot Bibliotheque Orientale under the heading
Cabil calls attention to the possibility that in the word Cabil the
derivation from قَبَلَ is kept to. Cf. Genesis, iv. 1.

[2] Genesis, iv. 3-9. Cf. Súra V. 30—36.

[3] Commonly called Pseudo-Jonathan.

[4] Pirke R. Eliezer, chapter xxi.

הָיוּ אָדָם וְעֶזְרוֹ יוֹשְׁבִים וּבוֹכִים וּמִתְאַבְּלִים עָלָיו וְלֹא הָיוּ
יוֹדְעִים מַה לַעֲשׂוֹת לְהֶבֶל שֶׁלֹּא הָיוּ נְחוּנִים בִּקְבוּרָה בָּא עוֹרֵב
אֶחָד שֶׁמֵת לוֹ אֶחָד מֵחֲבֵרָיו לָקַח אוֹתוֹ וְחָפַר בָּאָרֶץ וּטְמָנָה
לְעֵינֵיהֶם אָמַר אָדָם כָּעוֹרֵב אֲנִי עֹשֶׂה מִיָּד לָקַח נִבְלָתוֹ שֶׁל
הֶבֶל וְחָפַר בָּאָרֶץ וּטְמָנָה

body, scratched in the earth and hid it before their eyes; then said Adam, I shall do as this raven has done, and at once he took Abel's corpse, dug in the earth and hid it." In the Qurán a verse follows [1] which, without knowledge of the source from which it has come, seems to stand in no connection with what has gone before, but which will be made clear by the following explanation. The verse according to my translation runs thus : " Wherefore we commanded the children of Israel, that he who slayeth a soul, without having slain a soul, or committed wickedness in the earth, shall be as if he had slain all mankind; but he who saveth a soul alive, shall be as if he had saved the lives of all mankind." One perceives here no connection at all, if one does not consider the following Hebrew passage: [2] " We find it said in the case of Cain who murdered his brother: The voice of thy brother's bloods crieth. [3] It is not said here *blood* in the singular, but bloods in the plural, *i.e.,* his own blood and the blood of his seed. Man was created single in order to show that to him who kills a single individual, it shall be reckoned that he has slain the whole race ; but to him who preserves the life of a single individual it is counted that he hath preserved the whole race." By this comparison it is made clear what led Muḥammad to this general digression ; he had evidently received this rule from his informants when they related to him this particular event. Another

---

[1] Súra V. 35.   [2] Mishna Sanhedrin IV. 5.

מָצִינוּ בְּקַיִן שֶׁהָרַג אֶת אָחִיו נֶאֱמַר בּוֹ קוֹל דְּמֵי אָחִיךָ צֹעֲקִים אֵינוֹ אֹמֵר דַּם אָחִיךָ אֶלָּא דְּמֵי אָחִיךָ דָּמוֹ וְדַם זַרְעִיוֹתָיו לְפִיכַךְ נִבְרָא אָדָם יְחִידִי לְלַמֶּדְךָ שֶׁכָּל הַמְאַבֵּד נֶפֶשׁ אַחַת מִיִּשְׂרָאֵל מַעֲלֶה עָלָיו הַכָּתוּב כְּאִלּוּ אִבֵּד עוֹלָם מָלֵא וְכָל הַמְקַיֵּם נֶפֶשׁ אַחַת מִיִּשְׂרָאֵל מַעֲלֶה עָלָיו הַכָּתוּב כְּאִלּוּ קַיֵּם עוֹלָם מָלֵא

[3] Genesis, iv. 10, not דם (singular), but דְּמֵי (plural). Compare the translation of Onkelos.

L

allusion to Cain is found in the Qurán in a passage where he is called the man "who has seduced among men." [1] No one else is mentioned in this period excepting Idrís [2] who, according to the commentators, is Enoch. This seems probable from the words, [3] "And we uplifted him to a place on high," and also from a Jewish writing in which he is counted among the nine who went to Paradise alive. Jalálu'ddín brings this point even more prominently forward: [4] "He lived in Paradise where he had been brought after he had tasted death; he was quickened however, and departed not thence again." He appears to have gained his name [5] on account of the knowledge of the Divine Law attributed to him. Elpherar remarks: "He was called Idris (searcher) on account of his earnest search in the revealed Scriptures." It is remarkable that in both these passages of the Qurán [6] he is mentioned after Ishmael.

---

[1] Súra XLI. 92. ٱلَّذِى أَمَّلَ مِنَ ٱلْأَنْسِ

[2] إِدْرِيسَ Súras XIX. 57, 58 ; XXI. 85, 86.

Elpherar on Súra XIX. 57 says : وهو جد ابى نوح واسمه اخنوخ

"He is the grandfather of the father of Noah, his name is Enoch;" which name Abulfeda (Hist. Anteislámica page 14) spells حنوخ and expressly remarks : بحاء مهملة و نون و واو و حاء معجمة " With an unpointed ha, nun, waw, and a pointed ha;" and later he adds و امّا حنوخ وهو ادريس

[3] Súra XIX. 58. وَرَفَعْنَاهُ مَكَانًا عَلِيًّا. Compare Genesis, v. 24 and the Tract Derech Erez cited in Midrash Yalkut, chap. XLII.

[4] In Maraccio. هو حيى فى الجنة ادخلها بعد ان اذيق الموت وأحيى ولم يخرج منها

[5] إِدْرِيسَ is derived from تَدَرَّسَ Elpherar on XIX. 57. وسمى ادريس لكثرة درسة الكتب

[6] Súras XIX. 55, 56 ; XXI. 85.

B.—From Noah to Abraham.

The corruption which spread in the time of Noah is not
described with any details in the Qurán, and one event
which is stated by the Rabbis to have taken place at this
period is transferred by Muḥammad to Solomon's time,
to which he considered it better suited, as it treats of
angels and genii. The Rabbinical passage runs thus:[1]
" Rabbi Joseph was asked by his scholars:' What is Azael?'
and he answered: When men at the time of the Flood
practised idolatry, God was grieved at it, and two angels,
Shamhazai and Azael, said to him : ' Lord of the world, did

---

[1] Midr. Abhkhir quoted in Midr. Yalkut Chap. XLIV.

שָׁאֲלוּ תַלְמִידָיו אֶתְרַב יוֹסֵף מַחוּ עֲזָאֵל אָמַר לָהֶם כֵּן שֶׁעָמְדוּ
דוֹר הַמַּבּוּל וְעָבְדוּ עֲבוֹרָה זָדָה הָיָה הַקָּדוֹשׁבָּרוּךְ חוּר מִתְעַצֵּב
מִיַד עָמְדוּ שְׁנֵי מַלְאָכִים שִׁמְחַזַי וַעֲזָאֵל וְאָמְרוּ לְפָנָיו רִבּוֹנוֹ
שֶׁל עוֹלָם הֲלֹא אָמַרְנוּ לְפָנֶיךָ כְּשֶׁבְּרָאתָ אֶת עוֹלָמֶךָ מָה אֱנוֹשׁ
כִּי תִזְכְּרֶנּוּ אָמַר לָהֶם וְעוֹלָם מַה יְהֵא עָלָיו אָמְרוּ לוֹ רְבּ' שׁ'
ע' הָיִינוּ מְסַתְּפָּקִין בּוֹ אָ' עָ' בָּלוּי וְיָדוּעַ לְפָנַי אִם אַתֶּם שְׁרוּיִין
בָּאֶרֶץ הָיָה שׁלֵט בָּכֶם יֵצֶר הָרָע וִהְיִיתֶם קָשִׁים מִבְּנֵי אָדָם ל'
הֵן לָנוּ רְשׁוּת וְנָדוּר עִם הַבְּרִיוֹת וְתִרְאֶה אֵיךְ אָנוּ מְקַדְּשִׁין שְׁמֶךָ
א' ל' רְדוּ וְתָדוּרוּ עִמָּהֶם מִיַד רָאָה שִׁמְחַזַי רִיכָה אַחַת וּשְׁמָה
אִסְטְהַר נָתַן עֵינָיו בָּהּ אָמָא הִשָׁמְעִי לִי אָמְרָה לוֹ אֵינִי שֹׁמַעַת
לֹךְ עַד שֶׁתִּלַמְדֵנִי הַשֵׁם מְפֹרָשׁ שֶׁאַתָּה עֹלֶה בּוֹ לָרָקִיעַ בְּשָׁעָה
שֶׁאַתָּה זֹכְרוּ לְמָדָהּ אוֹתוֹ שֵׁם הַזִכִּירָה אוֹתוֹ שֵׁם וְעָלְתָה לָרָקִיעַ
יְלֹא הִקְלְקָלָה אָמַר הַקָּ' בָּ' ח' הוֹאִיל וּפֵרְשָׁה עַצְמָהּ מִן הָעֲבֵרָה
לְכוּ וְקִבְעוּהָ בֵּיו שִׁבְעָה כוֹכָבִים הַלָלוּ כְּדֵי שֶׁתִּזְכּוּ בָּהּ לְעוֹלָם
וְנִקְבְּעָה בַּפִּימָה מִיַד קִלְקְלוּ עִם בְּנוֹת הָאָדָם שֶׁהָיוּ יָפוֹת וְלֹא
וְכְלֹא לִכְבּוֹשׁ אֶת יִצְדָן עָמְדוּ וְנָשְׂאוּ נָשִׁים וְהוֹלִידוּ בָּנִים הֵנָּא
וְהִיָא וַעֲזָאֵל הָיָה עַל מִינֵי צִבְעוֹנִים וְעַל מִינֵי תַכְשִׁיטִין שֶׁל
נָשִׁים שֶׁמְּסַפָּתִין אֶת בְּנֵי אָדָם לְהַרְחוּר עֲבֵרָה

Compare Yoma 67. 2. and Rashi, Zohar on Genesis, i. 26.

we not say unto Thee at the creation : 'What is man that
Thou art mindful of him?'[1]   But He said : 'What shall
become of the world?' They answered : 'We would have
made use of it.' 'But it is well-known to Me that, if you
lived on the earth, lust would overcome you, and you would
become even worse than man.' 'Then give us permission
to live with men, and Thou wilt see how we shall sanctify
Thy name.' 'Go and live with them.' Then Shamhazai
saw a maiden by name Istahar. He cast his eyes on her
and said : 'Listen to me ;' to which she replied : 'I will not
listen to thee until thou teachest me the explicit name
of God, through the mention of which thou risest to
heaven.' He taught her this name which she then uttered
and rose unspotted to heaven. Then God said : 'Because
she turned herself from sin, well! fasten her between
the seven stars, that ye may enjoy her for ever'; and so
she was fastened into the Pleiades. But they lived in
immorality with the daughters of men, for these were
beautiful, and they could not tame their lusts. Then they
took wives and begat sons, Hiwwa and Hiyya. Azael was
master of the meritricious arts and trinkets of women
which beguile men to immoral thoughts." It is evident
that this story is alluded to in the passage in the Qurán,[2]
where the two angels Hárút and Márút are said to have
taught men a charm by which they might cause division
between a man and his wife.[3] During this state of

---

[1] Psalm, viii. 5.

[2] Súra II. 96. هَارُوتُ وَ مَارُوتُ

[3] This connection and comparison which might well appear very doubtful, and which seemed even to me at first nothing more than a conjecture,
receives full corroboration from that which later Arabian authors, quite
in harmony with the Mid. Yalkut, say about the angels. We find in
Maraccius Prodromi iv. 82, the following :

و قال مجاهد عجبت الملائكة من ظلم بنى ادم وقد جاءتهم الرسل فقال
لهم ربهم اختاروا منكم اثنين انزلهما يحكمان في الارض فكانا هاروت و ماروت

corruption of morals Noah appears, teaching men and
seeking by exhortation to turn them from their evil
ways. He builds himself the Ark and is saved, while the rest
of the people perish.[1] His whole appearance as an admonisher and seer is not Biblical but Rabbinical, and serves
Muḥammad's ends perfectly, as Noah in this way is a type
of himself. According to rabbinical writings,[2] Job, xii. 5
refers to Noah, " who rebuked them and spake to them
words as severe as flames, but they scorned him and said :
' Old man, for what purpose is this ark ?' He, however, said:
' God is going to bring a flood upon you.'" Other particulars

---

فحكما فعدلا حتى نزلت عليهما الزهرة احسن فى صورة امراة تخاصم زوجها فافتتنا
بها و ارادا على نفسها فطارت الزهرة فرجعت حيث كانت .... قال محمد
وقد ذكر يحيى من غير مجاهد ان المراة التى افتتنا فيها كانت من اهل الدنيا *

"Mujáhid says: The angels wondered at the wickedness of the sons
of Adam, for Apostles had already been sent to them ; then their Lord
(God) said to them : 'Choose out two of you, and I will send them that
they may judge upon earth.' Then Hárút and Márút were chosen, and
they judged righteously, till Zahrah (the star Venus, just like the
Yalkutish אסְטְהַר, like אֶסְתֵּר the Persian ستاره and the Greek
ἀστήρ). In Job xxxi. 26 the Targum puts אסתהר for the Hebrew (אוֹר
came in the form of a most beautiful woman and complained about her
husband. They were led astray by her and lusted after her, but she fled
and went back to where she was before . . . . Muḥammad says: 'Yaḥya
states on another authority than that of Mujáhid, that the woman through
whom they were led astray was a human woman.' The union of these
two views is to be found in the passages quoted from Midrash Yalkut.

[1] Súras VII. 57—63, X. 72—75, XI. 27—50, XXII. 43, XXIII. 23—32.
XXV. 39, XXVI. 105—121, XXIX. 13. 14, XXXVII. 73—81, LIV. 9—18,
LXXI. 1—end.

[2] Sanhedrin 108. (Comp. Midrash Rabbah on Genesis, paras. 30 and
33, also on Ecclesiastes, ix. 14.)

מַה דִּכְתִיב לַפִּיד בּוּז לְעַשְׁתּוּת שַׁאֲנָן נָכוֹן לְמוֹעֲדֵי רָגֶל
שֶׁהָיָה נֹחַ הַצַּדִּיק מוֹכִיחַ אוֹתָם וְאוֹמֵר לָהֶם דְּבָרִים קָשִׁים כְּלַפִּידִים
וְהָיוּ מַבְזִין אוֹתוֹ רָמְרִי לוֹ זָקֵן תֵּיבָה זוֹ לָמָּה אָמַר לָהֶם הַקָּ'
בָּ' חַ' מֵבִיא עֲלֵיכֶם אֶת הַמַּבּוּל

also accord with Rabbinical tradition, *e.g.*, "The people laughed at the ark,"[1] accords with "They mocked and laughed at him in their words." "The waters of the Flood were hot,"[2] with "The generation of the deluge was punished with hot water." Still many inaccuracies and perversions are to be found; for instance, Muḥammad makes Noah to have lived 950 years before the Flood,[3] whereas this is really the whole term of his life; and he represents one of Noah's sons as disobedient to him, and states that this same son did not follow him into the Ark, but believed himself safe on a mountain peak.[4] This idea probably arose from a misunderstanding of Ham's evil conduct after the Deluge.[5] Muḥammad also makes out Noah's wife to have been unbelieving,[6] although he is silent as to wherein her unbelief consisted; and I can find no reason for this statement, which is not mentioned either in the Bible or in the Rabbinical writings.

---

[1] Súra XI. 40 Cf. Midr. Tanchuma, Section Noah.

הָיוּ מְשַׂחֲקִין מִמֶּפוּ וּמַלְעִיגִין בִּדְבָרִים

[2] Súra XI. 42. and XXIII. 27. وَفَارَ ٱلتَّنُّورُ

Cf. Rosh Hashanah 16. 2. and Sanhedrin 108.

דּוֹר הַמַּבּוּל בְּרוֹתְחִין נִדּוֹנוּ

The Arabic Commentators seem to me to have quite misunderstood these passages, since they assume fabulous references. Our explanation, which is justified by a figurative interpretation of the words 'And the oven glows,' appears to me sufficiently confirmed by a comparison with the Talmudic utterance. Also D'Herbelot (Bib. Orient. Noah, page 671,) understands وَفَارَ ٱلتَّنُّورُ in this way.

[3] Súra XXIX. 13. Cf. Genesis, ix. 29.
[4] Súra XI. 44, 45, 48.
[5] Genesis, ix. 22 ff.

The commentators actually call this son Canaan, كنعان (compare Genesis, ix. 25 ff) although they, like the Bible, do not reckon any son of this name in their enumeration of the sons, but count these three only, viz. سام وحام ويافث

[6] Súra LXVI. 10.

Perhaps Muḥammad was misled by the analogy of the wife of Lot, who is mentioned in the same context. While these variations are due to errors and to the confusion cf different times and events, others are to be ascribed to deliberate[1] alteration and elaboration. And of this kind are those details not mentioned in Jewish History, which represent Noah as one occupying the same position as Muḥammad and speaking in his spirit. This applies particularly to that which is put into his mouth as admonisher. This is the case not only with Noah, but with all who appear in the character of the righteous in any evil age. Thus he puts into the mouth of Luqmán, as a wise man known to the Arabs,[2] words suitable to his own circumstances and opinions, and the same thing happens in the case of Noah and the other preachers of Jewish history to whom he alludes. Noah although he worked no miracle, was saved in a miraculous way, and so Muḥammad cannot put into his mouth the same words which he uses of himself, as well as ascribes to other forerunners of himself after Noah's time, viz., that he is a mere preacher; yet he makes him say everything which is not clearly contrary to the historical facts related about him. He was only an unimportant man,[3] and did not pretend to be any one wonderful or supernatural.[4] But he was divinely commissioned to warn the people, and for this he asked no reward.[5] O sancta simplicitas! one would exclaim in considering this last point, if Muḥammad had written it down with full consideration of Noah's position as one threatening the world with punishment, and if it had not been rather that he saw everything from his own distorted point of

---

[1] The word "deliberate" is to be understood in the sense already sufficiently explained in the First Division, Third Section, so that we may use it from now on without further explanatory comment.

[2] Súra XXXI. 11 ff.   [3] Súra VII. 61.   [4] Súra XI. 33.
[5] Súra XI. 31. and XXVI. 109.

view, and was determined to make every thing accord with
his ideas. In another place he goes so far as to interpolate
a verse into Noah's discourse, which is entirely character-
istic of his own, and in which the little word (translated
" speak ")[1] actually occurs, which is always regarded
as a word of address to Muḥammad from God (or Gabriel).
The same thing will be noted further on in the case of
Abraham.

After Noah the next mentioned is Húd[2] who is evidently
the Biblical Eber.[3] This seems a striking example of the
ignorance of Muḥammad, or, as it appears to me more
probable here, of the Jews round about him. According
to the Rabbinical opinion[4] the name Hebrew is derived
from Eber, but in later times this name was almost
entirely forgotten and the name Jew[5] was commonly used.
The Jews, to whom it was known that their name was
derived from an ancestor, believed that the name in
question was that in use at the time, and that the ancestor
therefore was this patriarch Húd.[6] His time is that in
which a second punitive judgment from God on account
of bold, insolent behaviour is mentioned in the Scripture,

---

[1] قَلْ XI. 37. Cf. XXIX. 19·   [2] هُودٌ

[3] עֵבֶר   [4] עִבְרִי from עֵבֶר

Compare Mid. Rabbah on Genesis, para. 42.

לְאַבְרָם הָעִבְרִי שֶׁהוּא מִבְּנֵי בָנָיו שֶׁל עֵבֶר

" Abram was called the Hebrew because he was descended from Eber."
(Genesis, xiv. 13.).

[5] יְהוּדִי Yahúdi. Among the Arabs sometimes يَهُودٌ Yahúd, more

often هُودٌ Húd.

[6] Elpherar (on Súra VII. 63) gives along with an incorrect genealogy
the following correct one, بن سالح بن ارفخشد بن سام بن نوح, and
the author of the book اعلام الهدى says directly " Húd is عابر·"
(Mar. Prod. iv. 92.)

and this is treated of in several chapters of the Qurán.[1]
In order to have the right to refer what is said about Húd
to the time of the confusion of tongues, or, as the Rabbis
call it, the Dispersion,[2] we must adduce some particulars
which point to this reference, for the statements are very
general in their tenour and might be referred to other
occurrences. The following verse [3] possibly refers to the
building of the Tower : " And ye erect magnificent works,
hoping that ye may continue for ever." The Arabic commentators take it that the buildings would afford them a
perpetual dwelling-place, but the verse might also mean,
" make by building it an everlasting name for yourselves."
The neighbourhood is called in the Qurán the " Possessor
of Pillars.[4] In one passage[5] there appears to be a reference
to Nimrod, who lived at this time and in this region, since
the children of Ad are here reproached for obeying the
command of every contumacious hero.[6] The idea that
they were idolators, which is brought up against them in
all the passages in the Qurán, agrees perfectly with the
Rabbinical view expressed as follows : [7] " And it came to

---

[1] Súras VII. 63—71, XI. 52—64, XXII. 43, XXIII. 83—44, XXV. 40,
XXVI. 123—141, XXIX. 37, XXXVIII. 11, XL. 32, XLI. 12—16, XLVI.
20—25, L. 13, LI. 41, 42, LIII. 50, LIV. 18—22, LXIX. 4 –9, LXXXIX.
5—9.

[2] דּוֹר הַפְּלָגָה

[3] Súra XXVI. 129. وَ تَتَّخِذُونَ مَصَانِعَ لَعَلَّكُمْ تَخْلُدُونَ

[4] Súra LXXXIX. 6. ذَاتِ ٱلْعِمَادِ Cf. Genesis xi. 4.

[5] Súra XI. 62. وَٱتَّبَعُوا أَمْرَ كُلِّ جَبَّارٍ عَنِيدٍ

Compare Genesis, x. 8, 9, where Nimrod's surname is always גִּבּוֹר

[6] D'Herbelot, under the heading Nimrod, asserts that the Arabians
connect Nimrod with the building of the Tower.

[7] Midr. Rabbah on Genesis, xi. 2, par. 38.

וַיְהִי בְּנָסְעָם מִקֶּדֶם הִסִּיעוּ עַצְמָן מִקַּדְמוֹנוֹ שֶׁל עוֹלָם

M

pass when they journeyed from the beginning (East),
that is to say, when they withdrew themselves from Him
Who is the beginning of the world." Muḥammad says
of these people [1] that they built an (idolatrous) symbol on
every high place in order to play there (i.e. to practice
idolatry). And the Rabbis tell us [2] that the race of the
dispersion contemplated building a tower and putting an
idol on its summit. Resemblances are also to be found
with reference to the punishment which overtook them.
Muḥammad tells us [3] they were followed in this world by a
curse, and that they shall be followed by the same on the
day of resurrection, and the Rabbis say [4] that the race
of the dispersion had no part in the next world, for the
twice-mentioned dispersion applies to this world and the
other. In Muḥammad's treatment the essential point of
the punishment is lost sight of, for instead of describing
it as a simple dispersion and confusion of tongues, he
speaks of an absolute annihilation of the sinners by a
poisonous wind. [5] One sees at once the mistaken source
from which this change is derived. We recognize partly
from our knowledge of Muḥammad's motives in making
the alteration, and partly from the minuteness with which

---

[1] Súra XXVI. 128. تَعْبَثُونَ آيَةً رِيعٍ بِكُلِّ أَتَبْنُونَ Compare לִצְחֵק

to play, Exodus, xxxii. 6.

[2] דּוֹר הַפְלָנָה אָמְרוּ בֹּאוּ וְנַעֲשֶׂה לָנוּ מִגְדָל וְנָשִׂים עֲבוֹדָה
זָרָה בְּרֹאשׁוֹ

[3] Súra XI. 63. وَأُتْبِعُوا فِى هَذِهِ ٱلدُّنْيَا لَعْنَةً وَيَوْمَ ٱلْقِيَامَةِ

[4] Mishna Sanhedrin X. 3.   Genesis, xi. 8, 9.

דּוֹר הַפְלָנָה אֵין לָהֶם חֵלֶק לָעוֹלָם הַבָּא שֶׁנֶּאֱמַר וַיָּפֶץ ח'
אוֹתָם מִשָּׁם עַל פְּנֵי כָל־הָאָרֶץ וַיָּפֶץ ח' אוֹתָם בָּעוֹלָם הַזֶּה
וּמִשָּׁם הֱפִיצָם ח' בָּעוֹלָם הַבָּא

[5] Súras XLI. 15, XLVI. 23 ff. LI. 41, LIV. 19, LXIX. 6 ff.

the new punishment is described, which would not have
been accorded to a fiction. It appears therefore that the
history reached this development in the mouth of the
people, who delight in minute descriptions of punishment.
The remaining deviations and additions, particularly the
latter, are caused, as we have already remarked in the case
of Noah, by confusion with Muḥammad's own time and
person. This is the case when he transfers 'unbelief in
the resurrection to the time of Húd and counts it among
the sins of that time which were worthy of punishment.[1]
This is seen too especially in the great importance assigned
to Eber and to his desire to turn the people from their evil
ways. Decided traces of this are certainly to be found in
Jewish writings,[2] where we are told that Eber was a great
prophet, who by the Holy Spirit called his son Pelag,
because in his days the earth was divided[3] (which Eber
had known beforehand). Much also is said of the school
of Eber, and Rebekah is said to have gone there; for
it is written: "She went to enquire of the Lord,"[4] and
Jacob is supposed to have stayed there for fourteen years.
But of the fact that Eber preached to the people, he being
their brother (on which Muḥammad places great stress,
because he himself was sent as an Arab to the Arabs),
not a trace is to be found, still less of the fact that he took
no reward from them.[5] One point still remains to be
cleared up, why the race under discussion is called in the

---

[1] Súra XXIII. 87.

[2] Seder 'Olam quoted in Midrash Yalkut, Chap. 62.

נָבִיא גָּדוֹל הָיָה עֵבֶר שֶׁקָּרָא אֶת־שֵׁם בְּנוֹ פֶּלֶג בְּרוּחַ הַקֹּדֶשׁ
שֶׁנֶּ' כִּי בְיָמָיו נִפְלְגָה הָאָרֶץ

[3] Genesis, x. 25.

[4] Genesis, xxv. 22. Midr. Rabbah on Genesis, par. 63. Also par. 68. for
Jacob's sojourn in the home of Eber.

[5] Súra XI. 53, XXVI. 127.

Qurán the people of Ád.[1] The commentators state that Ád
was the son of Uz, the son of Aram, the son of Shem, the
son of Noah; and Muḥammad seems also to have been of
this opinion, whence it comes that he transfers the events
to the land of Aram or Iram.[2] Nevertheless it seems to
have come about chiefly from the fact that all these occurrences are described with an Arabian colouring, and so
they were attributed to Arab tribes, amongst which an
ancient extinct one had the name of Ád;[3] perhaps in it
there is also an etymological reference to a "return" to
the early evil conduct of the generation of the Deluge. In
another passage there is an allusion to this occurrence,[4]
where the fact itself is brought forward much more in
accordance with the Biblical account, but quite without
specification of time or persons: "Their predecessors
devised plots heretofore, but God came into their building
to overthrow it from the foundation, and the roof fell on
them from above and a punishment came upon them which
they did not expect." On this Elpherar remarks:[5] "These
are Nimrod, the son of Canaan, who built a tower in Babel
in order that he might mount to heaven"; and further:
"And when the tower fell the language of men became
confused, and so they could not finish it; then they spoke
seventy-three languages, on this account the city was
called Babel (confusion), before this the language of men
was Syriac." The Rabbis, too, assert that before this

---

[1] عَادٌ

[2] Súra LXXXIX. 6. اِرَم

[3] Poc. Spec., p. 3.

[4] Súra XVI. 28.

[5] .... وهم نمرود بن كنعان بنى الصرح ببابل ليصعد الى السماء
ولما سقط الصرح تبلبلت لسان الناس من الفرغ يومئذ فتكلموا بثلاثة وسبعين
لسانا فلذلك سميت بابل وكان لسان الناس قبل ذلك بالسريانية *

men spoke in Hebrew, but afterwards in seventy languages.
Jalálu'd-dín says the same thing,[1] and adds that Nimrod
built the Tower "in order that he might mount out of it
into heaven to wage war with the inhabitants thereof."[2]
But the identity of this narrative with that of Húd and Ád
is no more accepted by Abulfeda[3] than it is by Elpherar
and Jalálu'd-dín, even on the view that Húd is the same
as Eber. Although the colouring of this narrative as
given in the Qurán differs much from that of the
Biblical account, yet the identity of the two can be
shown by putting this and that together, and by explaining the way in which the individual differences
arose. But in the case of another narrative which
follows this one in almost all the passages of the Qurán,[4]
it is very difficult to find out the subject of which it treats
and the Bible characters to which it refers. This narrative
is about Ṣamúd,[5] which like Ád is an ancient extinct Arab
tribe,[6] to whom their brother Sálih was sent when they fell
into sin.[7] Sálih is said to have exhorted the Ṣamúdites
to righteousness and to have commended to them a
certain she-camel as especially under divine protection;

---

[1] Maracc. on the passage.

[2] ليصعد منه الى السماء ليقاتل اهلها

[3] Hist. Anteislámica, pp. 18 and 20.

[4] Except in Súras L. 12, and LXIX. 4, where it precedes. In the former
of these two passages it precedes the story of the Midianites also, and
thus no chronological order is followed. In Súras LI. 43 and LIII. 51, it
actually precedes the story of the Deluge, and in Súra LXXXV. 18,
Pharoah is placed before Ṣamúd on account of the rhyme.

[5] ثَمُود Ṣamúd, مَالِح Sálih.

[6] Poc. Spec., p. 3.

[7] The passages which treat of this are the following :—Súras VII.
71—78, XI. 64—72, XXII. 43, XXV. 40, XXVI. 141—160, XXVII. 46—55,
XXIX. 37, XXXVIII. 12, XL. 32, XLI. 12—18, L. 12, LI. 43—46, LIII.
51, LIV. 23—33, LXIX. 4—6, LXXXV. 18, LXXXIX. 8, XCI. 11—16.

he even bade them share water with her.[1]　But the unbe-
lievers of his time (according to one passage [2] only nine in
number) hamstrung her, and so divine punishment overtook them.　I find no similar occurrence in Jewish writings,
but the likeness of the name points to Shelah [3] who however, as the father of Eber, would have deserved mention
before him.[4]　On the whole, the word is so general in its
meaning of " a pious man " that we cannot treat it here
with certainty as having been originally a proper name.[5]
Perhaps the story of the houghing is founded on the
words in Jacob's blessing of his sons,[6] and the sharing
of the water on the etymology of the name Ṣamúd.[7]
Moreover Ṣamúd was, according to the commentators,
the son of Gether the son of Aram, the son of Shem,
the son of Noah, which fits in fairly well with the date
already assigned to Shelah.[8]　It is however impossible

---

[1] Súra LIV 28, XCI. 12.

[2] Súra XXVII. 49.

[3] שֶׁלַח See Genesis, x. 24. This is also D'Herbelot's view. See his
Bib. Orient. under Sálih.

[4] Ismá'íl ben 'Ali asserts however that Sálih lived after Húd. (Maracc.
Prodr., iv. 93).

[5] Later Arabians call Shelah also سالح as in the passage quoted above
from Elpherar, who gives however a different genealogy for Sálih in his
comment on Súra VII. 71. Still, in a copy of the Samaritan Arabic
translation of the Pentateuch שֶׁלַח, is translated by صالح. (Compare
De Sacy in Eichhorn's Bibliothek der Bibl. Liter., X, pp. 47, 110, 111.)

[6] Genesis, xlix. 6. וּבִרְצֹנָם עִקְּרוּ שׁוֹר

[7] From ثَمَدَ " to demand water."

[8] The أَصْحَابُ ٱلْحِجْر mentioned in Súra XV. 80 are supposed to be the
same as the Ṣamúdites, as Elpherar also says; but this opinion has no
foundation and appears improbable, because in this passage where chronological order seems to be observed, the stories of Abram and the Angels,
of Lot in connection with Abram, and of the Midianites are given earlier.

for me to give any more exact explanation from Jewish writings.

C.—Abraham to Moses.

Though the saints mentioned earlier bore some likeness to Muḥammad, and though their condition, so similar to his own, encouraged him as well as verified his statements, yet Abraham [1] was his great prototype, the man of whom he thought most highly, and the one with whom he liked best to compare himself and to make out as one with himself in opinion. Abraham's faith [2] is that which is preached in the Qurán.[3] He was a believer in the unity of God.[4] He was neither Jew nor Christian for it is written:[5] "Abraham was not a Jew, nor a Christian, but he was a believer in the unity of God, given up to God (a Muslim)."[6]

---

[1] اِبْرَاهِيمُ   [2] مِلَّة   [3] Súra XVI. 124.

[4] حَنِيفٌ   Súra II. 129, III. 60, VI. 79, XVI. 121, 124.

[5] Súra II. 134. مَاكَانَ اِبْرَاهِيمُ يَهُودِيًّا وَلَا نَصْرَانِيًّا وَ لَكِنْ كَانَ حَنِيفًا مُسْلِمًا

[6] On this Baidháwi has the following :

تنازعت اليهود والنصارى فى ابراهيم و زعم كل فريق انه منهم وترافعوا الى رسول الله صلعم فنزل والمعنى ان اليهودية والنصرانية حدثت بنزول التورية والانجيل على موسى وعيسى *

"The Jews and the Christians disputed about Abraham, and each party believed they could count him on their side. They appealed to Muḥammad and thereupon came this revelation. The meaning is, that Judaism and Christianity first came into existence by the sending of the Law through Moses and the Gospel through Jesus." That this is the Jewish view is shown by the following passage :—

קִיֵּם אַבְרָהָם אָבִינוּ אֶת כָּל הַתּוֹרָה כֻּלָּה שֶׁנֶּאֱמַר עֵקֶב אֲשֶׁר שָׁמַע אַבְרָהָם בְּקוֹלִי

"Our forefather Abraham observed the whole Law, for it is written (Genesis, xxvi. 5.): "Because Abraham obeyed My voice, and kept My charge, My commandments, My statutes and My laws." (Yoma, xxviii. 2).

He is represented as the friend of God,[1] and this is
his name throughout the East.[2] Abraham's importance
and the rich legendary material concerning him, which
Judaism offered, lead us to expect much about him in
the Qurán, and our expectation is not disappointed. It is
to him that the founding of the Ka'bah is traced back.[3]
He is supposed to have lived in the Temple,[4] and to have
composed books.[5] This opinion is also held by the Rabbis,
many of whom attribute to Abraham the well-known
cabalistic and undoubtedly very ancient Sepher Jazirah.
Passing to the events of his life, we first come across the
beautiful legend of his attaining to the true knowledge of
God. We are told also how he tried to persuade his
father and his people thereto. A special instance of this
was when he destroyed the idols, and, putting the staff into
the hand of the largest, attributed the action to him. He
sought thus to convince the people, who quite perceived
the impossibility of the idols having done it, since they
could not move, but they were not thereby persuaded.[6]
Abraham is represented as praying in vain that his father
might be released from the punishment of hell.[7] We are
told too that the people, embittered by Abraham's conduct
towards the idols, wanted to have him burnt alive, but that
he was rescued from that fate by divine intervention.[8]
The whole story is taken from the Rabbinical writings,
where we read as follows.[9] "Terah was an idolator: once

---

[1] خَلِيلُ آللّٰه   [2] Súra IV. 124.   وَٱتَّخَذَ ٱللّٰهُ اِبْرَاهِيمَ خَلِيلًا

[3] Súra II. 119 ff.   [4] Súra XIV. 40.   [5] LXXXVII. 19.

[6] Súras VI. 74--82, XIX. 42—51, XXI. 52—69, XXII. 43, XXVI. 69—
105, XXIX. 15—23, XXXVII. 81—95, XLIII. 25—28, LX. 4—6.

[7] Súras IX. 115, XXVI. 86—104, LX. 4. Sunna 395.

[8] Súras II. 260, XXI. 69—74, XXIX. 23—27, XXXVII. 95—99.

[9] Midrash Rabba on Genesis, para. 38.

תֶּרַח עֹבֵד לִצְלָמִים הָיָה חַד זְמַן נְפַק לְאֲתַר הוֹשִׁיב לְאַבְרָהָם

he went away and left Abraham to sell his idols. Whenever a buyer came, Abraham asked him his age. If he
replied, I am fifty, or sixty years old, Abraham said : ' Woe
to the man of sixty who desires to worship the work of a
day, so that the buyer went away ashamed.'[1] Once a woman
came, with a dish of wheat and said, ' Here, put this before
them ;' but Abraham took a stick and beat down all the

מֹכֵר תַּחְתָּיו הֲוָה אָתֵי בַּר אֶנָשׁ בָּעֵי דְּיִזְבַּן וַהֲוָה אָמַר לֵהּ
בַּר כַּמָּה שְׁנִין אַתְּ וַהֲוָה אָמַר לֵהּ בַּר חַמְשִׁין אוֹ שִׁתִּין וַהֲוָה
אָמַר לֵהּ וַי לֵהּ לַחֲהוּא גַבְרָא דַהֲוָה בַּר שִׁתִּין וּבָעֵי לְמִסְגַד
לְבַר יוֹמֵי וְהָוָה מִתְבַּיֵּשׁ וְהָלֵךְ לוֹ חַד זְמַן אֲתַת חֲדָא אִתְּתָא
טְעִינָא בִּידָהּ חֲדָא פִּינַךְ דְּסֹלֶת אֲמֶרֶת לֵהּ הֵא לָךְ קָרֵב
קֳדָמֵיהוֹן קָם וְנָסַב בְּחֻקְלְסָא בִּידֵהּ וְתַבְּרִינְחוֹן לְכָלְהוֹן פְּסִילַיָּא
וִיהַב בְּחֻקְלְסָא בִּידָא דְרַבָּא דַהֲוָה בֵּינֵיהוֹן כַּד דַאֲתָא אֲבוּהִי
אָמַר לֵהּ מָן עֲבַד לְהוֹן כְּדֵין אָ' לֵ' מָה נִכְפַּר מִנָּךְ אֲתַת חֲדָא
אִתְּתָא טְעִינָא לָהּ חֲדָא פִּינַךְ דְּסֹלֶת וַאֲמֶרֶת לִי הֵא לָךְ קָרֵב
קֳדָמֵיהוֹן קָרֵבִת לְקֳדָמֵיהוֹן הֲוָה דֵין אָמַר אֲנָא אֵיכַל קַדְמֵי וְדֵין
אָמַד אֲנָא אֵיכַל קַדְמֵי קָם הָדֵין רַבָּא דַהֲוָה בֵּינֵיהוֹן נָסַב בְּחֻקְלְסָא
וְתַבְּרִינוֹן אָ' לֵ' מָה אַתְּ מַפְלַח בִּי וְיָדְעִין אִינּוּן אָ' לֵ' וְלֹא
יִשְׁמְעוּ אָזְנֵיךְ מַה שֶׁפִּיךָ אֹמֵר בַּסְבָה וּמִסְרַח לְנִמְרֹד אָ' לֵ' נִסְגֻּד
לְנוּרָא אָ' לֵ' אַבְרָהָם וְנִסְגֻּד לְמַיָּא דְּמַטַּפִּין נוּרָא אָ' לֵ' נִמְרֹד
נִסְגֻּד לְמַיָּא אָ' לֵ' אִם כֵּן נִסְגֻּד לַעֲנָנָא דְּטָעֵין מַיָּא אָ' לֵ' נִסְגֻּד
לַעֲנָנָא אָ' לֵ' אָ' כֵּ' נִסְגֻּד לְרוּחָא דִמְבַדַּר עֲנָנָא אָ' לֵ' נִסְגֻּד
לְרוּחָא אָ' לֵ' וְנִסְגֻּד לְבַר אֲנָשָׁא דְּסָבֵל רוּחָא אִם מִלִּין אַתְּ
מִשְׁתָּעֵי אֲנִי אֵינִי מִשְׁתַּחֲוֶה אֶלָּא לָאוֹר הֲרֵי אֲנִי מַשְׁלִיכְךָ בְּתוֹכוֹ
וִיבֹא אֱלֹהַּ שֶׁאַתָּה מִשְׁתַּחֲוֶה לוֹ וְיַצִּילְךָ מִמֶּנּוּ יָרַד אַבְרָהָם
לְכִבְשַׁן הָאֵשׁ וְנִצּוֹל

[1] Abulfeda (*Hist. Anteislámica*, page 20) says :

وكان ازر ابو ابراهيم يصنع الاصنام و يطيعها و جعل ابراهيم ليبيعا فكان ابراهيم
يقول من يشترى ما يضره ولا ينفعه *

" Azar the father of Abraham made idols and served them and bade
Abraham sell them, but Abraham, said : ' Who would buy that which
harms him and does him no good ? ' "

N

idols, and put the stick into the hands of the largest idol.
When his father returned, he said, ' Who has done this ?'
On which Abraham replied, ' Why should I deny it ? ' A
woman came with a dish of wheat and bade me set it in
front of them. I had scarcely done so when each wanted
to eat before the other, and the greatest beat them all
down with the stick which he had in his hand. Terah
said: ' What art thou inventing for me ? Have they then
understanding ? ' Abraham replied. ' Do thine ears not
hear what thy mouth says ? ' Then Terah took him and
gave him over to Nimrod, who said: ' We will worship
fire.' Abraham said: ' Rather water, which extinguishes
fire.' Nimrod replied : ' Water then.' ' Rather the cloud
which carries water.' ' The cloud then.' ' Rather the wind
which scatters the cloud.' ' The wind then.' ' Rather
men, who endure the wind.' Nimrod at this became angry
and said: ' Thou art only making a speech. I worship
fire and will throw thee into it. The God whom thou dost
worship may come and save thee out of it.' Abraham
was then thrown into a glowing furnace, but was saved
from it." The intercession for his father is not mentioned in Jewish writings; and that this was fruitless,
yea that Abraham, arriving at a clearer understanding,
desisted from his attempt,[1] seems to directly contradict
the Jewish view as expressed in the following passage.[2]
" By the words, thou shalt go to thy fathers in peace, it was
shown to Abraham that his father was a partaker in eternal life." Further, a Rabbinical saying [3] declares as a
general rule that " the son makes the father clean, but not
the father the son." But Muḥammad very often combats

---

[1] Súra IX. 115.　　　　　[2] Midrash Rabba on Genesis, para. 38.

וְאַתָּה תָּבוֹא אֶל אֲבוֹתֶיךָ בְּשָׁלוֹם בְּשׂוֹרוֹ שֶׁיֵּשׁ לְאָבִיו חֵלֶק
לְעוֹלָם הַבָּא　　　See Genesis, xv. 15.

[3] Sanhedrin 104.　בְּרָא מְזַכֵּי אַבָּא אַבָּא לָא מְזַכֵּי בְּרָא

this view and the similar one that the merits of ancestors count for good to their posterity.[1] For example he says : "That people (the Patriarchs) are now passed away ; they have what they gained and ye shall have what ye gain, and ye shall not be questioned concerning that which they have done." [2] That Muḥammad brings forward a dialogue between Abraham and the people, where the Midrash has one with his father only, is explained by the fact that Abraham is intended to be a type of Muḥammad, and so it is necessary that he should be represented as a public preacher. Another circumstance which is mentioned in the Qurán, viz., that Lot became a believer with and through Abraham,[3] may possibly have arisen from a passage in the Midrash immediately following that quoted above, which says that Haran the father of Lot was at first irresolute, but turned to Abraham's opinion after the deliverance of the latter. Haran however failed in the ordeal of fire to which he was then subjected. The idea of Lot's conversion, however, is chiefly derived from the account given of his subsequent life, in which he shows himself to be a pious man ; and it is probably for this reason that Muḥammad connects him with the event just related. Muḥammad appears sometimes to have so confounded himself with Abraham that, in the middle of speeches ascribed to the latter, he indulges in digressions unsuitable to any but himself, and thus falls from the part of narrator into that of admonisher. In one passage [4] a long description of Hell and Paradise is found, and in another,[5] the declaration that those who came before had also been charged with imposture. No doubt Abraham might have said this with reference to Noah, Húd and Sálih; still the words here seem rather forced into his speech, and indeed in one verse we find the word "say" which is to be regarded in the Qurán as the stand-

---

[1] זכות אבות   [2] Súra II. 128, 135.   [3] Súras XXI. 71, XXIX. 25.
[4] Súra XXVI. 88—104.   [5] Súra XXIX. 17—23.

ing address of God (or Gabriel) to Muḥammad.[1] This view renders it unnecessary to adopt the desperate expedient of Wahl, who supposes a transposition of verses, or an interpolation. The true explanation is rather Muḥammad's entire identification of Abraham with himself. Further, he is not content with making Abraham preach against idolatry, he represents him also as teaching the doctrine of the Resurrection of the dead.[2] The lack however of full certainty about this doctrine[3] caused Abraham, according to the Muḥammadan view, to pray for a tangible proof of it, and then was vouchsafed to him what the Rabbis call[4] the " covenant between the divided pieces."[5]

He was convinced through the fact that the divided birds came together again and became living,[6] a view which is foreign to Judaism. How Muḥammad came to call Abraham's father, (whose name is given in the Bible as Terah,[7] Azar[8] is at first sight not clear, but is completely explained when we consider the source[9] of his information, namely Eusebius. In his Church History, Eusebius calls him Athar[10] which is an easy transition from Thara,

---

[1] Compare above on Noah.　　　　[2] Súras II. 260, XXVI. 81.
[3] Baidhâwi says on Súra II. 262 :

قيل لما قال نمرود انا احيى واميت قال ان الاحيا برد الروح الى بدنها فقال هل عاينته فلم يقدر ان يقول نعم وانتقل الى تقرير اخر ثم سال ربه ليريه ليطمئن قلبه فى الجواب ان سئل عنه مرة اخرى *

" It is said that, after Nimrod had said : ' I make alive and I kill,' (II. 260), Abraham answered : ' Quickening is brought about by the return of the spirit to the body.' Nimrod replied : ' Hast thou then seen that ? ' Abraham could not answer in the affirmative and had to pass over to another argument. On this he prayed to the Lord for some revelation, in order that his mind might be easy about an answer to this question, if it were put to him again."

[4] בְּרִית בֵּין הַבְּתָרִים　　　[5] Genesis, xv. 9. ff.　　　[6] Súra II. 262.

[7] תֶּרַח　　　[8] Súra VI. 74.　اَزَر　　　[9] Pointed out by Maracc. Prodr., iv. 90.

[10] Ἀθαρ from Θαρα, hence Arabic. اَزَر

and then the Greek Athar was easily converted into the
Arabic Azar.[1] The reason which is given by some Arabic
commentators [2] is ridiculous. They maintain that Azar is
like Yázzar,[3] and that this means : [4] " O, perverted one,
O, erring one ;" and Abraham is supposed to have thus
addressed his idolatrous father.[5] We now pass on to the
more mature married life of Abraham and come to his
meeting with the angels,[6] whom he receives as guests.[7]
Abraham took them for Arabs, was much surprised that
they did not eat and stepped back in fear, whereupon they
announced to him that he would have a son and told him
also of the coming destruction of Sodom. In one passage
of the Talmud [8] we read : " They appeared to him nothing
else but Arabs ;" and in another passage [9] it is said

---

[1] According to the Tárikh Muntakhab, Azar was the father of Tharah
(D'Herbelot Bib. Orient. under Abraham, page 11).

[2] Vide Maracc. on the passage.   [3] يازّر   [4] يا معوج يا ضال

[5] But later Arabs know the right name تارخ , too, though strange to
say whenever they speak of Abraham they use the name آزر ; but when
on other occasions they mention Abraham's father, they call him by
the other name. Thus Elpherar on Súra VII. 78 : لوط بن هاران بن تارخ
ابن اخى ابراهيم The last ابن here refers again to Lot, (which is
shown by the manner of writing ابن with an alif) just as later Abraham
is called the عم , uncle of Lot. Also on Súra XXI. 71. Elpherar has
the following : وهو لوط بن هاران بن تارخ وهاران هو اخو ابراهيم وكان لهما
اخ ثالث يقال له ناحورا بن تارخ

Attention is more rarely called to the fact that both names are
the same. See Elpherar on Súra XXXI. 11 where in giving the genealogy
of Luqmán. He says تارخ وهو آزر . See also Abulfeda Hist. Anteislámica,
pp. 18 and 20.

[6] Súra XI. 72. رسلنا , on which Elpherar remarks : أزاد بالرسل الملائكة
" By messengers he means Angels."

[7] Genesis, xviii. Súras XI. 72–79, XV. 51–61, XXIX. 80–82, LI. 24–38.

[8] Qiddushin 52. לא נדמו לו אלא לעֲרְבִיִּים

[9] Baba Mezia, 86. 2. מַלְאֲכֵי הַשָּׁרֵת יָרְדוּ לִמְטָּה וְאָכְלוּ
לֶחֶם אָבְלוּ סָלְקָא דַעְתָּךְ אֶלָּא אִימָא נִרְאֶה כְּמָה שֶׁאָכְלוּ וְשָׁרְתוּ

" The angels descended and ate. They ate? No, but it appeared as though they ate and drank." There is only one error to be found in the account as given in the Qurán. The doubt as to whether in the advanced age of the pair a son could come into the world (which in other passages and in the Bible is put into the mouth of Sarah) is here uttered by Abraham, but in very mild words.[1] It is true that in the other Biblical account of the promise to Abraham, he himself is represented as doubting God's word.[2] In other passages the position of words and clauses might give rise to many errors, if we did not know the story better beforehand from the Bible. Thus in one passage [3] the laughter of Abraham's wife is given before the announcement is made, which leads the Arabic commentators to manifold absurd guesses. Elpherar by the side of these explanations (many of them quite wanting in truth) gives the right one in the following words: [4] " Bin 'Abbás and Wáhib say : ' she laughed from astonishment that she should have a child, for both she and her husband were of a great age.' Then the verse was transposed, but it ought to run thus : ' And his wife stood while We promised him Isaac, and after Isaac, Jacob, and then she laughed.' " It might seem that this son who was promised to Abraham was with deliberate forgery identified with Ishmael, because he is regarded as the ancestor of the Arabs ; and so too the ensuing temptation [5] connected with the sacrifice of his son is made to refer to Ishmael.

---

[1] Súra XV. 54 ff.　　　[2] Genesis, xvii. 17.　　　[3] Súra XI. 74.

[4] وقال بن عباس ووهب محكت تعجباً من ان يكون لها ولد على كبر
سنها وسن زوجها وعلى هذا القول تكون الاية على التقديم والتاخير تقديره
و امراته قائمة فبشرناها باسحاق و من وراء اسحاق يعقوب فضحكت *

[5] This is referred to in general terms in Súra II. 118, thus :

اِبْتَلَى اِبْرَاهِيمَ رَبُّهُ بِكَلِمَاتٍ

Cf. Mishna Aboth. v. 3.

עֲשָׂרָה נִסְיוֹנוֹת נִתְנַסָּה אַבְרָהָם אָבִינוּ

Ground for this acceptation is given in another passage,[1] when after the dispute about the idols has been related, we read from v. 99 as follows: " Wherefore We acquainted him that he should have a son who should be a meek youth, and when he had attained to years of discretion . . . . . Abraham said unto him : ' O, my son ! I saw in a dream that I should offer thee in sacrifice.' " He declared himself ready, on which Abraham heard a voice telling him that he had already verified the vision ; and a noble victim ransomed him. And then the passage continues : [2] " And We rejoiced him with the promise of Isaac, a righteous prophet ; and We blessed him and Isaac ; and of their offspring were some righteous doers, and others who manifestly injured their own souls." That the announcement of Isaac first appears here is a proof that the preceding context [3] refers to Ishmael. It is therefore evident that according to Muḥammad's representation the sacrificial action was performed on Ishmael, and further on this will be shown more in detail. But it is not clear that the announcement of the angels refers to him, seeing that in one of the three places where the same word [4] is used of this angelic announcement, it is explicitly applied to Isaac. That the angels had a two-fold mission—(1) to Abraham, in order to show him his fatherhood and the destruction of Sodom, and (2) to Lot, in order to remove him from Sodom before the destruction was accomplished, is Biblical and Muḥammad follows the Bible narrative. We have already mentioned that Lot is supposed to have

---

[1] Súra XXXVII. 99—114.   [2] Súra XXXVII. 112, 113.

وَبَشَّرْنَاهُ بِإِسْحَقَ نَبِيًّا مِنَ ٱلصَّالِحِينَ وَبَارَكْنَا عَلَيْهِ وَعَلَى إِسْحَقَ وَمِنْ ذُرِّيَّتِهِمَا مُحْسِنٌ وَظَالِمٌ لِنَفْسِهِ مُبِينٌ *

[3] As also عَلَيْهِ and ذُرِّيَّتِهِمَا in v. 113.

[4] بَشَّرَ Súra XI. 74 ; Cf. other two passages, Súra XXXVII. 99 and 112.

become a believer through Abraham. The visitation of
the angels, which is related in Genesis, xix. 1—27, is
mentioned in several passages in the Qurán.[1] On the
whole the narrative is fairly true, but the details are not
entirely free from embellishment. For example, in some
passages [2] the warning addressed to the people of Sodom on
account of their unchaste use of men is treated quite
separately from the narrative of the angels, and Muḥammad makes out that the angels told Lot [3] and even
Abraham [4] beforehand that Lot's wife should not be saved.
The unbelief of Lot's wife receives particular notice in one
passage,[5] while the destruction of the cities is mentioned
in many passages.[6] Muḥammad especially attributes to
Lot the distinguishing mark common to all preachers, viz.,
that they ask for no reward.[7]

It has already been remarked that, according to Muḥammad's showing, Ishmael * was the son whom Abraham was

---

[1] Súras VII. 78—83, XI. 79—85, XV. 61—78, XXII. 43, XXVI. 160—176,
XXVII. 55—60, XXIX. 27—35, XXXVII. 133—137, LIV. 33—39.

[2] Compare especially Súra XXIX. 27—30.

[3] Súras XI. 83, XXIX. 32. According to the reading امراتك in the
Acc. (Súra XI. 83), Lot did not even once ask her to accompany him,
but left her with the people of Sodom. This reading is not only adopted
by Hinckelmann, but by almost all the Arabic commentators quoted in
Elpherar; which reading, as he remarks, is confirmed by the variant
reading of Ben Mas'úd, who puts the word امراتك before الّ.

[4] Súras XXIX. 31, XV. 60.   [5] Súra LXVI. 10.

[6] Súra XXV. 42, and other passages.   [7] Súra XXVI. 164.

* On the passage quoted above (Súra XXXVII. 101) Elpherar
remarks as follows :

واختلف العلماء من المسلمين فى هذا الغلام الذى امر ابراهيم بذبحه بعد
اتفاق اهل الكتابين على انه اسحاق وقال قوم هو اسحاق *

"The learned among the Muslims are divided about the lad whom
Abraham was commanded to sacrifice; whereas the people of the Book
on both sides (Jews and Christians) are agreed that he was Isaac, and
common people are at one with them." Many commentators are then
quoted, who also share this opinion. وقال اخرون هو اسمعيل "Others,

commanded to sacrifice; and the reasons have been given
which persuaded Muḥammad to represent Ishmael as a

---

however say that he was Ishmael," and for this opinion the authorities
are now cited :

و كلا القولين يروى عن رسول الله صلعم ومن ذهب الى ان الذبيح اسحاق
احتج من القران بقوله فبشرناه بغلام حليم فلما بلغ معه السعى امره بذبح من
بشرة وليس فى القران انه بشر بولد سوى اسحاق كما فى سورة هود فبشرناه
باسحاق ومن ذهب الى انه اسمعيل احتج بان الله تعالى ذكر البشارة باسحاق
بعد الفراغ من قصّة المذبوح فقال فبشرناه باسحاق نبيا فدل على ان المذبوح غيره
و ايضا فان الله تعالى قال فى سورة هود فبشرناه باسحاق ومن وراء اسحاق يعقوب
كما بشرة باسحاق بشرة بابنه يعقوب فكيف يامره بذبح اسحاق وقد امره بنافلة منه*

"Both views are supported by the words of Muḥammad. Those who
maintain that Isaac was the one sacrificed prove it from Súra XXXVII. 99 :
'We brought him the joyful news that he should have a meek son.'
And when he was grown up, then God commanded Abraham to offer up
him who had been announced to him. But we do not read in the Qurán
that any son except Isaac was foretold to him, as it is written in the Súra
entitled Húd : 'And we announced to him Isaac.'—Súra XI. 74. Those
however who maintain that Ishmael was the one sacrificed prove it from
the fact that the announcement of Isaac comes after the completion of
the story of the sacrifice, when we read for the first time : 'And
we rejoiced him with the promise of Isaac, a righteous prophet.'—
Súra XXXVII. 112. This shews that the sacrificed person was another
than Isaac. (The same view is given in detail by Jalálu'd-dín as quoted by
Maracc.) Further it is said in Súra Húd (XI. 74) : 'We promised him
Isaac and after Isaac, Jacob. As he had announced Isaac, so he also
announced to him Isaac's son Jacob.' How could he then have commanded
the sacrifice of Isaac, when he had promised seed through him ?' This
last proof is truly not to be ranked very high, for a similar contradiction
in Holy Scripture in the case of Genesis, xxi. 12, and Genesis, xxii. would
then have to be explained. Beyond the first proof adduced, there is no
necessity either for this argument, or for still another argument which
immediately afterwards is cited in the commentary, viz., that the horns
of the ram are preserved in Mecca, the dwelling-place of Ishmael. It
will have been noted that in the text I have independently decided in
favour of the view that Muḥammad believed that it was Ishmael whose
sacrifice was ordered of God.

Doubtless all Arabian authorities would have come to this same
conclusion, had not the Jews and Christians expressed their opinion so
decidedly in favor of Isaac (in which they were followed by the common

O

very righteous man,[1] to include him in the ranks of the
patriarchs and prophets,[2] to mention him as the righteous
son of Abraham,[3] and to make out that he laid the foundation stone of the Ka'bah in connection with his father.[4]

---

people). This fact prevented many from giving to the text of the Qurán
sufficiently impartial consideration, and hence led them to abandon
Muḥammad's real view. The method by which these attempted to
weaken the proof for the opposite opinion is clear from Elpherar's comment on Súra XXXVII. 112 :

(من) جعل الذبيح اسمعيل قال بشر بعد هذه القصة باسحاق نبيا جزا طاعته

ومن جعل الذبيح اسحاق قال بشر ابراهيم بنبوة اسحاق رواه عكرمة عن ابن عباس

قال بشربة مرتين حتى ندى و حتى نبى *

" He who takes it that Ishmael was the one sacrificed explains that it
was after this event that Isaac a prophet was promised to Abraham as
a reward for his obedience; he who takes it that Isaac was the one
sacrificed explains that it was only the prophetic gift of Isaac which was
announced to Abraham. Akhrama in the name of Ibn 'Abbás explains
that Isaac was announced to his father twice, once before his birth and
again at the attainment of the prophetic gift." In the following verse,
however, which upholds our view still more strongly, Elpherar gives
an erroneous explanation of one part of the verse, and about the rest
maintains a significant silence. Thus he explains عليه as follows:—

يعنى على ابراهيم فى اولاده " That is to say, to Abraham in his children ; "

but the word ذُرِّيتِهِمَا, which is inexplicable on this interpretation of
عَلَيْهِ, he does not explain at all. In the legends of Islám, as Elpherar has
already remarked in his comment on the word قوم, Isaac is almost
without an exception spoken of as the one led to sacrifice. So also in
Elpherar on Súra XII. 36, where Joseph relates his history to his fellow-
prisoners, and on Súra XII. 86, where mention is made of a letter written
by Jacob to the king who was keeping his son in prison. Here Isaac is
always called ذبيح الله " The sacrificed of God." And when Jacob in the
course of the letter (quite according to the version of Sepher Hayyáshár)
alludes to the special protection of God enjoyed by his family he says :

و اما ابى فشدت يداه ورجلاه ووضع السكين على قفاه فغداه الله

" As for my father, both his hands and his feet were bound, and the
knife was put to his throat, but God ransomed him." Compare also
Abulfeda Hist. Anteislámica, page 22.

[1] Súras XIX. 55, 56, XXI. 85, 86.   [3] Súra XIV. 41.
[2] Súras II. 130, 134, III. 77, VI. 86, XXXVIII. 48.   [4] Súra II. 119.

This view is certainly not Jewish, but at the same time it is not contrary to Judaism, for the Rabbis tell us [1] that by the utterance: "Thou shalt be buried in a good old age (Genesis, xv. 15.) God showed Abraham that Ishmael would repent." And in the Talmud it is said [2] that Ishmael repented during his father's life-time. From his habit of reckoning Ishmael among the patriarchs, Muḥammad fell into the error of counting him as an ancestor of Jacob. Thus in one passage [3] he says: "The God of thy fathers, Abraham and Ishmael and Isaac," which Baidháwi attempts to explain in the following manner; [4] " He counts Ishmael among his ancestors, connecting him with the father—the grand-father also is the same as the father—and as Muḥammad says, The uncle is a part of the father. Then pointing to 'Abbâs, his uncle, he said, This is the survivor of my forefathers."

As he hereby transfers to Ishmael the action, which as the most worthy, is attributed by the Jews to Isaac, viz., readiness to be sacrificed, the latter remains simply a pious man, about whom there is little to relate and who is quite destitute of all legendary adornment. In consequence of this, Isaac appears only in the lists of the patriarchs, and almost always in those passages where Abraham's deliverance from the fire is mentioned and also his reward for his piety. In these passages Muḥammad following more the popular tradition mentions Isaac and Jacob but not Ishmael.

---

[1] תִּקָּבֵר בְּשֵׂיבָה טוֹבָה בִּשׂוֹרוֹ שֶׁיִּשְׁמָעֵאל עָשָׂה תְּשׁוּבָה
Mid. Rab. on Genesis, para. 38.

[2] Baba Bathra 16. יִשְׁמָעֵאל עָשָׂה תְּשׁוּבָה בְּחַיֵּי אָבִיו

[3] Súra II. 127.

[4] وعدّ اسمعيل من ابائه تعليبا للاب والجد كالاب لقوله عليه الصلاة
والسلام عم الرجل ‬‮‬فو ابيه كما قال فى العباس رضى الله عنه هذا بقية ابائى *

We are now struck by the strange confusion which
seems to have existed in Muḥammad's mind about Jacob.[1]
He seems to have been uncertain whether he was Abraham's son, or his grandson, the son of Isaac.   While there
is no passage which says explicitly that he was Abraham's
son, yet this idea is conveyed to all who have not learned
differently from the Biblical history.   In the angel's
announcement [2] it is said, " after Isaac, Jacob; " [3] and in
other passages [4] we read: "We gave to him (i.e. to
Abraham) Isaac and Jacob."   In the Sunna, however,
Joseph is called clearly the grandson and Jacob the son of
Abraham.[5]   Although these passages do not prove the
point absolutely, yet those passages which can be brought
forward in support of the opposite view are much less
powerful.   For if it must be allowed that in two passages [6]
Abraham and Isaac, and in one of these Jacob also, are
mentioned as the forefathers of Joseph, we can also shew
another passage [7] where Ishmael is mentioned as a forefather of Jacob without any continuous genealogy having
been given.   And further, since in the passage last cited
Abraham, Ishmael and Isaac are counted as the fathers
of Jacob, it is clear from the mention of Ishmael among
the others how great was the confusion which reigned in
Muḥammad's mind about Jacob's parentage.

We by no means assert that Muḥammad took Jacob for
the son of Abraham, but it is evident that the relationship

---

[1] يَعْقُوب   [2] Súra XI. 74.   وَمِنْ وَرَآءِ اِسْحَقَ يَعْقُوبُ

[3] The Arabic commentators, who may not and will not understand
these words as we do, are obliged to seek some other reasons for the
unsuitable allusion to Jacob.   Thus Elpherar says:—

تبشرت انها تعيش حتى ترى ولَدَ ولدها

"It was announced to her that she would live till she saw her
son's son."

[4] Súras VI. 84, XIX. 50, XXI. 72, XXIX. 26.
[5] Sunna 398 and 400.   [6] Súra XII. 6, 38.   [7] Súra II. 127.

between the two was not clear to him. This error did not spread; on the contrary, the later Arabs were better acquainted with these relationships. Thus, *e.g.*, Zamakh-shári says:[1] " It is related of the prophet that he said, ' If you are asked, who is the noble one ? ' answer : ' The noble one, the son of the noble one, the son of the noble one, the son of the noble one is Joseph, the son of Jacob, the son of Isaac, the son of Abraham.' "[2] But this is no testimony to the full certainty of Muḥammad himself, for often the traditions spread among the later Arabs are more correct than those given in the Qurán, as we said before in the case of the sacrifice of Isaac. Only a little is given of Jacob's life. There is an allusion to his wrestling with the Angel in the following words :[3] " All food was allowed to the children of Israel before the revelation of the Law, except what Israel (as he is here called)[4] forbade himself." This is evidently an allusion to the Biblical passage where the prohibition against eating the sinew of the thigh[5] is mentioned,[6] which Baidháwi[7] also gives, but assigns a wrong reason for it. Beyond this allusion and the history of Joseph, in which he is also involved and which we will give later on, the only other thing told about Jacob is his admonition before his death. This is

---

[1] On Súra XII. 4.

وعن النبى صلّى الله عليه اذا قيل من الكريم فقولوا الكريم ابن الكريم ابن الكريم ابن الكريم يوسف بن يعقوب بن اسحق بن ابراهيم *

(See de Sacy Anthologie Grammaticale, 125).

[2] Elpherar has nearly the same words, with the addition however of a long chain of traditions.

[3] Súra III. 87. مَا حَرَّمَ اِسْرَآئِيْلَ عَلَى نَفْسِهِ

[4] Israel is يعقوب Baidháwi.

[5] גִּיד הַנָּשֶׁה   [6] Genesis, xxxii. 33.   عرق النسا [7]

given in accordance with rabbinical sources as follows : [1]
" And Abraham commanded this to his sons,[2] even to
Jacob: ' My children, verily God hath chosen this religion
for you, therefore die not unless ye also be resigned.'
Were ye present when Jacob was at the point of death ?
When he said to his sons, ' Whom will ye worship after
me ? ' they answered: ' We will worship thy God and
the God of thy fathers Abraham and Ishmael and Isaac,
one God, and to him will we be resigned.' " We find
something similar in the Rabbinical writings : [3] " At the
time when Jacob was leaving the world, he called his
twelve sons and said to them : ' Hear your father Israel,[4] is
there any doubt in your hearts about God ? ' they said :
' Hear Israel our father, as in thy heart there is no doubt
about God, so also there is in ours ; but the Lord is our
God, the Lord is one.' [5] Then he spoke out and said :
' Praised be the name of his glorious kingdom, for ever.' " [6]
The sons of Jacob are not individually mentioned, but they
appear in the list of the Patriarchs as "the tribes," [7] so
called because of the subsequent division into tribes ;
Joseph [8] alone enjoying an honorable exception.   Besides

---

[1] Súra II. 126—7.   [2] Compare perhaps Genesis, xviii. 19.

[3] Midr. Rab. on Genesis, para. 98, and on Deuteronomy, para. 2.

בְּשָׁעָה שֶׁהָיָה יַעֲקֹב אָבִינוּ נִפְטַר מִן הָעוֹלָם קָרָא לְשְׁנֵים
עָשָׂר בָּנָיו אָמַר לָהֶם שִׁמְעוּ אֶל יִשְׂרָאֵל אֲבִיכֶם שֶׁמָּא יֵשׁ
בְּלִבְבְכֶם מַחֲלֹקֶת עַל הַקָּדוֹשׁ בָּרִיךְ הוּא אָמְרוּ לוֹ שְׁמַע יִשְׂרָאֵל
אָבִינוּ כְּשֵׁם שֶׁאֵין בְּלִבְּךָ מַחֲלֹקֶת עַל הַקָּ' בּ' ח' כַּךְ אֵין
בְּלִבֵּנוּ מַחֲלֹקֶת אֶלָּא ח' אֱלֹהֵינוּ ח' אֶחָד אַף הוּא פֵּרֵשׁ
בִּשְׂפָתָיו וְאָמַר בָּרוּךְ שֵׁם כְּבוֹד מַלְכוּתוֹ לְעוֹלָם וָעֶד

[4] Genesis, xlix. 2.   [5] Deuteronomy, vi. 4.

[6] Comp. the two recensions of the Jerusalem Targum on Deuteronomy,
vi. 4 ; also Tract Pesachim, page 56.

[7] הַשְּׁבָטִים, ٱلْأَسْبَاط   [8] يُوسُف

being alluded to in one other passage,[1] Joseph forms the
theme of almost the whole of the twelfth Súra,[2] which
is named after him. This Súra contains the narrative
given us in Genesis,[3] with many abbreviations it is true, but
also with many additions and alterations, which must be
pointed out. We must first mention the additions which
are derived from Jewish legend. Among these is the
statement that Joseph was inclined towards Potiphar's
wife, but that a sign warned him from her.[4] The Rabbinical comment on the words "He went into the house
to do his work"[5] runs as follows:[6] "Both intended to
commit sin;" and on the words "She caught him by his
garment saying, 'Lie with me,'" Rabbi Yohánán remarks,
"Both had got on to the bed, when the form of his father
appeared to Joseph at the window and said: "Joseph,
Joseph, one day the names of thy brethren will be graven
on the stones of the Ephod, also thine; wilt thou that it
shall be effaced?"[7] The fable that the Egyptian women

---

[1] Súra XL. 36.   [2] Súra XII. 4—108.

[3] Genesis, xxxvii. 9—36 and chapters, xxxix to xlvi.

[4] Súra XII. 24. وَهَمَّ بِهَا لَوْلَا أَنْ رَأَى بُرْهَانَ رَبِّهِ

[5] Genesis, xxxix. 11.   [6] Sotah, XXXVI. 2.

וַיְהִי כְּהַיּוֹם הַזֶּה וַיָּבֹא הַבַּיְתָה לַעֲשׂוֹת מְלַאכְתּוֹ אָמַר רַבִּי
יוֹחָנָן שְׁנֵיהֶם לִדְבַר עֲבֵרָה נִתְכַּוְּנוּ וַתִּתְפְּשֵׂהוּ בְּבִנְדּוֹ לֵאמֹר
שִׁכְבָה עִמִּי מְלַמֵּד שֶׁעָלוּ לַמִּטָּה שְׁנֵיהֶם עֲרֻמִּים בְּאוֹתָהּ שָׁעָה
בָּאתָה דְּיֶקְנָא שֶׁל אָבִיו וְנִרְאֵית לוֹ בַּחַלּוֹן אָמַר לוֹ יוֹסֵף יוֹסֵף
עֲתִידִין אַחֶיךָ שֶׁיִּכָּתְבוּ עַל אַבְנֵי אֵפוֹד וְאַתָּה בֵּינֵיהֶם רְצוֹנְךָ
שֶׁיִּמָּחֶה שִׁמְךָ מִבֵּינֵיהֶם

[7] Elpherar in his comment on the verse quoted gives some of these
particulars:

فروى عن بن عباس انه قال حل الهميان وجلس منها مجلس الخائن

"It is said on the authority of Ben 'Abbás that he said he had undone
his girdle and approached her with a sinful purpose." قال قتادة واكثر

mocked at Potiphar's wife, were invited in by her, and in contemplating Joseph's beauty [1] were so absorbed that they cut their own hands, is found in an old Jewish writing [2] which, though not genuine, is certainly very ancient, and is written is very pure Hebrew. This work is sometimes referred to in the Midrash Yalkut under the name of "The Great Chronicle." [3] In an old Jewish German translation however, it bears another title.[4] It is this translation which I have before me as I write, and for this reason I will not quote the actual words.[5] Also the discussion about the

---

المفسرين الله رأى صورة يعقوب وهو يقول يا يوسف تعمل عمل السفهاء وانت مكتوب فى الانبياء *

"Ketáda and the greater number of the commentators say that he saw the form of Jacob, who said: 'O Joseph, though thy name is written among the prophets yet thou behavest like the fools.'"

[1] Elpherar on xii. 31, agreeing with the Sepher Hayyáshár, gives, contrary to Wahl's forced interpretation, the correct meaning as follows:

اى جززن بالسكين التى معهن ايديهن وهن يحسبن انها يقطعن الاترج ولم يجدن الالم لشغل قلوبهن بيوسف *

"They cut themselves with the knife which they had in their hands, thinking they were cutting the orange, but they did not feel the pain on account of their absorption in the contemplation of Joseph."

הם וישר [4]   דברי חיַמים הארוך [3]   סֵפֶר הַיָשָׁר [2]

[5] An allusion to this fable is found in a passage from the Midrash Abhkir quoted in the Midr. Yalkut, chapter 146.

The Qurán story is seen to be still more like the narrative in Sepher Hayyáshár, when one adds the following details. The word مُتَّكَأً (verse 31) comes from وَكَأ (viii) to lean against, like the Rabbinical סְעוּדָה from סָעַד to support, prop; and like the Hebrew מֵסַב from סָבַב it signifies a meal, not on account of the new strength and support which food gives (to which one might easily be led by the expression סְעָד לֵב, compare especially Psalm, civ. 15), but on account of the oriental method of leaning against supports at meals, as Elpherar rightly observes:

قال بن عباس وسعيد بن جبير والحسن وقتادة ومجاهد متكاء اى طعاما

tearing of the clothes, whether they were torn in front or at the back,[1] is found in the same way in the Sepher Hayyáshár. In the words, " and a witness bore witness," [2] which we here do not take strictly according to the meaning of the context, but rather in the sense of an " arbitrator decided,"[3] others see an allusion to a witness

---

بسماه متكاه لان اهل الطعام اذا جلسوا يتكون على الوسائد فسمى متكاه على الاستعارة *

" Several Arabic commentators say that متكا means food, because the people when they sit eating lean against pillows. Therefore food is called by way of metonomy متكا." On this word the same Elpherar further comments as follows : و يقرا فى الشـواذ متكا بسكون التا واختلفوا فى معناه قال بن عباس هو الاترج وروى عن مجاهد مثله وقيل هو الاترج بالحبشة وقال الضحاك الزماورد وقال عكر متكا شى يقطع بسكين وقال ابو زيد الانصارى كلما يجز بالسكين فهو عند العرب متك والمتك والبتك القطع بالميم والبا *

" In the copy of Shuwáz مُتْكاً is written with a vowelless te(ت). Opinions are divided as to the meaning of this word. Ben 'Abbás says it is an orange. Mujáhid asserts the same thing. Some say an orange is thus called in Abyssinia. Dhuḥák says it is the Indian fruit Zumáward. 'Akr says مُتَكٌ is every thing which is cut with a knife. Abú Zaid the Christian, says that whenever anything is cut with a knife it is called by the Arabs مُتَكٌ, since مُتَكٌ and بَتَكٌ with mim (م) and be, (ب) mean among the Arabs cutting." According to the reading مُتَكٌ which some adopt, it would mean an orange or أُتْرُجٌ, and we are told expressly in Sepher Hayyáshár that Joseph's mistress offered this fruit to the women visiting her. Now our reading seems to me the right one, and the meaning given to مُتَكٌ very doubtful, for the Arabic commentators themselves are much divided in opinion, and their explanations are derived only from the passage itself, as often happens. Nevertheless from their words this much is clear, that the whole legend as it is found in the above-mentioned Jewish book has passed over to the Arabs, so that later commentators have tried to discover every detail in the words of the Qurán.

[1] Súra XII. 25.   [2] وَشَهِدَ شَاهِدٌ, Súra XII. 26.

[3] وحكم حاكم So also Elpherar.

who was present at what occurred between Joseph and the
woman, and some of the commentators quoted in Elpherar
express themselves quite in harmony with the Sepher
Hayyáshár as follows:[1] "Sa'íd Ben Jubair and Dhuḥák
say it was a child in the cradle which God permitted to
speak. This is the tradition of the Uphite commentator
according to 'Abbás." In the Sépher Hayyáshár it is also
asserted that there was present a child of eleven months
who till then could not talk, but then attained to speech.
But there is a difference in that the Jewish book makes the
child confirm the utterance of Joseph, while the Arabic
commentator puts into its mouth the decision about the
rent clothing, which other Arabic writers reject as highly
unsuitable. Many commentators say that this was no
child,[2] but rather a wise man full of penetration. It follows
from this that Muḥammad either mixed the two legends
inappropriately, or else that the second one came later
into Arabic tradition and was read by the Arabs into
the words of the Qurán. The words[3] which Wahl
translates: "But the devil would not allow it[4] that he
(the cup-bearer) thought of him (Joseph)," are explained
by the following passage:[5] "The talk of the lips tendeth
only to penury,[6] because although Joseph reminded the

---

[1] قال سعيد بن جبير والضحاك كان صبيا فى المهد افظة الله و هو روايۃ
العوفى عن عباس *

[2] وقال الحسن وعكرمة ومجاهد وقتادة لم يكن صبيا لانه كان رجلا
حكيما ذا راى *

[3] Súra XII. 42. فَآنْسَاهُ ٱلشَّيْطَانُ ذِكْرَ رَبِّهِ

[4] Wahl does not explain what ربه means here.

[5] וּדְבַר שְׂפָתַיִם אַךְ לְמַחְסֹר עַל יְדֵי שֶׁאָמַר לְשַׂר הַמַּשְׁקִים
זְכַרְתַּנִי וְהִזְכַּרְתַּנִי וְתוֹסֶף לוֹ שְׁתֵּי שָׁנִים שֶׁנֶּאֱמַר וַיְהִי מִקֵּץ
שְׁנָתַיִם יָמִים (Midr. Rabbah on Genesis, para. 89.)

[6] Proverbs, xiv. 23.

cup-bearer twice [1] that he should remember him, yet he
had to remain two more years in prison; for it is written,
' And it was after two years.' " [2]   The seeking of protection
from the butler is here regarded as sinful, and therefore
Muḥammad says: " And Satan made him (Joseph) forget
the remembrance of his Lord (God)," in that he trusted
not in God but in man.[3] In the same Súra [4] Jacob
recommends his sons to enter by different gates; in like
manner we read in the Rabbinical writings [5] that Jacob
said to them: " Do not enter by the same door." [6]
The statement [7] that the brothers said, when they found
the cup in Benjamin's sack: " If he be guilty of theft his
brother hath also been guilty," is evidently an erroneous
change in the words of a passage found in the Midrash
quoted above,[8] according to which they said, " See a

---

[1] Genesis, xl. 14.   [2] Genesis, xli. 1.

[3] Elpherar has the following :

قيل انس الساقى ذكر يوسف للملك تقديرة فانساه الشيطان ذكره لربه قال بن
عباس و عليه الاكثرون انسا الشيطان يوسف ذكر ربه حتى اتبع الفرج من غيرة
و استغاف بمخلوق و تلك غفلة عرضت ليوسف من الشيطان *

" It is said that the butler did not remember to mention Joseph to
the king. The virtual meaning of this is that Satan made him forget
ذكرة لربه the mention of him to his Lord (Pharaoh). But Ben 'Abbás and
most authorities after him say that Satan made Joseph forget the
remembrance of his Lord, so that he sought help apart from Him and
protection from a creature, and this was an omission to which Satan
tempted Joseph." Then he quotes many other passages which represent
this step of Joseph's as sinful.

[4] Súra XII. 67.   [5] Midr. Rabbah on Genesis, para. 91.

אָמַר לָהֶם יַעֲקֹב אַל תִּכָּנְסוּ כֻּלְּכֶם בְּפֶתַח אֶחָת

[6] The same reason is given alike by the Arabic commentators and in the
Midrash, viz. מִפְּנֵי הָעַיִן—(Cf. Elpherar on the verse) خاف عليهم العين
" For fear of envious looks," which the ancients regarded as very
disastrous in their consequences.

[7] Súra XII. 77.   [8] Mid. Rab., para. 92. חָא גּוְבָא בַּר נַּוְבְתָא

thief, son of a thief," with reference to Rachel's having
stolen the Teraphim.[1] From the Qurán it appears[2] that
Jacob knew by divine communication that Joseph still
lived, which is opposed to one Jewish view,[3] but agrees
with another,[4] which runs as follows: " An unbeliever.
asked our teacher, ' Do the dead live on ? Your fathers did
not accept this, and will you accept it ? It is said of Jacob,
that he refused to be comforted.[5] If he had believed that
the dead live on, would he have refused comfort ?' Then
he answered him. ' Foolish one ! he knew through the
Holy Ghost that he still lived (in the flesh), and one does
not take comfort concerning the living.' " The story that
Joseph told Benjamin beforehand who he was, is common
to the Qurán[6] and the Sepher Hayyáshár. Besides these
additions from Jewish legends there is also other matter
which owes its origin to error, or possibly to traditions
unknown to us. Muhammad's statement[7] that the brothers
asked their father to send Joseph with them contradicts
the Biblical account;[8] and the statement that one of the

---

[1] Genesis, xxxi. 19. The Arabian commentators give the most varying
accounts. One of these confirms our view of an erroneous confusion
with Rachel, viz., the following in Elpherar: قال سعيد بن جبير

وقتادة كان لجده ابى امه صنم يعبده فاخذه سرا

Sʻaid Ben Jubair and Katáda say that his grand-father, his mother's
father, had an image which he worshipped. This he stole secretly."

[2] Súra XII. 86, 97.   [3] Pirke Rabbi Eliezer, section 38.

[4] Mid. Tanchuma quoted in Mid. Yalkut, chapter 143.

שָׁאַל אֶפִּיקוֹרוֹס אֶחָד לְרַבֵּנוּ אֶפְשָׁר שֶׁהַמֵּתִים חַיִּים אֲבוֹתֵיכֶם
אֵינָם מוֹדִים וְאַתֶּם מוֹדִים מַה־כְּתִיב בְּיַעֲקֹב וַיְמָאֵן לְהִתְנַחֵם
אִלּוּ הָיָה יָדַע שֶׁהַמֵּתִים חַיִּים הָיָה מְמָאֵן לְהִתְנַחֵם אָמַר לוֹ
שׁוֹטֶה לְפִי שֶׁהוּא יָדַע בְּרוּחַ הַקֹּדֶשׁ שֶׁהוּא חַי וְאֵין מְקַבְּלִיו
תַּנְחוּמִין עַל הֶחָי

[5] Genesis, xxxvii. 35.   [6] Súra XII. 69.
[7] Súra XII. 11 ff.   [8] Genesis, xxxvii. 13 ff.

Ishmaelites who went to draw water found Joseph in
the pit is against the clear word of the Scripture that
the pit was dry.[1] Muḥammad makes Joseph expound
Pharaoh's dream, and only afterwards does he have
him fetched from prison,[2] in contradiction to the Bible
narrative.[3] He asserts that Jacob became blind from
grief, but that he recovered his sight by the application
of a shirt to his eyes. He was perhaps thinking of
Jacob's loss of sight[4] later on, or possibly the idea is
based on some legend unknown to me. According to
the Qurán Joseph's parents[5] came to him in Egypt, in
spite of the fact that according to the testimony of the
Scriptures[6] Rachel was long since dead. Muḥammad's
idea probably was to bring about a complete fulfilment
of the dream, which mentions both parents.[7]

On this, however, some of the Rabbis remark that this
is a sign that no dream is without a mingling of some vain
matter, while others say that Bilhah, Joseph's subsequent
foster-mother, is alluded to. Something like this is quoted
by Zamakhshári, to the effect that " this means his
father and his aunt ; "[8] while Elpherar has[9] still more
clearly : " Katáda and Sada say that by the moon is
meant his aunt, because his mother Rachel was already
dead." Thus it is possible that Muḥammad means
this aunt here, even as Elpherar remarks on another

---

[1] Genesis, xxxvii. 24. וְהַבּוֹר רֵיק אֵין בּוֹ מָיִם

[2] Súra XII. 47, 50. [3] Genesis, xli. 14 ff.

[4] Súra XII. 84, 93, 96. Cf. Genesis, xlviii. 10.

[5] Súra XII. 100, 101. أَبَوَيْهِ [6] Genesis, xxxv. 18 ff.

[7] Súra XII. 4. Cf. Genesis, xxxvii. 10. אֲנִי וְאִמְּךָ

[8] On Súra XII. 4. وقيل ابوه وخالته (De Sacy Anth. Gramm, page
127.)

[9] قاله قتادة وقال السدى القمر خالته لان امه راحيل كانت قد ماتت

passage,[1] to wit, that " Most commentators say that by
these are meant his father and his aunt Leah, his mother
having died at the birth of Benjamin." It is quite in
accordance with Muḥammad's usual procedure to put into
Joseph's mouth a long discourse on the unity of God and
the doctrine of a future life. This is given before the
interpretation of the dreams of his two fellow-prisoners.[2]
With Joseph we finish the first period, for between Joseph
and Moses Muḥammad mentions no one else. It almost
seems as if, with Justin, Muḥammad regarded Moses as
Joseph's son, although of course we cannot seriously
attribute such an opinion to him.

SECOND CHAPTER.

Second Part.

Moses and his Time.

The history of the earlier times was preserved only in
brief outlines, and was not so important either in itself,
or in the influence which it exerted on the subsequent

---

[1] Súra XII. 100.   قال اكثر المفسرين هو ابوه و خالته ليا وكانت امه
قد ماتت فى نفاس بنيامين

[2] The Arabian commentators, who are quite conscious of this
unsuitability explain it away very cleverly by saying that Joseph made
this digression, because it grieved him to be obliged to foretell evil to
one of his fellow-prisoners. Elpherar comments on verse 37 as follows :

فلما قصّا عليه الرُّويا كره يوسف ان يعبر لهما ما سالاه لما علم فى ذلك من
المكروه على احدهما فاعرض عن سؤلهما واخذ فى غيره من اظهار المعجزة والدعا
الى التوحيد *

" After they had told him the dream, he was unwilling to give them
the explanation for which they had asked him, because he recognised
in it something that would be disagreeable to one of them. For this
reason he put aside their question, and began a different discourse, in
which he taught them about the gift of miracle-working and exhorted
them to belief in the Unity of God.

ages; therefore Muḥammad adopted from it only such
legends as were edifying in themselves and to which he
could append pious reflections. In the period of which
we are now going to treat, there is certainly still a long
array of legends, but historical facts are preserved for us
with greater distinctness and clearer detail, and these
facts are of greater religious importance The giving of
the Mosaic Law and the eventful life and noble personality
of Moses himself afford Muḥammad plenty of material for
his narrative. Here we will first put together the whole
life of Moses as represented in the various passages of the
Qurán, and then we will go on to consider the details to
be commented upon. Among the oppressive enactments
of Pharaoh against the children of Israel was an order
that their children should be thrown into the water.
Moses [1] the son of Amram [2] was laid by his mother
in an ark; Pharaoh's wife, who saw the child there,
saved it from death and had it nursed by its mother.
When Moses was grown up he tried to help his oppressed
brethren, and once killed an Egyptian; the next day
however he was reminded by an Israelite of his yesterday's
deed. This made him afraid, and by the advice of a
friend he fled to Midian,[3] and married there the daughter
of a Midianite.[4] When he wished to leave Midian he saw
a burning bush, approached it, and received a command
to go to Egypt to warn Pharaoh [5] and to perform some
miracles to make him believe; he asked for his brother
Aaron as an assistant in this work.[6] He obeyed the
command and accomplished his mission, but Pharaoh
remained unbelieving and assembled his magicians, who

---

[1] مُوسَى [2] عَمْرَان [3] مَدْيَن

[4] Súras XX. 37—44, XXVIII. 2—29. [5] فِرْعُون

[6] Súras XX. 8—37, 44—51, XXVI. 9—17, XXVIII. 29—36, LXXIX.
15—20.

indeed imitated the wonders, but were so far surpassed by
Moses and Aaron that they themselves became believers
in spite of the threats of Pharaoh.[1]   But a mighty
judgment overtook Pharaoh and his people, who remained
stubborn in their unbelief; and at last the Egyptians
were drowned in the sea, while the Israelites were saved.[2]
Nothing is related of the journey of the children of
Israel before the giving of the Law, except the striking
of the rock with the staff so that water flowed out, and
this comes in only incidentally in two passages; [3] in the
former of which however other facts about the stay in the
wilderness are related.   Moses then received the Law,[4]
and prayed to see God's glory.[5]   During his absence the

---

[1] Súras VII. 101—125, X. 76—90, XI. 99—102, XX. 50—79, XXIII.
47—51, XXVI. 15—52, XXVII. 13—15, XXVIII, 36—40, XL. 24—49,
XLIII. 45—54, LXXIX. 20—27.

[2] Súras II. 46—47, VII. 127—139, X. 90—93, XX. 79—82, XXVI. 52—
69, XXVIII. 40—43, XLIII. 55.

[3] Súras II. 57, VII. 160.

[4] הַלֻּחוֹת اَلْاَلْوَاح Súra VII. 142 and 149. On the first passage
Elpherar has : قال بن عباس يريد الالواح التوراة " Ben 'Abbás says that
by Alwáḥ he means the Toráh;" and on the second passage he says
more correctly : التى فيها التوراة " Wherein is the Toráh."

[5] Súras VII. 135—147, 170, II. 52—55, 60, 87, IV. 152. In the Qurán
Mount Sinai is never mentioned in connection with the giving of the law,
although it is so mentioned by commentators, e.g., Elpherar on VII. 140.
But it was not unknown to Muḥammad, seeing that it is mentioned on
other occasions. Thus it is used as an oath in Súra XCV. 2 (طُورِ سِينِينَ
probably on account of the rhyme. Compare (الَّيَاسِينَ). Again it is mentioned in the account of the creation of the olive tree. Súra XXIII. 20 :
"And a tree springing from the طُورِ سَيْنَآء," in which passage the commentators cited by Elpherar take the name as an appellation. Among many
diverging explanations one is adduced which appears to me right, viz.,
وقيل هو بالسريانية الملتف بالاشجار " It is said that in Syriac it means a
place thickly planted with trees;" so that סִינַי would be connected with

Israelites made the golden calf, which Moses on his return dashed into pieces and gave to the Israelites to drink;[1] and after that he appointed seventy men:[2] Later on he sent spies to Canaan, but they all except two were godless. The people let themselves be deceived by them and in consequence were obliged to wander for forty years in the wilderness.[3] Further, Moses had a dispute with Korah, whom the earth swallowed up,[4] and he was wrongly accused.

This last statement may be either a reference to the matter of Korah, or to the dispute with Aaron and Miriam. These are the main events of Moses's life as they are given in the Qurán, and we have arranged them partly according to the order of their mention in that book, but more with reference to our better source. Besides all this, a wonderful journey which Moses is said to have taken with his servant[5] is given, about which we shall speak further on. To pass on now to details. Haman[6]

סְנֶה. Compare Ben Ezra, who in his comment on Exodus, iii. 2 admits a connection between סִינַי and סְנֶה. It is to be noted that those mentioned above who take Sinai as an appellation do not regard it as identical with the mountain on which Moses received the Law, which identification is merely cited as a possible view:

وقال بن زيد هو الجبل الذى نودى منه موسى " Ben Zaid says that this is the mountain from which Moses was addressed."

D'Herbelot (Biblio. Orient. under Sina, page 793) says: The Arabs sometimes call this mountain Sinaini سِنَيْن, (which however should be سِنَان, Sináni) with reference to its two peaks Horeb and Sina; in this way Sinína might perhaps be taken as the genitive of the Arabic word Sinúna سِنُون.

[1] Súras II. 48—52, 87, VII. 148—155, XX. 82—99.
[2] Súra VII. 154.
[3] Súra V. 23—29.
[4] Súra XXVIII. 76—83.
[5] Súra XVIII. 59—81.
[6] هَامَان Súras XXVIII. 5, 7, 38, XXIX. 38, XL. 25.

and Korah [1] are mentioned as counsellors of Pharaoh and
persecutors of the Israelites. The latter is alluded to in
this capacity by the Rabbis,[2] who say : " Korah was the
chief steward over Pharaoh's house." As to the former,
Muḥammad must at some time have heard him mentioned
as the Jew's enemy,[3] and therefore have put him in
here, although later Arabians do not thus designate the
Haman [4] who lived in the time of Ahasuerus. The Rabbis
also say a good deal about Pharaoh's advisers, amongst
whom they sometimes mention Balaam, Job and Jethro.
Of these the first agreed with Pharaoh and for this reason
he was afterwards killed by the Israelites ; the second
remained silent, therefore he had to endure sufferings ;
the third fled, and so the happiness of being the father-in-
law of Moses fell to his lot. The two chief magicians,[5]
who are also mentioned in a letter of the apostle Paul,
are specially named as abettors. Fear on account of some
dream [6] is given as the greatest cause of persecution ;
and this is in accord with the statement of the Rabbis that
it was foretold to Pharaoh by the magicians [7] that a boy
would be born who would lead the Israelites out of Egypt ;
then he thought, if all male children were thrown into the
river, this one would be thrown with them.[8] The finding

---

[1] قَارُون Súras XXIX. 38, XL. 25.   [2] Midr. Rabb. on Numbers, par. 14.

קֹרַח הָיָה קַתּוֹלִיקוֹס לְבֵיתוֹ שֶׁל פַּרְעֹה

[3] הָמָן

[4] Not هَامَان but هَيْمَون. (compare Makarizi in De Sacy's Chrest. Arabe.
page 143, line 9 of the first edition).

[5] ממרא and יוחני   [6] Súra XXVIII. 5.

[7] Pirke Rabbi Eliezer, Section 48.

[8] אָמְרוּ הַחַרְטֻמִּים לְפַרְעֹה עָתִיד נַעַר לְהִוָּלֵד וְהוּא לְהִנָּלֵד וְהוּא יוֹצִיא
אֶת יִשְׂרָאֵל מִמִּצְרַיִם וְחָשַׁב וְאָמַר בְּלִבּוֹ הַשְׁלִיכוּ כָּל הַיִּלוֹדִים
הַזְּכָרִים אֶל דִּיאוֹר וְהוּא מֻשְׁלָה עִמָּהֶם

of Moses is attributed to Pharaoh's wife,[1] and she is
mentioned as a believer,[2] evidently having been confounded
with Pharaoh's daughter, by whom Moses was found
according to the Scriptures,[3] and in the same way the
name[4] given to Pharaoh's wife by the commentators is a
corruption of the name[5] by which his daughter was known
among the Jews. The words of the Bible: " Shall I go
and call thee a nurse of the Hebrew women ? "[6] give rise
to the following Rabbinical fable:[7] " Why must the nurse
be a Hebrew women ?" This shows that he refused the
breast of all the Egyptian women. For God said: " Shall
the mouth that is one day to speak with me suck an unclean
thing ? "[8] According to Muḥammad Moses regarded his
slaying of the Egyptian as sinful and repented thereof,[9]
which is contrary to the Jewish view,[10] expressed as
follows; "The verse in the 24th Psalm (according to the
reading of the Kethíbh; ' Who took not away his soul out
of vanity ') refers to the soul of the Egyptian, which Moses
did not take away, until he had investigated his case judi-
cially and had found that he deserved death." That the
Hebrew whom he released strove again on the following day
with an Egyptian,[11] and that he betrayed Moses, because he
would not uphold him, but on the contrary reproved him

---

[1] Súra XXVIII. 8. [2] Súra LXVI. 11. [3] Exodus, ii. 5.

[4] أَسِيَة [5] בִּתְיָה 1 Chron. iv. 18. [6] Exodus, ii. 7.

[7] Sotah 12, 2. מַה שְׁנָא עִבְרִיּוֹת מְלַמֵּד שֶׁהֶחֱזִירוּהוּ עַל כָּל

הַמִּצְרִיּוֹת כֻּלָּן וְלֹא יָנַק אָמַר הַקָּדוֹשׁ בָּרוּךְ הוּא פֶּה שֶׁעָתִיד

לְדַבֵּר עִמִּי יִינַק דָּבָר טָמֵא

[8] There is an allusion to this also in Súra XXVIII. 11.

[9] Súras XXVI. 19, XXVIII. 14.

[10] Midr. Rabb. on Exodus, para. 5

אֲשֶׁר לֹא נָשָׂא לַשָּׁוְא נַפְשׁוֹ זֶה נַפְשׁוֹ שֶׁל מִצְרִי שֶׁלֹּא הָרַג

אֶת הַמִּצְרִי עַד שֶׁעָמַד עָלָיו בְּדִין וְרָאָה שֶׁחַיָּב מִיתָה

[11] Súra XXVIII. 17 ff.

for his quarrelsome temper is mere embellishment, as is also the very happy invention of a man who warned Moses to flee.[1] There is a mistake to be found in the very brief account of Moses' flight to Midian and his residence there, for Muḥammad speaks of two [2] instead of seven [3] daughters of the Midianite. Instead of letting the vision in the bush be the occasion of Moses' leaving Midian, as it is in the Bible,[4] Muḥammad erroneously makes out that Moses had formed the resolution to leave the country before this event, and that the vision appeared to him on the way.[5] The appearance of Moses before Pharaoh is connected in a remarkable way with the divine commission to the former. So closely are the two circumstances bound together that in many places Pharaoh's answer follows immediately upon God's command, without its having first been mentioned that Moses and Aaron had gone in obedience to God to Egypt, had done wonders before Pharaoh and had admonished him. But on the other hand in those passages where only the admonitions given by Moses to Pharaoh are related, without the preceding events being given, the part elsewhere omitted is of course supplied, but as we might expect with changes. Pharaoh is said to have reproached Moses with the murder of the Egyptian.[6] This is a very simple invention, which however is contrary to the literal sense of the Scriptures,[7] unless we accept the Rabbinical explanation [8] of the words, " the king of Egypt died," [9] that is, " he became leprous and a leper is as one dead ; " and also of the words, " for all are died who sought

---

[1] Súra XXVIII. 19.   [2] Súra XXVIII. 23.

[3] Exodus, ii. 16.   [4] Exodus, iii.

[5] Súra XXVIII. 29.   [6] Súra XXVI. 17 ff.

[7] Exodus, ii. 23. iv. 19.   [8] Midr. Rabb. on Exodus, par. 1.

וַיָּמָת מֶלֶךְ מִצְרַיִם שֶׁנִּצְטָרַע וְהַמְצֹרָע חָשׁוּב כְּמֵת

[9] Exodus, ii. 23.

thy life " [1] which is as follows : " Were they dead ? They were Dathan and Abiram, who were involved in the dispute of Korah. This only means that they had become powerless."* Further, Moses is supposed to have shewn the sign of his leprous hand before Pharaoh,[2] which is not mentioned in Scripture,[3] but which agrees with the following statement in the Rabbinical writings : [4] " He put his hand into his bosom, and drew it out as white as snow from leprosy ; they also put their hands into their bosoms and drew them out as white as snow from leprosy." The magicians who were summoned asked at first, in distinction from God's messengers, for their reward ; [5] but when they had seen their serpents swallowed by that of Moses, they believed, praised God and were not intimidated by Pharaoh's threats. This is quite contrary to the Bible, in which such a confession is found only after the plague of lice,[6] and there too only in the form of a mere hint. Among Moses' own people only his own tribe is said to have believed on him,[7] and the Rabbis say [8] that " the tribe of

---

[1] Midr. Rabb. on Exodus, par. 5.

כִּי מֵתוּ כָּל הָאֲנָשִׁים וְכִי מֵתוּ וַהֲלֹא דָתָן וַאֲבִירָם הֵם וְהֵם
הָיוּ עִם קֹרַח בְּמַחֲלָקְתּוֹ אֶלָּא מָי מֵתוּ שֶׁנִּתְעַנּוּ

[2] Súras VII. 108, XXVI. 32.   [3] Exodus, vii. 8 ff.

[4] Pirke Rabbi Eliezer, Section 48.

הִכְנִיס יָדוֹ לְחֵיקוֹ וְחוֹצִיאָהּ מְצוֹרַעַת כַּשֶּׁלֶג וְגַם הֵם הִכְנִיסוּ
יָדָם לְחֵיקָם וְהוֹצִיאוּ אוֹתָם מְצוֹרָעוֹת כַּשֶּׁלֶג

[5] Súras VII. 110, XXVI. 40.   [6] Exodus, viii. 15.

[7] Súra X. 83. The suffix refers to Moses, as some Arabic commentators cited by Baidháwi (Henzii Fragm. Arab. page 103) and by Elpherar take it.

[8] Midr. Rabb. on Exodus, para. 5.

שִׁבְטוֹ שֶׁל לֵוִי פָּנוּי הָיָה מֵעֲבוֹדַת פֶּרֶךְ

* According to Midr. Rabb. on Exodus, para 1, Dathan and Abiram were the two disputants, one of whom reproached Moses with the murder of the Egyptian.

Levi was exempt from hard labour." Pharaoh himself was also a magician, and this he claims, according to my opinion, in his address to the other magicians.[1] This is in accord with the Rabbinical statement [2] that the Pharaoh who lived in the days of Moses was a great magician. In other passages of the Quran,[3] Pharaoh claims for himself divinity, which assumption no doubt is intended to be accepted by the people. This trait is also developed in Jewish legend,[4] where we read: " Pharaoh said to them : ' From the first have ye spoken an untruth, for lord of the world am I, I created myself and the Nile ; as it is written : [5] my river is mine own and I have made it for myself.' " In another passage [6] Muhammad puts the following words into Pharaoh's mouth : " Is not the kingdom of Egypt mine and these rivers which flow beneath me ? " Elpherar, with others,[7] remarks on the words " beneath me," that they mean " by my command." A quite new but charming fiction is that of a pious Egyptian, who warned his countrymen not to despise the teaching of Moses and not to persecute him.[8] Certain features of this story sound familiar. For instance, the words in verse 29 : " If he be a liar, on him will the punishment of his falsehood light ; but if he speaketh the truth, some of those judgments with which he threateneth you will fall upon you," bear a resemblance to the words of

---

[1] Súras XX. 74, XXVI. 48.   [2] Midr. Yalkut, chapter 182.

שֶׁהָיָה בִּימֵי מֹשֶׁה אַמְגּוּשִׁי נָדוֹל הָיָה

[3] Súras XXVI. 28, XXVIII. 38.   [4] Midr. Rabb. on Exodus, para. 5.

אָמַר לָהֶם מִתְּחִלָּה שֶׁקֶר אַתֶּם אוֹמְרִים כִּי אֲנִי הוּא אֲדוֹן
הָעוֹלָם וַאֲנִי בָּרָאתִי עַצְמִי וְאֶת נִילוֹס שֶׁנֶּאֱמַר לִי יְאֹרִי וַאֲנִי
עֲשִׂיתִנִי

[5] Ezekiel, xxix. 3.   [6] Súra XLIII. 50.

[7] قال الحسن بامري " Al Hasan says by my command."

[8] Súra XL. 29 ff.

Gamaliel in the New Testament. The allusion to Joseph in verse 36 is found in a very dissimilar Jewish tradition, as follows;[1] "If Joseph had not been, we should not be alive." Muḥammad is not clear about the plagues. In some passages[2] he speaks of nine plagues. In another passage[3] he enumerates five, which stand in the following order: Flood, Locusts, Lice, Frogs and Blood. Although we cannot here find fault with the want of order in the plagues and with the omission of some of them since Muḥammad here is not, any more than is the Psalmist,[4] to be considered as a strict historian, yet the mistaken inclusion of a flood, which is not to be confounded with the overthrow in the sea,[5] may fairly be considered as a proof of the want of reliable information on the subject. The fear of the Israelites[6] at the approach of the Egyptians by the Red sea is also mentioned by Muḥammad.[7]

Now we come to a circumstance, which is also taken from Jewish legend, but which has been almost entirely misunderstood, from ignorance of its origin. The passage[8] may be translated as follows: " And we caused the children of Israel to pass through the sea, and Pharaoh and his army followed them in a violent and hostile manner, until when he was drowning, he said: 'I believe that there is no God but He on Whom the Children of Israel believe, and I am now one of the resigned;' on which God said, (or perhaps this is to be read in the first person, so that this verse too expresses Pharaoh's penitence, and the next verse begins the expression of God's answer); 'Thou hast been hitherto one of the rebellions and wicked doers. This

---

[1] Midr. Rabba on Exodus, para. 1

אִלּוּלֵי יוֹסֵף לֹא הָיִינוּ חַיִּים

[2] Súras XVII. 103, XXVII. 12.   [3] Súra VII. 130.
[4] E. g. in Psalm, cv. 28 ff.   [5] first mentioned in v. 132.
[6] Exodus, xiv. 10 ff.   [7] Súra XXVI. 61 ff.
[8] Súra X. 90 ff.

day, however will we save thee with thy body, that thou
mayest be a sign to those who shall be after thee.'"[1]   This
is the quite simple meaning of the words, which has been
turned and twisted about by others, because they were
ignorant of the following Jewish legend:[2] "Recognize
the power of repentance! Pharaoh King of Egypt rebelled
excessively against the Most High saying: 'Who is God
that I should hearken to His voice?'[3] but with the same
tongue he repented saying: 'Who is like Thee, O Lord,
among the Gods?'[4] God delivered him from the dead, for
it is written: 'For now I had put forth my hand and

---

[1] Not one Arabic commentator among those quoted in Elpherar appears
to have had a suspicion of the explanation given above, which is so well
suited to the words; still it is not quite unknown to Baidháwi. Along
with other explanations he gives (Henzii Fragm. Arab., page 201) the

following : فَٱلۡيَوۡمَ نُنَجِّيكَ نُنقِّذُكَ مما وقع فيه قومك من قعر البحر

و نجعلك طافيا *

'And to-day we save thee i.e., we will bring thee back from where thy
people are sunk,—even from the depth of the sea, and we will put thee
on dry land."   And further on: بِبَدَنِكَ كاملا سويّا   "With thy body, i.e.,

whole and unharmed."   But on the other hand the words: "That thou
mayest be a sign to those who shall come after thee," are explained by
him only in the ordinary way, viz. that he should be a horror and a
warning to them.

[2] Pirke Rabbi Eliezer, Section 43.

תֵּדַע לְךָ כֹּחַ הַתְּשׁוּבָה מִפַּרְעֹה מֶלֶךְ מִצְרַיִם שֶׁמָּרַד בְּצוּר
עֶלְיוֹן הַרְבֵּה מְאֹד שֶׁנֶּ' מִי ה' אֲשֶׁר אֶשְׁמַע בְּקוֹלוֹ וּבְאוֹתוֹ לָשׁוֹן
שֶׁחָטָא בּוֹ בַּלָּשׁוֹן עָשָׂה תְּשׁוּבָה שֶׁנֶּ' מִי כָּמֹכָה בָּאֵלִים ה'
וְהִצִּילוֹ הַקָּ' בָּ' ה' מִבֵּין הַמֵּתִים וּמִנַּיִן שֶׁלֹּא מֵת שֶׁנֶּ' כִּי עַתָּה
שָׁלַחְתִּי אֶת־יָדִי וָאַף אוֹתְךָ וְהֶעֱמִידוֹ הַקָּ' בָּ' ה' מִבֵּין הַמֵּתִים
לְסַפֵּר כֹּחוֹ וּגְבוּרָתוֹ וּמִנַּיִן שֶׁהֶעֱמִידוֹ שֶׁנֶּ' וְאוּלָם בַּעֲבוּר זֹאת
הֶעֱמַדְתִּיךָ

Comp. also Midrash on Psalm, cvi. and Midr. Yalkut, chapter 238.

[3] Exodus, v. 2.   [4] Exodus, xv. 11.

smitten thee,'[1] but God let him live to proclaim His power and might, even as it is written in Exodus, ix. 16."

On the occasion of the striking of the Rock Muḥammad makes twelve streams gush out, so that each individual tribe[2] had its own particular stream. Apparently this is a confusion of the events at Raphidim, where the rock was struck,[3] with those at Elim where the Israelites found twelve wells.[4] On these wells the commentator Rashi, probably following earlier expositors says:[5] "They found them ready for them, in number as the twelve Tribes." When it came at last to the giving of the Law, the Israelites are said to have rebelled; but God threatened them that He would overturn the mountain[6] upon them if they would not accept the Law. The Jews also say that God threatened to cover them with the mountain as with a basin turned upside down.[7] But now the Israelites demanded that they themselves should see God; they died at the sight of Him, but were afterwards raised again.[8] The corresponding Rabbinical statement may be translated as follows:[9] "The Israelites desired two things of

---

[1] Exodus, ix. 15.

[2] أُمَّة, not سِبْط, although the twelve sons of Jacob are also called الأَسْبَاط by Muḥammad. Still in Súra VII. 160 أَسْبَاط and أُمَم are used side by side in an entirely similar sense, so that one recognizes the identical meaning of the two, and therefore one may with perfect right translate أُمَّة as "tribe."

[3] Exodus, xvii. 6.

[4] Exodus, xv. 27. Comp. also the two recensions of Jerusalem Targum.

[5] כְּנֶגֶד שְׁנֵים עָשָׂר שְׁבָטִים נִזְדַּמְּנוּ לָהֶם

[6] Súras II. 60, 87, VII. 170.

[7] Abodah Zarah II. 2. כֹּפֶה אֲנִי עֲלֵיכֶם אֶת־הָהָר כְּגִינִית

[8] Súra II. 52 ff. IV. 152.

[9] שְׁנֵי דְבָרִים שָׁאֲלוּ יִשְׂרָאֵל מִלִּפְנֵי הַקָּ'בָּ'ה' שֶׁיִּרְאוּ כְבוֹדוֹ
וְיִשְׁמְעוּ קוֹלוֹ וְהָיוּ רוֹאִין אֶת־כְּבוֹדוֹ וְשׁמְעִין אֶת־קוֹלוֹ שֶׁנֶּ' הֵן הֶרְאָנוּ

God, that they might see His glory and hear His voice ; and
both were granted them, as it is written: [1] ' Behold the
Lord our God hath shewed us His glory and His greatness,
and we have heard His voice out of the midst of the fire.'
Then they had no power to bear it, for when they came to
Sinai and He appeared to them, their soul departed at His
speech, as it is written: [2] ' My soul went forth when he
spake.' The Law (the Torah) however interceded with
God for them saying: ' Would a king marry his daughter
and slay all his household ? ' The whole world rejoices
(on account of my appearance), and shall thy children
(the Israelites) die ? At once their souls returned to them,
therefore it is written: [3] ' The Law of the Lord is perfect,
restoring the soul.' " The story of the calf is also one
of those which Muḥammad, following the Rabbis, has
found it easy to embellish. He says that the people would
have killed Aaron, if he had not made them a calf; [4]
and the Rabbis say: [5] " Aaron saw Hur (who had wished to oppose them) killed; then he thought: if I do not
listen to them they will do with me as with Hur."
According to another statement of the Qurán [6] one of

ח' אֱלֹהֵינוּ אֶת־כְּבוֹדוֹ וְאֶת־גָּדְלוֹ וּכְתִיב וְאֶת־קֹלוֹ שָׁמַעְנוּ מִתּוֹךְ
הָאֵשׁ וְלֹא הָיָה בָּהֶם כֹּחַ לַעֲמוֹד כְּנֶן שֶׁבָּאוּ לְסִינַי וְנִגְלָה לָהֶם
פְּרְחָה נִשְׁמָתָם עַל שֶׁדִּבֵּר עָמָהֶם שֶׁנֶ' נַפְשִׁי יָצְאָה בְּדַבְּרוֹ אֲבָל
הַתּוֹרָה בִּקְשָׁה עֲלֵיהֶם רַחֲמִים מִלִּפְנֵי הַקַּבַּ'ה' יֵשׁ מֶלֶךְ מַשִּׂיא
בִתּוֹ וְהוֹרֵג אַנְשֵׁי בֵיתוֹ כָּל־הָעוֹלָם כֻּלּוֹ שְׂמֵחִים וּבָנֶיךָ מֵתִים מִיָּד
חָזְרָה נִשְׁמָתָן שֶׁנֶ' תּוֹרַת ח' תְּמִימָה מְשִׁיבַת נָפֶשׁ

[1] Deuteronomy, v. 24 (Heb., v. 21).   [2] Canticles, v. 6.
[3] Psalm, xix. 8.   [4] Súra VII. 150.

[5] Sanhedrin 5 אַהֲרֹן רָאָה חוּר שֶׁזָּבוּחַ לְפָנָיו אָמַר אִם לָא
שָׁמַעְנָא לְהוֹן הָשַׁתָּא עָבְדִי לִי כִּדַעֲבַדוּ בְחוּר

Rashi makes the same remark on Exodus, xxxii. 4.

[6] Súra XX. 87, 90, 96.

the Israelites, named Sámiri,[1] led them astray and also made the calf. This arose perhaps from Samáel,[2] the name of one who is supposed by the Jews to have been helpful at the making of the calf; but at any rate the tale has been differently developed by Muḥammad. According to him this was one of the Israelites who was present, and whom Moses condemned to everlasting wandering,[3] so that he was compelled to say perpetually, "Touch not."[4] One recognises that this legend is composed of different elements. It is not foreign to Jewish tradition that another Israelite, not Aaron, made the calf, and according to one legend, Micah,[5] who is mentioned in Judges, helped in the making;[6] whence it comes that many Arabians assert that Sámiri and Micah are one and the same person.[7] Perhaps Muḥammad formed the word Sámiri from a confusion with the name Samáel.

Sámiri was the name for Samaritan, and according to the Arabians the Samaritans said, "Touch us not."[8] With how much reason the Arabians hold this is indeed unknown, perhaps only from confusion with a sect of the Pharisees described as bad in the Talmud, where it is named "The set-apart, touch me not;"[9] but I have only a dim recollection of the passage. In short the Samaritans were certainly known to later Arabians by this name, and

---

[1] السَّامِرِيُّ   [2] סַמָּאֵל

[3] Súra XX. 97. Compare the wandering Jew in the Christian legend.

[4] لَا مِسَاسَ   [5] Judges, xvii.

[6] Rashi on Sanhedrin 101. 2.

[7] Cf. Aḥmad Ben Idris in Hottinger's Hist. Orient., page 84.

[8] Cf. Makarizi (in De Sacy, Chrest. Arabe, i. 113 in the second edition, 189 in the first edition): ويذكر انهم الذى يقولون لا مساس and further: قال ابو ريحان محمد بن احمد البيرونى ان السامرة تعرف بالا مساسية on which passage De Sacy quotes the Súra, along with Baidháwi's comment.

[9] פָּרוּשׁ אַל תִּמוּשֵׁנִי

Muḥammad doubtless knew them by it too ; and since he
gave the name of Samaritan [1] to the maker of the calf, this
man must have seemed to him to be the founder of the
sect, and the " Touch me not " must have originated with
him, which as a punishment was known to Muḥammad
from the similar story of the wandering Jew.   Muḥammad
says that the calf lowed as it come forth.[2]   With this is to
be compared the Rabbinical statement : " There came forth
this calf [3] lowing, and the Israelites saw it.   Rabbi Je-
huda says that Samáel entered into it and lowed in order to
mislead Israel." [4]   In the Qurán it is said [5] that among the
people of Moses there was a tribe which kept to the truth.
This seems to refer to the tribe of Levi and especially to
their behaviour about the calf, although possibly it may
refer also to their belief in Moses's mission to Pharaoh of
which we have spoken before.   In the biblical account a
statement is made,[6] which is explained by the Rabbis as
follows : [7] " From Exodus, xxxii. 26, it is clear that the
tribe of Levi was not implicated in the matter of the
golden calf." The Arabian commentators produce the most
unedifying fables about this passage.

In the events which follow abbreviations are to be found,
but neither changes nor embellishments, except in the
story of the dispute with Korah, which gives rise to some.
Korah is said to have had such riches that a number of

---

[1] السَّامِرِيّ   [2] Súras VII. 147, XX. 90.

[3] Exodus, xxxii. 24.   [4] Pirke Rabbi Eliezer, section 45.

וַיֵּצֵא הָעֵגֶל הַזֶּה גֹּעֶה וְרָאוּ אוֹתוֹ יִשְׂרָאֵל רַבִּי יְהוּדָה אֹמֵר
סַמָּאֵל נִכְנַס לְתוֹכוֹ וְהָיָה גֹעֶה לְהַתְעוֹת אֶת־יִשְׂרָאֵל

[5] Súra VII. 159.   [6] Exodus, xxxii. 26.

[7] Pirke Rabbi Eliezer, section 45.

שֵׁבֶט לֵוִי לֹא שִׁתֵּף עַצְמוֹ בְּמַעֲשֵׂה הָעֵגֶל שֶׁנֶּ' וַיַּעֲמֹד מֹשֶׁה
בְּשַׁעַר הַמַּחֲנֶה וַיֵּאָסְפוּ אֵלָיו כָּל־בְּנֵי לֵוִי

strong men were required to carry the keys of his treasure-
chamber,[1] and the Rabbis tell us,[2] " Joseph buried three
treasures in Egypt, one of which became known to Korah.
Riches kept by the owner to his hurt[3] may be applied
to the riches of Korah. The keys of Korah's treasure-
chamber were a burden for three hundred white mules."
It is implied in the same Talmudic passage that he became
overbearing and quarrelsome from the possession of such
riches, and Muḥammad embellishes this idea in a fine
manner. One passage in the Qurán may refer to this
dispute, for it says there that some persons had accused
Moses, but that God cleared him from the charge which
they had brought against him.[4] Some of the commentators also refer the passage to this event, while they bring
forward the following story, which we give in Elpherar's
words :[5] " Abu'l-'Álíah says that it refers to the fact that
Korah had hired a bad woman, who accused Moses before
all the people of bad conduct with herself. God made her
dumb, cleared Moses of the accusation, and destroyed
Korah." This is actually supposed to have happened after
Moses had made known the law about adultery, and after
the enquiry as to whether it applied to him also had been
answered by him in the affirmative.[6] The Rabbis also
allude to this in the following words :[7] " And when Moses

---

[1] Súra XXVIII. 76.

[2] שָׁלֹשׁ מַטְמֹנִיּוֹת הִטְמִין יוֹסֵף בְּמִצְרַיִם אַחַת נִתְגַּלָּה לְקֹרַח
עֹשֶׁר שָׁמוּר לִבְעָלָיו לְרָעָתוֹ זֶה עָשְׁרוֹ שֶׁל קֹרַח מַשּׂוֹי שָׁלֹשׁ
מֵאוֹת פְּרָדוֹת לְבָנוֹת הָיוּ מִפְתְּחוֹת בֵּית גְּנָזָיו שֶׁל קֹרַח

[3] Ecclesiastes, v. 12.   [4] Súra XXXIII. 69.

[5] وقال ابو العالية هوان قارون استاجر بغية تقذف موسى بنفسها على
رأس الملا فعصمها الله وابرا موسى من ذلك واهلك قارون *

[6] Cf. Abulfeda Hist. Anteislámica, page 32.

[7] וַיִּשְׁמַע מֹשֶׁה וַיִּפֹּל עַל פָּנָיו מַה־שְּׁמוּעָה שָׁמַע מְלַמֵּד
שֶׁחֲשָׁדוּהוּ בְּאֵשֶׁת אִישׁ

See Numbers, xvi. 4.

heard it, he fell on his face.   What did he hear ? That he
was blamed for being intimate with the wife of another ; "
and in another passage we read : [1] " Each man suspected
his wife on account of Moses."   Other commentators
understand that the accusation was that Moses had killed
Aaron, because the two were alone together when Aaron
died on Mount Hor ; but Moses was cleared from this by
the angels, who produced Aaron's corpse.[2] This is also a
Rabbinical idea, for we read in the Midrash Tanchuma : [3]
" All the congregation saw that Aaron was dead.[4]   When
Moses and Eleazar came down from the mountain, the
whole congregation came together against them asking
them : ' Where is Aaron ?' They said : ' He is dead.' They replied : ' How can the death angel come to a man who has once
resisted him and held him back ? for it is written : [5] He
(Aaron) stood between the dead and the living and the
plague was stayed. If you produce him, well ; if not, we
will stone you.'   Moses then prayed : ' Lord of the world,
clear me from this suspicion.' Then God immediately opened

---

[1] Sanhedrin 110.   כָּל־אֶחָד קִנֵּא לְאִשְׁתּוֹ מִמּשֶׁה

[2] Elpherar has : وقال قوم ايذاوهم اياه انه لمامات هارون فى التيه
ادعوا على موسى انه قتله فامر الله الملائكة حتى مروا به على بنى اسرايل
Comp. Abulfeda Hist. Anteislámica, pp. 32 and 34. فعرفوا ان لم يقتله
فبراه الله مما قالوا *

[3] וַיִּרְאוּ כָּל־הָעֵדָה כִּי גָוַע אַהֲרֹן כְּוָן שֶׁיָרְדוּ משֶׁה וְאֶלְעָזָר
מִן הָהָר נִתְקַבְּצוּ כָּל־הַקָּהָל עֲלֵיהֶם אָמְרוּ לָהֶם הֵיכָן אַהֲרֹן
אָמְרוּ לָהֶם מֵת אָמְרוּ לָהֶם הֵיאַךְ מַלְאַךְ הַמָּוֶת יָכוֹל לַפְגּוֹעַ
בְּאָדָם שֶׁעָמַד בְּמַלְאַךְ הַמָּוֶת וַעֲצָרוֹ דִּכְתִיב וַיַּעֲמֹד בֵּין הַמֵּתִים
וּבֵין הַחַיִּים וַתֵּעָצַר הַמַּגֵּפָה אִם אַתֶּם מְבִיאִין אוֹתוֹ מוּטָב וְאִם
לֹא נִסְקַל אֶתְכֶם בְּאוֹתָהּ שָׁעָה עָמַד משֶׁה בִּתְפִלָּה וְאָמַר
רִבּ'שֶׁ'ע' הוֹצִיאֵנִי מִן הַחֲשָׁד מִיַּד פָּתַח הַקָּ' בָּ' ח' אֶת־הַמְעָרָה
וְהֶרְאָהוּ לָהֶם שֶׁנֶּ' וַיִּרְאוּ כָּל־הָעֵדָה כִּי גָוַע אַהֲרֹן

[4] Numbers, xx. 29.   [5] Numbers, xvi. 48. (Hebrew, xvii. 13.)

the grave and shewed Aaron to them, and to this refers the passage : ' The whole congregation saw, etc.' " Here I omit entirely a third very insipid fable which the commentators mention, and which seems to them to be the most probable occasion of the verse, but I cannot trace it to any Jewish source. The most correct view is, as Wahl has already remarked, that the verse refers to the reproaches of Aaron and Miriam.[1] In short the fifth verse of Súra LXI is about the answer of Moses to the disputants. Here the commentators give only the fable not quoted by us, just because here, as in the second passage, they repeat only the most universally accepted view. But this cannot prevent us from holding to our opinion. Of the journey described by Muḥammad [2] I could not find a trace in Jewish writings, although the colouring is Jewish.* Moses is said to have gone with his servant to see the place where two seas meet, and to have forgotten a fish, which they were taking with them for food and which sprang into the sea. When they went back to seek it, a servant of God met them and made the journey with them, telling them before hand that his actions would rouse their impatience. He sank a ship, killed a youth and propped up a wall ; and only when they parted did he give sufficient reasons for these actions. The story following this about Dhu-'l-

---

[1] Numbers, xii. 1 ff. [2] Súra XVIII. 59—81.

* The author adds the following note in the Appendix :

Zunz (die gottesdienstlichen Vorträge der Juden, historisch entwickelt, S. 130 u. Anm. d.) has pointed out the Jewish source of this story, in which the servant of God according to the Arabians is said to be Elias (cf. under Elias) ; only that, according to the Jewish source, the traveller is R. Joshua ben Levi, a man who plays a leading part in tales of marvel and adventure (cf. Zunz pp. 140—141) and whom this adventure suits much better than it does Moses, who stands on too high a plane. We may easily recognize therefore the Jewish origin of this legend, which has been embellished quite after the manner of the Qurán.

Qaruain [1] might well refer to Moses, the shining one,[2] if anything of the sort were known about him.

Of the individual laws which are mentioned historically in the Qurán,[3] only one, viz., that relating to the red heifer,[4] affords material for a narrative, and that is given [5] in very unnecessary fullness and with manifold errors. In the first place Muhammad confounds the red heifer [6] with the calf which is slain for one murdered by an unknown hand,[7] and he also makes the dead man live again [8] on being struck with a piece of the animal. In view of such great distortions we must not deal hardly with him for the following small one; he says that the cow must be of one year,[9] in contradiction to the rabbinical statement that she had to be a two-year old.[10]

As to those persons who come into the history of Moses, we have already disposed of Pharaoh, Aaron and Korah,[11] while we have only mentioned others and therefore must add more about them. Miriam [12] is praised in the scripture and called a prophetess,[13] but the Rabbis value her still more highly and say of her: [14] " The angel of death had no power over Miriam, but she died from the divine afflation, and therefore worms could not touch her." According to

---

[1] ذو ٱلْقَرْنَيْنِ, Súra XVIII. 82 ff.

[2] Exodus, xxxiv. 29 ff.

[3] See Appendix.

[4] Numbers, xix. 2 ff.

[5] Súra II. 63 ff.

[6] Súra II. 67.

[7] Deuteronomy, xxi. 2 ff.

[8] Súra II. 68.

[9] عَوَان Súra II. 63.

[10] Vid. Midr. Rabb. on Numbers, para. 19.

[11] قَارُون هَرُون فِرْعُون.

[12] مريم

[13] הַנְּבִיאָה

[14] Baba Bathra, 17.

מִרְיָם לֹא שָׁלַט בָּהּ מַלְאַךְ הַמָּוֶת אֶלָּא בִּנְשִׁיקָה מֵתָה וְלֹא שָׁלַט בָּהּ רִמָּה וְתוֹלֵעָה

Muḥammad [1] Miriam is the mother of Jesus.[2] Although Miriam's name is not mentioned in the passage where she is alluded to in the history of Moses,[3] yet there is not the slightest doubt that Muḥammad took both Marys for one and the same person; for the Talmudic utterance already cited, viz., that Miriam did not die through the angel of death, could easily be turned into a statement of a long, if not endless, life for her, especially by Muḥammad, who treats chronology pretty much according to his own pleasure. The other person who appears in the history of Moses is his father-in-law Jethro. Now it is true that his name, like that of Miriam, is not mentioned in the story of Moses,[4] hence the Muḥammadan tradition connects this Midianite (as the Qurán simply designates the father-in-law of Moses) with Shu'aib, the Arabic name for Jethro, and so they came to be considered as one and the same, not however without more or less opposition. Thus Elpherar says:[5] "Opinions are divided as to the name of Moses' wife's father. Many say he was the prophet Shu'aib; others that he was Jethro the nephew of Shu'aíb who died before him; others again that he was a man who believed on Shu'aib." But the most widespread tradition is that it was Shu'aib himself.

Thus Elpherar always calls him by this name, when mentioning him in connection with these events and

---

[1] مَرْيَم ٱبْنَتُ عِمْرَان وَأُخْتُ هَرُون Súras LXIV. 12, VII. 188.

[2] Cf. Súra III. title and verse 30 ff.; Súra XIX. particularly verse 29; Súra LXVI. 12, and Sunna 405.

[3] Súra XXVIII. 10. [4] Súra XXVIII. 28 ff.

[5] Elpherar on Súra XXVIII. 28.

واختلفوا فى اسم ابيها فقال مجاهد والضحاك والسدى والحسن هو شعيب النبى ملعم وقال وهب وسعيد بن جبير يثرون ابن اخى شعيب وكان شعيب قد مات قبل ذلك .... وقيل رجل من امن بشعيب *

Abulfeda[1] relates just this one t! ing about Shu'aib, viz.,
that he was the father-in-law of Moses, without giving any
other opinion.   Though his name is not mentioned in this
connection in the Qurán, other events independent of Moses'
life are related of him, particularly his admonition of
the Midianites, which is said by the Rabbis to have been
the cause of the hatred of that people towards him.[2]
Muḥammad took up the admonition without mentioning the
consequence which it entailed on Jethro, viz., the driving
away of his daughters, which was just the circumstance
which led to Jethro's connection with the life of Moses.
According to Muḥammad an immediate punishment fell on
the Midianites.[3]   The Rabbis have the following on the
subject:[4] "The priest of Midian had seven daughters.[5]
God hates idolatry and did He give Moses a refuge with an
idolater ? Concerning this our teachers tell us: Jethro was
priest of the idols, but knew their worthlessness, despised

---

[1] Hist. Anteislámica, page 30.   [2] Exodus, ii. 17.

[3] Súras VII. 83—92, XI. 85—98, XXII. 43, XXV. 40, XXVI. 176—92,
XXIX. 35—6, XXXVIII. 12, L. 12—3.

[4] Midr. Rabb. on Exodus, para. 1.

וּלְלַחֵן מִדְיָן שֶׁבַע בָּנוֹת וַהֲלֹא הַקָּ'בָּ'ח' שֹׂנֵא עֲבוֹדָה זָרָה
וְנֹתֵן מָנוֹס לְמֹשֶׁה אֵצֶל עֹבֵד עֲ' זָ' אֶלָּא אָמְרוּ רַבּוֹתֵינוּ יִתְרוֹ
כּוּמֶר הָיָה לַעֲ' זָ' וְרָאָה שֶׁאֵין בָּה מַמָּשׁ וּבִכֵּר עָלֶיהָ וְהִרְהֵר
לַעֲשׂוֹת תְּשׁוּבָה עַד שֶׁלֹּא בָּא מֹשֶׁה וְקָרָא לִבְנֵי עִירוֹ וְאָמַר לָהֶם
עַד עַכְשָׁיו הָיִיתִי מְשַׁמֵּשׁ אֶתְכֶם מֵעַתָּה זָקֵן אֲנִי בִּדְּרוּ לָכֶם
כּוּמֶר אַחֵר וְהוֹצִיא כְּלֵי תַשְׁמִישׁ עֲ' זָ וְנָתַן לָהֶם הַכֹּל עָמְדוּ
וְנִדּוּּהוּ שֶׁלֹּא יִזְדַקֵּק לוֹ אָדָם וְלֹא יַעֲשֶׂה לוֹ מְלָאכָה וְלֹא יִרְעֶה
אֶת־צֹאנוֹ וּבִקֵּשׁ מִן הָרֹעִים לִרְעוֹת לוֹ אֶת צֹאנוֹ וְלֹא קִבְּלוּ
וַיָּבֹאוּ הָרֹעִים וַיְגָרְשׁוּם אֶפְשָׁר חוּא כֹּהֵן מִדְיָן וְהָרֹעִים מְגָרְשִׁים
בְּנוֹתָיו אֶלָּא לְלַמֶּדְךָ שֶׁנִּדּוּּהוּ וְגֵרְשׁוּ בְּנוֹתָיו

[5] Exodus, ii. 16.

idolatry and had thought of being converted even before
Moses came. Then he called his fellow-townsmen and
said to them: ' Till now I have served you, but now I am
old, choose you another priest: and he gave them back the
vessels of service.' Then they put him under a ban, so that
no one conversed with him, no one worked for him, no one
tended his flocks; and when he asked this service from the
shepherds, they would not give it. The shepherds came
and drove them away.[1] Was it possible? Jethro was the
priest of Midian and the shepherds drove away his daughters? But this shews that they had put him under a ban,
and for this reason they drove his daughters away." In the
mouth of the people, or more probably from Muḥammad
himself, the legend received the embellishment that Jethro
wanted to convert his fellow-countrymen to the faith, and
that they were punished on account of their unbelief. A
reproach which is specially brought against them, or rather
the point of the exhortation, viz., to give just weight and
measure,[2] must be founded on some legend or other,
although I have not yet come across it in Jewish writings.[3]
Jethro shows himself as a preacher quite according to
Muḥammad's ideas. He preaches about the Last Day[4] and
asserts that he desires no reward;[5] on the other hand his
townspeople reproach him with working no miracles.[6] I
have presented the facts and quotations here as though
there were no doubt that all these passages refer to Jethro,
but exception might be taken to this. An altogether
different name[7] is found in the Qurán, and it is not easy to

---

[1] Exodus, ii. 17.   [2] Súras VII. 83, XI. 86.

[3] It seems as though Muḥammad had confounded the Midianites with
the inhabitants of Sodom, to whom such things are imputed by the
Rabbis.

[4] Súra XXIX. 35.   [5] Súra XXVI. 180.

[6] Súra XXVI. 186, 187.   [7] شعيب

explain how Jethro came by it. However, we must first try
to shew that Shu'aib and Jethro are identical, and then put
forward our conjectures as to how the many-named Jethro
added this name to his others. The identity is first shewn
by the fact that those to whom he was sent are called
" Midianites ; " [1] in the second place, the two first passages [2]
give the events concerning him between the story of Lot
and that of Moses.

Now if we can find among the Rabbis any intimation
favourable to this supposition, then nothing important will
remain to oppose its adoption [3] as a probable hypothesis.
Very little, however, can be adduced to shew how Shu'aib
and Jethro came to be one and the same person. Muḥammad may have confused the name Hobáb [4]—often used for
Jethro and probably pronounced Chobab—with Shu'aib.
Perhaps an etymological explanation may be thought of
here, for the Rabbis assert that the staff used later by
Moses and called the divine staff [5] grew in Jethro's garden. [6]
Now Sha'ba [7] means staff and Shu'aib [8] may be taken as the
possessor of the staff. If Shu'aib is the same as Jethro,

---

[1] Súras VII. 83, XI. 85, XXIX. 35. (مَدْيَنَ), XXII. 43 (أَصْحَابُ مَدْيَنَ,
where مَدْيَن is regarded as the name of a town).

[2] Súras VII. 83—92, XI. 85—98.

[3] It is all very well for Ahmad ben As Salím (quoted by Maracc. on
Súra VII. 83.) to assert that this is the opinion of طايفة من الجهال, " a heap
of fools." Some regard Jethro, as the father of Shu'aib, (as Elpherar on
Súra VII. 83 : وقيل هو شعيب بن يثرون); others, as his nephew (cf. the
passage quoted above from Elpherar on Súra XXVIII. 23.). The difference in the names confuses the commentators, and also their ignorance
of the source from which here, as often, Muḥammad drew.

[4] חוֹבָב

[5] מַטֵּה הָאֱלֹהִים

[6] That Moses obtained the staff from Jethro is asserted also by D'Herb.
B. O. under the word Shu'aib, p. 772, according to the Muḥammadan view.

[7] شَعْبَة

[8] شُعَيْب

there are passages [1] in which the former is mentioned, while those to whom he is sent are not called Midianites; and so we find a new name for these people,[2] viz., " men of the wood," [3] which name is evidently derived from the thorn bushes (סְנֶה) which were in the vicinity.

It remains for us to justify the bringing forward of two more passages, [4] and it is all the more difficult for us to do so, because in order to prove our point we must accuse Muḥammad himself of a misunderstanding. In these passages Shu'aib is not mentioned, but the people who are held up as a warning are called " men of the well," [5] without any other particulars being given about them. But further these " men of the well " [6] are mentioned in one passage along with the " men of the wood," and so it seems certain that Muḥammad regarded them as two different peoples; but nevertheless we allow ourselves to believe them to be really identical.

The real reason for bringing Jethro into the Qurán is, as we have already remarked, the quarrel of the shepherds with his daughters, although the fact itself is not mentioned in that book; and it is thus easy to understand that the Jews may have sometimes called the Midianites by this name i.e., " men of the well." No other circumstances related about these persons mentioned in the Qurán would authorize this appellation. The story of Jacob at the well (setting aside the fact that not the slightest allusion

---

[1] *E.g.* Súra XXVI. 176 ff.   أَصْحَابُ ٱلْأَيْكَةِ [2]

[3] Elpherar on Súra VII. 83 has: مدين وهم أصحاب الايكة ; but this same Elpherar will not allow this with regard to Súra XXVI. 177, because in connection with Midian Shu'aib is mentioned as أخوهم their brother, which is not the case with the أَصْحَابُ ٱلْأَيْكَةِ, " people of the wood."

[4] Súras XXV. 40, L. 12.   أَصْحَابُ ٱلرَّسِّ [5]

[6] Súra L. 12.

to it is to be found in the Qurán,) has in it no trace of hostility ; and so the conjecture is not too daring that, as a matter of fact, all these three,[1] viz., the Midianites, the people of the wood, and the people of the well, are the same, but that Muḥammad regarded the first two only as identical and looked on the last as different. Still this tradition seems to have been received even among the Arabs, for we find in Elpherar[2] among other explanations the following : " Wahb says that the people of the well sat beside it (the well), and the shepherds served idols. Then God sent Shu'aib, who was to exhort them to Islám, but they remained in their error, and continued their efforts to harm Shu'aib. While they sat round the well in their dwellings the spring bubbled up and gushed over them and their houses, so that they were all ruined." In like manner Jalálu'd-dín says :[3] " Their prophet is called by some Shu'aib, by others differently." This admission of the Arabic commentators strengthens our opinion considerably. Another person of some importance in the Mosaic age is said by some Arabic commentators to be alluded to in the Qurán,[4] but many others dispute the allusion. Elpherar quotes four different opinions on this passage. The first opinion is that it refers to Balaam, for which he quotes many authorities, and relates the history of Balaam in almost complete accord with the

---

[1] ‎أَصْحَابُ ٱلرَّسِّ ـ أَصْحَابُ ٱلْأَيْكَةِ ـ أَصْحَابُ مَدْيَنَ.

[2] On Surá XXV. 40.　‎قال وهب كانوا اهل بئر قعود عليها واصحاب مواشى يعبدون الاصنام فوجه الله عزوجل شعيبا عليه السلام يدعوهم الى الاسلام فتمادوا فى طغيانهم وفى اذى شعيب عم فبينماهم حول البئر منازلهم ان فارت البئر تخسف بهم وبديارهم فهلكوا جميعا *

[3] On Súra XXV. 40 (vid. Maracc.) ‎نبيهم قيل شعيب وقيل غيرة

[4] Súra VII. 174—5.

Bible narrative.[1] Jalálu'd-dín and Zamakhshári[2] refer
this to Balaam, and call him Balaam the son of Bá'úrá.[3]
Beyond these no other persons who come into the life of
Moses, or who were important in his time, are mentioned,
and thus our second part comes to an end.

SECOND SECTION.

Chapter II.

Third Part.

The three kings who ruled over undivided Israel.

The history following immediately on the time of Moses,
including the time of the Judges, must either have seemed
to Muḥammad unedifying, which is improbable, as the
story of that heroic age was quite in accord with his feelings
and aims; or else it must have been wholly unknown to
him, and this appears to have been the case from the fact
that he speaks of the choosing of a king as an event
happening after Moses,[4] in terms which can only mean
immediately or very soon after Moses. Saul stands very
much in the back ground; for on the one hand his history
was known to Muḥammad only in a very abbreviated form,
and on the other hand the Prophet had such an undefined
notion of Saul's personality that he attributes to him the
actions of others. Saul's history is related in the Qurán[5]
in the following manner: "After Moses the Israelites
desired a king, in order that they might go out under him
to the Holy War;[6] to which however only a few of them

---

[1] Elpherar calls him, following some authorities, بلعم بن عابور ; and
following others, بلعم بن باعر.

[2] Maracc. on the passage.

[3] بلعم بن باعورا

[4] Súra II. 247. مِنْ بَعْدِ مُوسَى

[5] Súra II. 247—53.

[6] 1 Samuel, viii. 20.

afterwards went. The prophet (Samuel) gave out that
Saul was sent of God, still he seemed despicable in the eyes
of the people.[1] As a sign that the rule pertained to Saul,
the prophet of Israel announced the return of the Ark of
the Covenant. Saul then proved his troops, and allowed
only those to belong to his army who drank water lapping
it with the hand; this was done by very few, and even
these were afraid of Goliath and his armies. David at
length overcame the Philistine and his hosts and gained the
dominion." The circumstance that through Saul the Ark of
the Covenant came back[2] is contrary to Scripture, according to which the Ark came back earlier. The story of
Saul's proving his troops is evidently a confusion with that
of Gideon, concerning whom this is related in the Bible,[3]
and has doubtless risen from the similar story of Saul's
forbidding food to the army.[4] This confusion with Gideon
accounts too for the saying that only a few mighty men
followed Saul. The name of the prophet is not given, and
later Arabians also are in ignorance about it.[5] Saul is
called Tálút,[6] a name probably given on account of his
height.[7] Muḥammad notices in the Qurán that Saul was
of great height,[8] and Baidháwi gives this derivation for
his name. Goliath is called Jálút.[9] The personality of
David [10] is certainly more clearly grasped in the Qurán,
but the actual historical events of his life are scarcely
touched upon. David's victory over Goliath is mentioned

---

[1] 1 Samuel, x. 27.

[2] Súra II. 249 must be thus understood, and perhaps it would also be
better to read ياتيكم التابوت here.

[3] Judges, vii. 5 ff.　　　　　　　　[4] 1 Samuel, xiv. 24 ff.

[5] Baidháwi says : وهو يوشع أو شمعون (شـمشـون؟) او اشمويل

[6] طَالُوت probably derided from طَال to be tall.

[7] 1 Samuel, ix. 2, x. 23.　　　　　[8] Súra II. 248.

[9] جَالُوت　　　　　　　　　　　[10] دَاوُد

incidentally in the history of Saul. Again, the story of David and Bathsheba is only distantly alluded to, in that (setting aside the passage[1] in which he is called "Penitent" probably with reference to her) the parable of the case in law devised by the Prophet Nathan[2] is narrated,[3] and to it is added[4] that David perceived that this was a sign; and after he had repented, he was received back into favour by God. According to the Qurán the case in dispute is not related by the prophet, but the two disputants themselves come before David. In another passage[5] mention is made of David's and Solomon's excellent judgment on the occasion of some quarrel unknown to us about shepherds tending flocks on strange fields at night. A remarkable circumstance is given in several passages,[6] where it is stated that David compelled the mountains and the birds to praise God with him, which, as Wahl rightly remarks, owes its origin to David's poetical address to all creatures, in which address he imagines them endowed with life and reason, and calls on them to join with him in extolling the Almighty. According to the Qurán[7] mankind is indebted to David for the invention of armour. This legend probably arose from David's warlike fame, although there is much said in the Bible about Goliath's armour. In another passage[8] we find a general mention of David. In one of the Sunnas[9] it is mentioned that David did with very little sleep; and Elpherar[10] in a long chain of tradition beginning with Ibn 'Abbás and ending

---

[1] Súra XXXVIII. 16. أَوَّاب   [2] Samuel, xii. 1 ff.

[3] Súra XXXVIII. 20—3.   [4] Súra XXXVIII. 23—6.

[5] Súra XXI. 78.

[6] Súras XXI. 79, XXXIV. 10, XXXVIII. 16—20.

[7] Súra XXI. 80.   [8] Súra XXVII. 15.

[9] Sunna 148.   [10] On Súra XXXVIII. 16.

with 'Amrú, says:[1] " The Apostle of God said : ' (David)
slept half the night, rose for a third, and then slept again
for a sixth.' " The Rabbis also speak of this, on the
strength of the [2] verse, " At midnight I will rise to give
thanks unto Thee," and they assert that David used to
sleep only during sixty respirations.[3] David is also known
to Muhammad as the author of the Psalms.[4] The affair
of the Sabbath-breakers, who were punished by being
changed into apes, is also supposed to belong to the time
of David, but the circumstance is mentioned [5] only in
general terms, and nothing definite is given about time or
details, except in verse 82, where the time is given, but not
the fact. Among the Jews there is no trace of this legend.

The life of Solomon [6] is in itself unimportant, and it
is only the wisdom for which he is famed in the Bible
which makes him the hero of the whole East, one might
therefore expect to find much more about him in the
Qurán than really exists there. Muhammad speaks of his
wisdom,[7] and especially brings forward the fact that
Solomon understood the language of the birds. This is
also asserted by the Rabbis, and is founded on the Biblical
statement: [8] " He spake of trees . . . . . . and birds." The
winds [9] also performed his will, and the Genii were found
in his following ; [10] this is also related, e.g., in the second

---

[1] قال رسول الله صلعم كان داود ينام نصف الليل و يقوم ثلثه و ينام سدسه

[2] Palms, cxix. 62.   [3] שְׁתִּין נִשְׁמֵי (Berachoth).

[4] زَبُور Súras IV. 161, XVII. 57.

[5] Súras II. 61, IV. 50, V. 65, VII. 166.

[6] سليمان   [7] Súra XXVII. 15, 16.

[8] 1 Kings, v. 13. וַיְדַבֵּר עַל הָעֵצִים.........וְעַל הָעוֹף

[9] رِيح here probably means the spirits of the air, like רוּחוֹת

[10] Súras XXI. 81, 82, XXXIV. 11, 12, XXXVIII. 35—9.

Targum on the Book of Esther,[1] thus: "To him were obedient demons of the most diverse sorts, and the evil spirits were given into his hand." This legend is derived primarily from a mistaken interpretation of a passage in Ecclesiastes.[2] Muḥammad relates the following tale:[3] "On one occasion the lapwing[4] was not found in attendance on Solomon, and the King regarding him as a truant threatened to kill him. Then the lapwing came with the news that he had discovered a land as yet unknown to Solomon, which was not subject to him, the land of Sheba, in which the people together with the Queen worshipped the sun. Solomon sent the bird back with a letter summoning these people to adopt the belief in the Unity of God. He himself went thither at once with his troops, and had the Queen's throne brought to him by a ministering angel. The Queen had been already converted, and she came into Solomon's camp; he had her brought before him into a hall, of which the flooring was glass, and she imagining it to be water, exposed her legs." This same story is to be found in the Targum[5] already referred to, together with some other circumstances which I shall omit here. The story runs as follows: "Thereupon the partridge was sought and not found among the birds, and the King commanded angrily that it should be fetched, and he wanted to kill it. Then the partridge answered the King: 'My lord and King, attend and hear my words, for three months I considered and flew about the whole world to find the town where thou wast not obeyed. Then I saw a town in the East called Kitor, where there are many

---

[1] On Esther, i. 2.

לֵהּ יִשְׁתַּמְּעוּן שֵׁדִים וּפִנְגְעִין וְחַיִּין וְרוּחִין בִּישִׁין אִתְמְסָרוּ בִּידֵהּ

[2] Ecclesiastes, ii. 8. שִׁדָּה וְשִׁדּוֹת

[3] Súra XXVII. 20—46.   [4] هدهد

[5] Second Targum on the Book of Esther.

people, but a woman rules over them; she is called the Queen of Sheba. If it please thee now, my lord King, I will go to that town and bind the Queen with chains and its nobles with iron fetters and bring them all here.' And it pleased the King, and Scribes were called who wrote letters and bound them to the wings of the partridge. When the bird came to the Queen she saw the letter tied on to its wing, she opened it, and these were the contents: 'From me, Solomon the King, greeting to thee and to thy princes! Thou knowest well that God hath appointed me King over the beasts of the field and the birds of the heaven, and over the demons, spirits and spectres of the night, and that the kings of all the countries under heaven approach me in submission. If thou also wilt do this, great honour will be shewn thee; if not, then I will send against thee kings and legions and horsemen. The kings are the beasts of the field; the horsemen, the birds of the air; the armies, demons and spirits; while the legions are nightmares, which will strangle you in your beds.' When the Queen had read this, she rent her clothes and sent for the elders and lords and said: 'Do you know what King Solomon has sent me?' They said: 'We neither know him, nor heed him.' But the Queen did not trust them, but called for ships and sent presents to the king, and after three years she went herself. When the king heard that she had come, he seated himself in a glass room. She thought the king was sitting in the water, and bared herself to go through it. When she saw his magnificence, she said:[1] 'Blessed be the Lord thy God, which delighted in thee, to set thee on the throne . . . . . to do judgment and justice.'" We must forgive Muḥammad the two slight changes he makes in the story, viz., that he turns the matter from one of government into one of

---

[1] 1 Kings, x. 9.

religion, and that he begins the letter [1] with the words : "In the name of the Merciful God," Solomon built the Temple also by the help of the spirits, who even went on building after his death, while he remained sitting on his throne till a worm gnawed him.[2]

Once when Solomon became arrogant he was driven from the kingdom, and a spirit reigned in his stead until he repented.[3] The Sanhedrin [4] gives the following brief account : "At first Solomon reigned even over the exalted ones, as it is written : [5] Solomon sat on the throne of the Lord ; but afterwards only over his own stick, as it is written : [6] What profit hath man of all his labour? and further,[7] this was my portion from all my labour." [8] When he repented, he gave up his useless extravagances, and had his horses disabled,[9] to which the following passage alludes : [10] "It is wisely ordained that the reasons for the commandments are not given ; they were given in two

---

[1] بِسْمِ آللهِ آلرّحْمٰنِ آلرّحِيمِ   Súra XXVII. 30.

[2] Súra XXXIV. 13. Cf. on this point Gittin, 68.

[3] Súra XXXVIII. 33—5.   [4] Sanhedrin, 20.

בַּתְּחִלָּה מָלַךְ שְׁלֹמֹה עַל הָעֶלְיוֹנִים שֶׁנֶּ׳ וַיֵּשֶׁב שְׁלֹמֹה עַל
כִּסֵּא ה' וְלַבְסוֹף לֹא מָלַךְ אֶלָּא עַל מַקְלוֹ שֶׁנֶּ׳ מַה־יִּתְרוֹן לָאָדָם
בְּכָל־עֲמָלוֹ וּכְתִיב זֶה הָיָה חֶלְקִי מִכָּל־עֲמָלִי

[5] 1 Chronicles, xxix. 23.   [6] Ecclesiastes, i. 3.

[7] Ecclesiastes, ii. 10.

[8] Cf. also Midr. Rabba on Numbers, par. 11 ; on Canticles, iii. 4 ; and on Ruth, ii. 14.

[9] Súra XXXVIII. 29—32.   [10] Sanhedrin, 21.

מִפְּנֵי מַה־לֹּא נִתְגַּלּוּ טַעֲמֵי תוֹרָה שֶׁהֲרֵי שְׁנֵי מִקְרָאוֹת נִתְגַּלָּה
טַעֲמָן וְנִכְשַׁל בָּהֶן גְּדוֹל הָעוֹלָם שֶׁנֶּ׳ לֹא יַרְבֶּה לוֹ סוּסִים
אָמַר שְׁלֹמֹה אַרְבֶּה וְלֹא אָשִׁיב וּכְתִיב וַתַּעַל מֶרְכָּבָה מִמִּצְרַיִם
בְּשֵׁשׁ מֵאוֹת

cases, and one of the greatest of men sinned. For it is written:[1] The king shall not multiply horses to himself, nor cause the people to return to Egypt, to the end that he should multiply horses. Then Solomon thought, I will get me many horses and not send to Egypt; but it is written:[2] And a chariot came up and went out of Egypt for six hundred shekels of silver." A story about spirits, which is said to have happened in Solomon's time,[3] has already been mentioned in connection with Noah. A story about the ants, which fled before Solomon's army, is related in the Qurán,[4] and remains to be noticed. It is evidently founded on the verse,[5] " Go to the ant thou sluggard ..... and be wise;" and based on this same foundation we have a beautiful fable in the Talmud,[6] but I could find there no trace of the story given in the Qurán.

The story of the lapwing[7] has gained a firm foot hold in Arabic legend, and a pretty myth about the bird is found in Fakihat Elcholafa.[8] For Muḥammad there were no very important personages between Moses and Jesus; and such as he does mention he merely alludes to. This is not to be wondered at when Solomon, the wise man of the East, who is endowed with all manner of legendary adornment comes, comparatively speaking, so little before us in the Qurán.

———

[1] Deuteronomy, xvii. 16.

[2] 1 Kings, x. 29.

[3] Súra II. 96.

[4] Súra XXVII. 18—9.

[5] Proverbs, vi. 6 ff.

[6] Chullin, 57. 2.

[7] هُدْهُد

[8] Page 91.

Second Chapter.

Fourth Part.

Holy Men after the time of Solomon.

Many important men might be mentioned here, but Muḥammad knew but few of them, and about those whom he does name he gives for the most part nothing special, but mentions them only with other pious persons. Some only are treated with a little more detail, and we will mention them here first, so as then to put the others together briefly. Of Elijah [1] his dispute with the people about the worship of Baal is related briefly. In the legends of Islám as well as in those of later Judaism Elijah plays a very important part. He is that mystical [2] person known under the name of Khizr. He is therefore the same as Phinehas, [3] erroneously called by some the nephew of Aaron [4] instead of his grandson, and, like Elijah the prophet [5] in later Jewish traditions, he is the mediator between heaven and earth. It is he who appears

---

[1] اِلْيَاس Súras VI. 85, XXXVII. 123. In one place he is called

اِلْيَاسِيَن (Súra XXXVII. 30) on account of the rhyme. We find among other opinions in Elpherar the following:

فقد قيل الياسين لغة فى الياس مثل اسمعيل و اسمعين و ميكايل و ميكاين

"It is said that Ilyásín is a dialectic change for Elyás, as Ism‘aíl for Ism‘aín and Míkháyil for Míkháyin." These examples are certainly unsuitable, for in them the change is only from ل to ن , while here the complete addition of the syllable ‑ين takes place. This the Arabs, in spite of the similar سِنِين mentioned before, seem to shrink from explaining as a change deliberately made on account of the rhyme.

[2] خِضر

[3] فِنْحَاص

[4] ابن اخى هرون

[5] אֵלִיָּהוּ הַנָּבִיא

to the pious under the most varied forms, who visits the
schools, and imparts to famous teachers that which God
communicates about this or that opinion expressed by them.
The Muslims too know him in this capacity, and they
recognize him in the servant of God who proposed himself
as a travelling companion to Moses,[1] and in these actions
they have the prototype of his ministry as one who appears
in a miraculous manner, has intercourse with men in human
fashion, and performs incomprehensible actions which
only receive true significance through knowledge which is
hidden from man.

Jonah is mentioned in several passages of the Qurán.[2]
His mission to Nineveh, his being swallowed by the fish,
his rescue from it, and the story of the gourd which shaded
him, are all given very briefly.[3]   Job's[4] sufferings and
healing are mentioned in two passages,[5] and in the latter
passage Muḥammad adds that Job produced a cooling
and refreshing fountain for himself by stamping on the
earth. We know of no parallel passage to this in the
Rabbinical writings.

We come now to a passage[6] hitherto wrongly referred
which translated runs thus:

> " Slain were the men of the pit of the burning fire,
>   When they sat around the same,

And were witnesses of what was done to the true believers,
and they wished to punish them only because they
believed in the mighty and Glorious God," &c.

---

[1] Súra XVIII. 59—82.

[2] يُونُس Súras VI. 86, X. 98, XXXVII. 139, XXI. 87 ذُو ٱلنُّون , LXVIII.
48 صَاحِبُ ٱلْحُوتِ.

[3] Súras X. 98, XXI. 87—8, XXXVII. 139—149, LXVIII. 48—51.

[4] أَيُّوبُ   [5] Súras XXI. 83—4, XXXVIII. 40—5.

[6] Súra LXXXV. 4 ff.

Commentators make this refer to the punishment of a Jewish Himyarite King who persecuted the Christians, but the appellation "believers" as applied to Christians has no parallel elsewhere in the Qurán, no detail bearing on this event is mentioned, and just this one form of persecution (burning) is not given by the martyrologists.

If we compare the passage with the story of the three children [1] all fits in perfectly.

The three believers would not bow themselves before an idol, and were thrown into the fiery furnace; those who threw them in were slain by the heat and the believers were saved. Evidently Muḥammad here alludes to this.[2]

It is possible that there is an allusion to the story of the revival of the dry bones [3] in a passage of the Qurán,[4] which tells us that many who left their habitations for fear of death were slain by God, but were afterwards restored to life.[5] The Talmud treats the narrative given in Ezekiel more in detail.[6]

Another biblical reference may perhaps be found in

---

[1] Daniel, iii. 8 ff.

[2] An intimation that this passage refers to this circumstance is given by the Arabian commentator Muqátil (cited by Elpherar), in that he asserts that there were in fact three "people of the burning fiery pit" (أَصْحَابُ ٱلْأُخْدُودِ); and of the pits one was in فارس , *i. e.* Persia, and indeed under نصر بخت Nebuchadnezzar; but he adds: ولم ينزل الله فيهما قرآن, God revealed nothing in the Súra about this or about the other event which took place in Syria, but only revealed about the one under Dhú-nawás. But this intimation is enough for the strengthening of our opinion.

[3] Ezekiel, xxxvii.   [4] Súra II. 244.

[5] The Arabian commentators know of this but dimly, for Ismail Ben 'Ali gives out in the name of Ibn Tálib that this event took place in the time of the Judge (?) حزقيل, *i.e.* Ezekiel, who came after برسياس, the son of Caleb, in this office. (Maraco: Prodr. IV. 83.)

[6] Sanhedrin 92.

U

the words : [1] "Dost thou not see how thy Lord stretches
(lengthens) out the shadow when he will, makes it quies-
cent, then sets the sun over it as an indicator." This I
think is perhaps an allusion to the sign given to Hezekiah.[2]

We find more in the Qurán about Ezra,[3] if not about his
history, yet about the way in which the Jews regarded
him. According to the assertion of Muḥammad the Jews
held Ezra to be the Son of God.[4] This is certainly a mere
misunderstanding which arose from the great esteem in
which Ezra was undoubtedly held. This esteem is expressed
in the following passage : [5] "Ezra would have been worthy
to have made known the law if Moses had not come before
him." Truly Muḥammad sought to cast suspicion on the
Jews' faith in the unity of God, and thought he had here
found a good opportunity of so doing.

This utterance as an expression of the Jewish opinion
of that time loses much in value when we consider the
personality of that Phineas the son of Azariah, to whom it
is attributed.

In the traditions of Islám there is a great deal about
Ezra as the compiler of the Law. In this character also

---

[1] Súra XXV. 47—8.

[2] 2 Kings, xx. 9—12.   [3] عُزَيْر

The Arabian grammarians dispute as to whether the word should
receive a nunnation or not, but it seems to me that the omission of it is
more suitable to the form of the word which is like a diminutive.
Several of the Arabians regard this as correct.

[4] Súra IX. 30. Sunna, 462.

In D'Herbelot (under the word "Ozair" page 691) much is adduced
from Muslim commentators and historians to explain this passage, which
however, in harmony with the Talmud, only asserts Ezra's renewing of
the Law.

[5] Sanhedrin 21. 2.

רָאוּי הָיָה עֶזְרָא שֶׁתִּנָּתֵן תּוֹרָה עַל יָדוֹ אִלְמָלֵא לֹא קִדְּמוֹ
מֹשֶׁה

he comes before us in Scripture, and the Jews believed this
of him; so the probability becomes great that Muḥammad,
on the one hand, intentionally exaggerated, and, on the
other hand, eagerly caught up the hasty and mocking
utterance of some individual to prove this point against
the Jews.

The Arabian commentators according to Maraccius [1]
refer another passage in the Quran [2] to Ezra, namely, the
one where it is related of some person that he passed by a
ruined city and doubted if it could ever be restored. God
let him die for one hundred years, then revived him and
imparted to him the assurance that one hundred years had
gone by, while he believed that but one day had passed.

The proof was that his food and drink had perished and
his ass was mouldering away. Then behold! God put
together the bones of the animal and clothed them with
flesh, so that the man acknowledged: "God is mighty
over all." The fable is derived, as Maraccius rightly
observes, from the ride round the ruined city of Jerusalem
made by Nehemiah,[3] who is often confused with Ezra.

Two other Biblical characters are merely mentioned:
Elisha [4] in two passages,[5] and each time strangely enough
immediately after Ishmael; and Dhú'l-Kifl,[6] who according
to his name which means the nourisher, and from the fact
related of him that he nourished a hundred Israelites in
a cave, must be Obadiah.[7] Perhaps however he may be
Ezekiel, who according to Niebuhr [8] is called Kephil by the
Arabs.[9]

---

[1] Prod. iv. 85,   [2] Súra II. 261.

[3] Nehemiah, ii. 12 ff.   [4] اَلْيَسَع

[5] Súras VI. 86, XXXVIII. 48.   [6] Súras XXI. 85, XXXVIII. 48.

[7] 1 Kings, xviii. 4.   [8] Reisebeschreibung II. 265.

[9] According to Khondemír (D'Herbelot Bibl. Orient. under Elisha ben
Akhthob) Dhú'l-Kifl was a follower of Elisha, but Obadiah was contemporary with Elijah.

Now all the historical allusions have been put together, and when we examine them we see unmistakably in them the verification of the hypothesis which we laid down at the beginning—namely, that Muḥammad borrowed a great deal from Judaism, that he learned that which he did borrow from oral tradition, and that he sometimes altered it to suit his purpose. We have tried to shew in the first part that external circumstances must have raised in Muḥammad the desire to borrow much from Judaism, that he had the means thereto within his reach, and that other circumstances, particularly his own main aim, offered no obstacle to, but rather fitted in with such a borrowing. In the second part, we have attempted to show that Muḥammad really did borrow from Judaism, and that conceptions, matters of creed, views of morality, and of life in general, and more especially matters of history and of traditions, have actually passed over from Judaism into the Qurán.

And now our task is practically ended. If a thorough demonstration has been made of all these points, then the questions as to whether Muḥammad *did* borrow from Judaism, and *what* and *how* he so borrowed, have been sufficiently answered. Now, as a supplementary note we add a summary of the passages in which Muḥammad's attribute towards Judaism seems to be negative and even hostile. Some of these passages oppose Judaism, some abrogate laws binding on the Jews, and some allude to Jewish customs without imposing them upon the Arabs. But since we consider the question, the answer to which forms the subject of our theme, as now fully answered, without giving the results of further investigation, we therefore do not give these results as a part of this work itself, but add them as an appendix.

APPENDIX.

Statements in the Quran hostile to Judaism.

Just as we tried before to shew from the personality of Muḥammad and from the spirit of his time that borrowing from Judaism had taken place, even so we wish here to shew that statements hostile to Judaism are to be found in the Qurán. Muḥammad's aim was to bring about a union of all creeds, and no religious community stood more in the way of the attainment of this end than the Jews with their many cumbersome laws, unknown to other religions. Further, Muḥammad's aim was to establish in and through this union such religious doctrines only as were in his opinion purified. The observance of individual laws did not seem to him of great importance, except in so far as such laws resulted immediately from those special doctrines; moreover, he loved the old Arabian customs and kept to them. The Jews on the contrary laid the greatest stress upon the punctilious fulfilment of the revealed law, and shewed not the slightest desire to depart from it. While these two causes of mutual separation were founded upon the difference in the fundamental opinions of Muḥammad and the Jews, another may be added which arose more from an external difference. As we have already remarked, the Jews pressed Muḥammad very hard, and often annoyed him with repartee and evasions, thus rousing in him an inextinguishable hatred. Governed by this he misunderstood their religious doctrines, putting false constructions upon them, and so justifying his own deviation from them. He wished therefore to make a final separation from these hateful Jews, and to this end he established entirely different customs. Later Arabians confess that he made changes[1] "from the

---

[1] كراهة لموافقة النفى التشبيد باليهود

necessity of abolishing resemblances to the Jews."[1] Thus, Muḥammad asserts that the Jews are the enemies of the Muslims,[2] that they slew prophets,[3] a probable reference to Jesus; further, that they in common with Christians thought themselves specially favoured by God,[4] that they believed that they alone should possess Paradise,[5] that they held Ezra to be the son of God,[6] that they trusted in the intercession of their self pious predecessors,[7] that they had perverted the Bible [8] because in its existing form that Book contained no allusions to him, and that the Jews built temples on the graves of the prophets.[9] Such accusations and the reasons given earlier supplied Muhammad with grounds on which to justify his departure from Jewish laws.

A. Prayer.—Supper precedes prayer.[10] This is in direct opposition to the Talmud, which lays down exactly how long before prayer one may eat that the hour of prayer may not be let slip. Truly in this Muḥammad wished to live so as to please his Arabs.

B. Laws about women.—Muhammad says :[11] "It is lawful for you on the night of the fast to go in unto your wives." This is clearly prescribed in opposition to the directly contrary ruling in the Talmudic law prohibiting cohabitation on the night before the fast day in Abb, that being counted as part of the fast day itself.

The laws of divorce [12] are probably identical with those of the ancient Arabs. There is a remarkable passage in the Qurán,[13] which says that the man after he has put away his wife for the second time cannot marry her again until she has married another man, and been divorced by him too. This is directly contrary to the teaching of the Bible.[14]

---

[1] Pocock notæ Misc., chap. 9, page 369.
[2] Súra V. 85.
[3] Súras II. 58, V. 74.
[4] Súra V. 21.
[5] Súras II. 88, LXII. 6.
[6] Súra IX. 30. Sunna 462.
[7] Súra II. 128, 135.
[8] Súra II. 73, and other passages.
[9] Sunna 70 ff.
[10] Sunna 97 ff.
[11] Súra II. 183.
[12] Súra II. 229 ff.
[13] Súra II. 230.
[14] Deuteronomy, xxiv. 1 ff.

The Muslims assert [1] that the Jews of that period laid down that cohabitation was to take place in the usual way. On this Muhammad to please himself and his Arabs says: [2] "Your wives are your tillage, go in therefore unto your tillage in what manner soever ye will," etc.

C. The most important and prominent change to be considered in this connection is the removal of the prohibition about food, concerning which Muhammad asserts that it was imposed upon the Jews only on account of their iniquity. [3] (It is interesting that Jesus states just the converse when he speaks of the abolition of divorce. [4]) Muhammad abolishes the law about meat in several passages, [5] but holds to part of it in others, [6] following it would seem the precedent of the apostles, to whom almost the same utterance is attributed in the New Testament. [7] Thus he forbids carrion, blood, swine's flesh, and that which has been slain for an idol; to which he adds in the first passage, that which is not properly killed, viz., that slain by strangling, or by a blow from an axe, that killed by a fall from a mountain, that which is gored, and that torn by wild beasts. These last rules, considering the total silence about them in other later passages, may be regarded as "abolished." [8] In another passage [9] Muhammad mentions particular meats which were forbidden to the Jews. [10]

D. Lastly, the following utterance [11] of Muhammad is decidedly combative: "We have therein commanded them that they should give life for life, and eye for eye, and nose for nose, and ear for ear, and tooth for tooth; and that wounds should also be punished by retaliation; but whoever should remit it as alms it should be accepted as an atonement for him. And whoso

---

[1] Sunna 460.

[2] Súra II. 223.

[3] Súra IV. 158.

[4] St. Matthew, xix. 8.

[5] Súras III. 44, 87, IV. 158, V. 89, 90.

[6] Súras V. 4, VI. 146, XVI.116.

[7] Acts, xv. 19—28.

[8] مَنْسُوخ

[9] Súra VI. 147.

[10] Leviticus, xi. 3, 7, 27, ff. and 39 ff.

[11] Súra V. 49.

judgeth not according to what God hath revealed they are unjust." The passage of Scripture which Muḥammad here has in mind is in Exodus ;[1] and those who do not observe it are the Jews, in that they extend to all cases the permission to make atonement with money, which is given only when the injured party agrees to it. The Mishna[2] runs as follows : "If a man has blinded another, or cut off his hand, or broken his foot, one must regard the injured person as though he were a slave sold in the market, and put a price upon him and reckon how much he was worth before the injury and how much now, etc."

These are about all the chief points showing a consideration of Judaism, and the collecting of them gives us another proof that Muḥammad had a personal knowledge of Judaism through acquaintance with the Jewish manner of life and through intercourse with the Jews.

If we now once more consider this treatise as a whole, we shall find that by the establishment of the fact which was to be demonstrated, viz., that Muḥammad borrowed from Judaism, we come to a clear understanding of the Qurán in general as well as of individual passages in it. Furthermore, the state of culture of the Arabians of that day, and especially of the Arabian Jews, is to some extent made clear, and light is thrown upon the plan of Muḥammad and upon his intellectual power and knowledge by many authentic documents. Then in collecting the passages which serve as proofs we are compelled to dismiss at once the ill-considered confidence with which people are apt to speak of each legend as a dream of the rabbinical Talmudists ; for although the author neither can nor will maintain that no passage bearing on his thesis has escaped him in the Rabbinical literature, still this must be accepted as a fact until it can be proved that this

---

[1] Exodus, xxi. 23 ff.   [2] Mishna Baba, Ramma viii. 1.

סֻמָּא אֶת־עֵינוֹ קִטֵּעַ אֶת־יָדוֹ שָׁבַּר אֶת־רַגְלוֹ רוֹאִין אוֹתוֹ כְּאִלּוּ
הוּא עֶבֶד נִמְכָּר בַּשּׁוּק וְשָׁמִין כַּמָּה הָיָה יָפֶה וְכַמָּה הוּא יָפֶה

or that has been omitted, and thus for the present we must attribute to some other source every thing of which the Jewish origin has not been proved. By this, however, I do not intend to say that everything which, according to our ideas, is mythical and for which a Jewish source appears to be forthcoming, may be laid upon Judaism; for, on the one hand, the opinion or legend may originally have had a different signification and it may have reached its present extravagant development in the mouth of the people, and, on the other hand, the source itself may have had no obligatory importance, and therefore does not hold the same place with regard to Judaism as the Qurán holds with regard to Islám. We must distinguish between Judaism and views derived from the Jews; this distinction, however, is unfortunately either from ill-will or ignorance often not made.

And now I submit this treatise to you, honoured readers, and your judgment will convince me of the correctness or falsity of my opinions, and as to whether my work fulfils its end or has failed in its purpose.

INDICES.

A.—List of Hebrew and Arabic words explained.

B.—List of Passages cited from the Qurán.

Y

C.—List of Passages cited from the Sunna.

D.—The Chief Authors cited.

Abulfeda, Annales Moslemitici.
   „   Historia Anteislamica.
   „   Vita Mohammedis.
Assemanni, Bibliotheca Orientalis.
Baidháwi, Commentary on Qurán.
Hamasa,—
D'Herbelot, Bibliotheque Orientale.
Hottinger, Historia Orientalis.
Ibn Arabscha, Fakihat Elcholafa.
Pococke, Notae Miscellaneæ.
   „   Specimen Hist. Arabum.